"In *Sacred Times*, Fr. Turner ha
understanding many of the ins
the Liturgy of the Hours and the Roman Missal, in particular the General
Roman Calendar and the Table of Liturgical Days. He meticulously
examines, for example, how one navigates the celebration of consecutive
solemnities and anticipated (Saturday) Masses. In the reform of the
liturgy, Turner reveals some of the tensions, at times, between the revisers
of the liturgy, the Congregation for the Doctrine of the Faith, and various
popes. Readers will find Turner's discussion on making the Roman
calendar truly universal and not a 'Mediterranean calendar,' why certain
saints were included or excluded from the General Calendar, and how the
Roman Rite came very close to losing Ash Wednesday fascinating indeed."

—Peter D. Rocca, CSC, general editor, Paulist Press Ordo

"Once again, Fr. Paul Turner invites his readers to break open the rites of
the Church with care. *Sacred Times* unpacks the logic of the reformed
General Roman Calendar, highlighting its emphasis upon the paschal
mystery as the heart of the liturgical year and explaining the pastoral and
theological reasoning regarding everything from the Proper of Saints to the
celebration of vigil masses. Replete with references and helpful appendices,
this volume offers clear distinctions and principles for those in professional
church ministry as they prepare for worship and a welcome compendium
of sources for academics and students of liturgical and pastoral studies."

—Katharine E. Harmon, project director,
    Obsculta Preaching Initiative, St. John's University School of
    Theology and Seminary, Collegeville, Minnesota

"The revision of the liturgical calendar was key to the reform of the
liturgy following the Second Vatican Council, not only in providing a
foundation for the work on the Missal, Lectionary, and Liturgy of the
Hours but also in expressing a renewed theology of time centered on
the Paschal Mystery. Fr. Paul Turner, with his customary diligence, is
a knowledgeable guide to the work of revision. This, however, is not
just a work of historical research; it also provides a guide to the current
liturgical year, calendar, and days of special prayer highlighting the origins
and history of each celebration, which will be a helpful resource to all
who plan and prepare liturgy."

—Martin Foster, director, Liturgy Office,
    Catholic Bishops' Conference of England and Wales

"Paul Turner's *Sacred Times* is an extraordinary resource for anyone with a question about or interest in the liturgical year. It should be on every priest's or liturgical minister's bookshelf. Not merely supplying information, in a conversational tone Turner takes the reader behind the scenes to discussions and decisions that have been made in developing the liturgical calendar, providing annotations to original documents. Every day is sacred in this volume, and the reader learns the origin of every saint's feast. A final chapter on the table of liturgical days explains the ranks of feasts which can often be confusing."

—Julia Upton, RSM, PhD, retired distinguished professor
of theology, St. John's University, New York

"Even those who have often traversed the liturgical year as revised by Vatican II will find new information and new contexts in Paul Turner's *Sacred Times*. A scholar's thoroughness, a teacher's clarity, and a pastor's care are combined and presented in an accessible manner. From the historical conciliar background of the calendar's revision to practical insight for current-day observances, this is a most useful book. It will be a gift for all whose ministry is connected to the sacred times, as well as the faithful who celebrate week by week or day by day."

—Alan J. Hommerding, pastoral musician, hymnwriter,
composer, author, liturgical publications editor,
GIA Publications

"Fr. Paul Turner's *Sacred Times* will be a most welcome addition to the office bookshelves of every liturgist and liturgical musician. The scope of the work is comprehensive and concise at the same time. It is also well structured, in a manner to both make for easy reading and comprehension as well as for finding just the miniscule detail one is looking for at a moment's notice. Especially helpful are the included tables and appendices, particularly the reminders of the variety of ranks of our liturgical celebrations and their hierarchy, and their significances for liturgical adaptations. Every pastor, liturgist, and liturgical musician should add this book to their collections of reference materials."

—Orin Johnson, director of music and liturgy,
St. Margaret of Scotland, in the Archdiocese of St. Louis,
and author of *Incarnate in Word and Song*

Sacred Times

A Guide to
the General Roman Calendar
and the Table of Liturgical Days

Paul Turner

LITURGICAL PRESS
Collegeville, Minnesota

litpress.org

Library of Congress Cataloging-in-Publication Data

Names: Turner, Paul, author.
Title: Sacred times : a guide to the general Roman calendar and the table of liturgical days / Paul Turner.
Description: Collegeville, Minnesota : Liturgical Press, [2024] | Includes index. | Summary: "What happens when the liturgical calendars clash? This is a common question that priests, deacons, and liturgists may have about the relative weight of days in the liturgical calendar. In Sacred Times, Paul Turner offers a practical commentary on the General Roman Calendar and the Table of Liturgical Days that explains what the calendar honors, how it came to be, and why these celebrations matter. Sacred Times also includes an alphabetical list of days and additional reference tools"— Provided by publisher.
Identifiers: LCCN 2024032027 (print) | LCCN 2024032028 (ebook) | ISBN 9780814689028 (trade paperback) | ISBN 9780814689035 (epub) | ISBN 9780814689639 (pdf)
Subjects: LCSH: Catholic Church—Liturgy—Calendar. | Church calendar. | Fasts and feasts—Catholic Church.
Classification: LCC BX4655.3 .T87 2024 (print) | LCC BX4655.3 (ebook) | DDC 263/.9—dc23/eng/20240806
LC record available at https://lccn.loc.gov/2024032027
LC ebook record available at https://lccn.loc.gov/2024032028

QVI BENE INTELLIGVNT
TEMPORA SACRA
ET AGRICVLTVRÆ ET GENERATIONVM HVMANÆ VITÆ
QVÆ TAM PLENA EST CELEBRATIONIS, PASSIONIS AC MYSTERII
QVAM CALENDARIVM LITVRGICVM
DEDICAT AVCTOR HVNC LIBRVM
CONSOBRINÆ ANNÆ MARIÆ
ET MARITO EIVS LAVRENTIO HALVORSONO

Contents

Abbreviations

DOL   International Commission on English in the Liturgy, *Documents on the Liturgy, 1963–1979: Conciliar, Papal, and Curial Texts*, ed. and trans. Thomas C. O'Brien (Collegeville, MN: Liturgical Press, 1982)

GILH   General Instruction of the Liturgy of the Hours (New York: Catholic Book Publishing, 1975)

GIRM   The General Instruction of the Roman Missal, Revised Edition (Washington, DC: United States Conference of Catholic Bishops, 2011)

ICEL   International Commission on English in the Liturgy

ILM   Introduction: *Lectionary for Mass* (Collegeville, MN: Liturgical Press, 2000)

OBC   *The Order of Baptism of Children* (Collegeville, MN: Liturgical Press, 2020)

OCIA   *The Order of Christian Initiation of Adults* (Collegeville, MN: Liturgical Press, 2024)

OCM   *The Order of Celebrating Matrimony* (Collegeville, MN: Liturgical Press, 2016)

ODCA   *The Order of the Dedication of a Church and an Altar* (Washington, DC: United States Conference of Catholic Bishops, 2018)

OM The Order of Mass, Roman Missal

OUI *Ordo unctionis infirmorum eorumque pastorales curæ* (Vatican City: Typis Polyglottis Vaticanis, 1975)

PCS Pastoral Care of the Sick: Rites of Anointing and Viaticum, *The Rites*, Volume I (Collegeville, MN: Liturgical Press, 1990)

SC Second Vatican Council, *Sacrosanctum Concilium* (Constitution on the Sacred Liturgy), 1963

UNLYC Universal Norms on the Liturgical Year and the General Roman Calendar, Roman Missal

USCCB United States Conference of Catholic Bishops

Chapter One

The General Roman Calendar

The Liturgical Year

The book of Genesis envisioned the creation of the entire cosmos within units of time. As God created space, so God created time. As certain spaces are especially sacred, so are certain times.

The Catholic Church arranges days on its liturgical calendar according to their sacred meaning. A secular calendar honors four seasons of the year. A school calendar arranges semesters, breaks, and vacations. Sports calendars have a pre-season, a regular season, and a post-season. The fiscal year marks its own origin and ending. The final days of any calendar year prompt observances of remembering, as the new year inspires resolutions.

The secular calendar's divisions into years, months, weeks, and days interact with the liturgical calendar. However, the principal annual references for a Christian are not spring, summer, autumn, and winter, but Advent, Christmas, Lent, and Easter. Most American workers have weekends off. Sunday anchors the Christian week.

The secular calendar in the United States marks certain days as holidays—New Year's Day, Martin Luther King Jr. Day, Presidents' Day, Memorial Day, Juneteenth, Independence Day,

Labor Day, Columbus Day, Indigenous Peoples' Day, Veterans' Day, Thanksgiving Day, and Christmas Day. The church calendar observes a cycle of saints. They populate the year alphabetically, from Adalbert to Wenceslaus, span ministries from early martyrs to contemporary writers, and died in places from Jerusalem to Futuna Island.

Colors apply to certain liturgical days. The priest and deacon vest in white for festive times and days, red for observances of the Lord's passion and of martyrs, green for Ordinary Time, violet for Advent and Lent, rose optionally for the Sundays marking the midpoints of Advent and Lent, gold or silver for solemn celebrations (GIRM 346).

Throughout the Catholic world, the calendar enjoys regional variations that integrate with the universal framework for the year. That framework establishes the principal times of the church year, as well as the saints whom all must honor. Together, the Proper of Time and the Proper of Saints make up the General Roman Calendar.

The Table of Liturgical Days

Not all days carry the same weight. Earth Day is widely observed in the United States, but it is not a federal holiday. Independence Day in one country is not the same date as in another. One couple marks their wedding anniversary with great celebration on a particular date when their neighbors in the same apartment building pass just another day.

The Table of Liturgical Days ranks the celebrations that pertain to the universal church and to smaller regions. The table helps people discern which celebration takes precedence when two coincide. In families, if someone has a birthday on December 25, all celebrate both a birthday and Christmas Day. When choosing the date for a funeral, the family may avoid scheduling it on a wedding anniversary. So in the liturgical year, the Table of Liturgical Days ranks the relative importance of days.

Renewed Vision

The General Roman Calendar underwent a rare, thorough revision following the Second Vatican Council. Changes happen repeatedly, but in the manner of new dwellers rehabbing an old house—adding features here and there. After a while, it seems prudent to freshen everything, to establish revised, comprehensive principles.

At the Second Vatican Council, the bishops approved the calendar's revision in their Constitution on the Sacred Liturgy (SC 102–11). Centering first on the resurrection of Jesus, the Constitution recommitted to the annual cycles that reveal the entire mystery of Christ from his incarnation and passion to the promised coming of the Holy Spirit. It noted the importance of days dedicated to Mary and the saints, as well as to various devotions of the people.

Even so, it called for a revision: "The liturgical year is to be revised so that the traditional customs and discipline of the sacred seasons shall be preserved or restored in line with the conditions of modern times" (SC 107).[1] Everything aimed to celebrate the paschal mystery without interference. The results produced a calendar that more capably expressed the universality of the church and of its beliefs.

The Revisers

To implement the 1963 Constitution on the Sacred Liturgy, Pope Paul VI established a Consilium to oversee the work. This group appointed various subgroups, one of which revised the liturgical year.

---

1. Austin Flannery, ed., *Vatican Council II: Constitutions, Decrees, Declarations; The Basic Sixteen Documents* (Collegeville, MN: Liturgical Press, 2014), pp. 150–51.

The Consilium assigned a number to each subgroup. The subgroup on the calendar was foundational to the revision of books like the Roman Missal and the Liturgy of the Hours, so it received the number one.

Annibale Bugnini, an Italian Vincentian and the secretary of the Consilium, served also as the chair of this subgroup, and Ansgar Dirks, a Dominican from the Netherlands teaching at the Dominican Liturgical Institute in Rome, was the subgroup secretary. Other members were Rembert van Doren, the Belgian Benedictine abbot of Mont-César; Johannes Wagner, the German priest who directed the Liturgical Institute at Trier; Canon Aimé-Georges Martimort of the Catholic Institute in Toulouse, France; the French professor Pierre Jounel of the Institut Supérieur de Liturgie in Paris; Agostino Amore, a Franciscan and church historian from the Antonianum in Rome; and Herman Schmidt, a Dutch Jesuit teaching liturgy at the Gregorian University in Rome. The members held their first meeting on January 23, 1965. Within two years Jounel replaced Bugnini as the chair.[2]

The revisers developed their work under the two major headings. Jounel was the specialist behind the Proper of Time, and Amore oversaw the Proper of Saints.

They were greatly helped by work conducted from 1948 to 1960 by the Pian Commission, established and named for Pope Pius XII. The ideas of the earlier group sparked conversation among the later one, which completed its work in 1969.

Terms: "Proper," "Ordinary," "Commons," "Time," "Season," and "Saint"

The liturgical calendar uses several words that appear easy to comprehend but are applied in a particular way. An

---

2. Annibale Bugnini, *The Reform of the Liturgy, 1948–1975*, trans. Matthew J. O'Connell (Collegeville, MN: Liturgical Press, 1990), pp. 305, 939, 944–46, 948–50.

understanding of these terms facilitates interpreting the calendar.

The Roman Missal, the main book for all the ministers at Mass, includes two divisions, each called "Proper," to distinguish them from what is commonly called the "Ordinary." The Ordinary scripts the dialogues, acclamations, and prayers for every celebration. The Propers specify the changeable parts: the antiphons, prayers, prefaces, and blessings, for example, that apply to one date on the calendar, but not to another. The Proper of Time and the Proper of Saints also constitute the main divisions for the calendar's norms.

The Missal and Liturgy of the Hours have sections called "Commons," distinct from "Propers." The Commons are generic texts that apply to a certain category, such as the Dedication of a Church, the Blessed Virgin Mary, and Martyrs, among many others.

People commonly speak of Advent, Christmas, Lent, and Easter as "seasons." However, the English translation of the Missal more specifically calls these "times." As there is Ordinary Time throughout most of the year, so there is Christmas Time and Easter Time. The Missal refers to the other two periods of time more simply: Advent and Lent.

The term "time" distances the liturgical calendar from the natural "seasons" of the year that shape secular calendars: spring, summer, autumn, and winter. The liturgical calendar rests on the paschal mystery, not on the rotation of the earth.

The word "Saints" refers to those whose memory is kept on certain days each year. However, one will also find within the Missal's Proper of Saints some devotional days and—at least in the United States—prayers that pertain to civil observances such as Independence Day.

Understanding these distinctions helps people find pertinent pages in the liturgical books. It also helps apply the key principles in the Table of Liturgical Days.

The Universal Norms on the Liturgical Year and Calendar revised the framework in 1969. Guidance for celebrating the various times and special days is found in the General Instruction of the Roman Missal, the Introduction to the Lectionary, and the General Instruction of the Liturgy of the Hours.

Chapter Two

Revising the Proper of Time

Paschal Mystery at the Center

Christians celebrate the resurrection of the Lord every week on Sunday. They also honor it with special devotion once a year (SC 102). The paschal mystery anchors the week and the year.

About a month before publishing the revised norms, Pope Paul explained their principles. He affirmed the importance of the paschal mystery in Christian worship, writing, "as to both the plan of the Proper of Seasons and of Saints and the revision of the Roman Calendar it is essential that Christ's paschal mystery receive greater prominence in the reform of the liturgical year."[1]

When the revised Universal Norms on the Liturgical Year and Calendar were published on March 21, 1969, the opening

---

1. Paul VI, *Mysterii paschalis*, "Approving the General Norms for the Liturgical Year and the New General Roman Calendar," 14 February 1969, in International Commission on English in the Liturgy (ICEL), *Documents on the Liturgy, 1963–1979: Conciliar, Papal, and Curial Texts*, ed. and trans. Thomas C. O'Brien (Collegeville, MN: Liturgical Press, 1982), 440 (3754), p. 1152.

section reflected this insight. "[T]hroughout the course of the year the Church unfolds the entire mystery of Christ and observes the [heavenly] birthdays of the Saints" (UNLYC 1).

Pope Paul reiterated this organizing principle the following month. "The criterion for [the calendar's] revision was that the elements making up the individual parts of each liturgical season would give clearer expression to the truth that Christ's paschal mystery is the center of all liturgical worship."[2]

The Proper of Saints also served to lift up the paschal mystery. The revisers reassigned many of the saints from their traditional day to the day of their death, their *dies natalis* or "heavenly birthday," when they entered fully into the paschal mystery. If some people thought that Catholics focused overmuch on the crucifixion of Christ, this principle formed an essential corrective: the whole paschal mystery, the death and resurrection of Christ, is the center of faith.

Proper of Time

For the Proper of Time, the revisers raised a number of questions stemming from the calendar then in force. If the paschal mystery is at the center, the end of Holy Week takes preeminence. But when does the Triduum start? And when does it end?

Easter Time culminates with Pentecost. But what should be done with the octave of Pentecost that seemed to expand Easter beyond fifty days?

Lent traditionally lasts forty days, but it embraces more than that. When should Lent begin? On Ash Wednesday? Or on its First Sunday?

---

2. Paul VI, "Address to a consistory," 28 April 1969, DOL 93 (676), p. 238.

Another penitential season preceded Lent. Should the Sundays of Septuagesima, Sexagesima, and Quinquagesima be kept?

The Constitution on the Sacred Liturgy said that Lent had a twofold character: penitential and baptismal (SC 109). How should this be recognized in the calendar?

When should Advent begin and end? How should its final weekdays be observed to underscore the approach of Christmas? Does Christmas Time begin on Christmas Day or with the Vigil of Christmas?

The Epiphany of the Lord was traditionally observed on January 6, but on a weekday very few people participated at Mass. Should Epiphany move to a Sunday?

The remaining Sundays of the year had been grouped as those "after Epiphany" and "after Pentecost." What changes when all of them become Ordinary Time?

In the past the church observed special days of prayer called Rogation and Ember Days. How do these fit inside a revised calendar?

The revisers felt the historic weight of these questions. Their resolution gave the church the Proper of Time in use today.

Sunday

Sunday starts and ends the week. The Constitution on the Sacred Liturgy calls it the eighth day (SC 106). Each Sunday celebrates the close of the previous week and launches the new one. It symbolizes the time outside of time for which Christians long at the end of their days—a completion of time, a perfection of time. The same paragraph of the Constitution urges Christians to observe Sunday with joy and rest.

The opening of the norms proclaims that the church commemorates the resurrection each week on the Lord's Day. Later they recall that the apostles honored the day. "Sunday must be considered the primordial feast day" (UNLYC 4).

Sunday has become the preferred date for different types of celebrations. The Order of Baptism of Children recommends it for the baptism of infants (OBC 9). The Order of Christian Initiation of Adults prefers Sundays for initiation apart from the Easter Vigil (OCIA 27).

The ordinations of priests and of deacons commonly take place on a Saturday, following a tradition predating the Second Vatican Council. However the ritual book recommends these events on a Sunday when great numbers of people may attend (9, 22, 109, 184, 250).[3]

Sunday Mass

Several features characterize a typical Sunday Mass as the primordial feast. All sing or recite the Gloria (GIRM 53), except for Sundays in Advent and Lent, and whenever All Souls' Day (November 2) falls on a Sunday. The celebratory nature of the words express the joy of the day.

The faithful hear three Scripture readings (ILM 66 §1). As weekdays feature only one reading before the gospel, the extra reading celebrates the Lord's Day: The faithful listen three times to the voice of God.

Homilies are expected on Sundays. Priests or deacons frequently deliver them on other days, but preaching especially befits Sunday. The Second Vatican Council declared that the Sunday homily "should not be omitted except for a serious reason" (SC 52).[4] The Sacred Congregation of Rites called for a homily on Sundays and holy days.[5] The Lectionary too

---

3. *Ordination of a Bishop, of Priests, and of Deacons* (Washington, DC: USCCB, 2021).

4. *Vatican II*, p. 136.

5. Sacred Congregation of Rites (Consilium), "Instruction (first) *Inter Oecumenici*: on the orderly carrying out of the Constitution on the Liturgy," no. 53, 26 September 1964, DOL 23 (345), p. 100.

requires a homily at Mass with a congregation on Sunday (ILM 25).

Each Sunday the community professes faith with the Creed (GIRM 68). Unlike the Gloria, the Creed belongs in every Sunday Mass of the year. Linking more closely to the paschal mystery than the Gloria does, the Creed unites the voices of the faithful in common belief. The Missal permits use of either the Nicene or the Apostles' Creed (OM 18–19).

Masses for Various Needs and Occasions are generally excluded from Sundays, but the diocesan bishop may authorize one in Ordinary Time for a good reason (GIRM 374). The same applies to the Second Sunday after the Nativity (Christmas) wherever the Epiphany remains on January 6, freeing up the preceding Sunday.

No other celebrations may be permanently assigned to Sundays (UNLYC 6). When dioceses or religious orders add their own observances, they create "particular calendars." These must harmonize with the general one. The same restriction applies to them: "On Sundays any permanent particular celebration is per se forbidden" (*Calendaria particularia* 2a).[6]

Sunday Liturgy of the Hours

Clergy, others in religious life, and many of the faithful pray the Liturgy of the Hours every day. Formerly known as the Roman Breviary, the Liturgy of the Hours offers a daily suite of prayer services for communal or personal use. These consecrate not only the times of the year and the days of the week, but also several hours of the day.

Psalms are arranged across a four-week cycle. For Christians, the Sunday psalms of the various offices foreshadow

6. Sacred Congregation for Divine Worship, "Introduction *Calendaria particularia,* on the revision of particular calendars and of the propers for office as Masses," no. 2, 24 June 1970, DOL 481 (3997), p. 1245.

the paschal mystery (GILH 129). The same applies to the canticles, antiphons, readings, and prayers. Psalm 118 serves as the responsorial for many Masses in Easter Time, especially during the octave. It is one of the psalms for Daytime Prayer on Sundays.

Although the norms do not draw similar attention to Fridays, the Liturgy of the Hours does, featuring penitential psalms each week (GILH 129). Each Friday puts Psalm 51 at Morning Prayer. Friday recalls the death of the Lord and prepares the faithful for Sunday.

Sunday's Liturgy of the Hours begins on Saturday with Evening Prayer I. It replaces Saturday Evening Prayer and commemorates the belief that the Lord rose from the dead during the night between Saturday and Sunday morning.

People may gather in common to pray any of the offices on any day, but they most appropriately gather for Evening Prayer II on Sundays (GILH 207). Some churches summon the faithful who earlier participated at Mass to praise God again at the close of this holy day.

Each office of the day concludes with a prayer. Often the words pertain to the hour—praising God for the morning or seeking protection at night, for example. But on Sundays the collect from Mass reappears in the Liturgy of the Hours to conclude the offices of Readings, Morning Prayer, Daytime Prayer, and Evening Prayer.

The *Te Deum*, a classic hymn of praise to God, is sung or recited near the end of Sunday's Office of Readings outside Lent. The faithful may expand this office into Vigils, adding three Old Testament canticles and a gospel passage about the resurrection of Jesus. A priest or deacon may preach a homily on that gospel (GILH 73). Although many people who pray the Liturgy of the Hours are unfamiliar with Vigils, it securely links Sunday with the resurrection.

Many parts of the liturgy come with options, but on Sundays certain elements of the Liturgy of the Hours are fixed: antiphons, hymns, readings, responsories, prayers, and psalms, for example (GILH 247). Regarding the psalms, a set used on one Sunday may be replaced with another Sunday set. This may facilitate singing. However, people should move toward a greater understanding of the psalms (247), and, presumably, a wider repertoire of music. In the second edition of the Liturgy of the Hours, the Sunday antiphons for the *Benedictus* and *Magnificat* come from the gospels of the three-year cycle at Mass.

Saturday Evening Mass

In 1965, just before the close of the Second Vatican Council, a growing number of individual bishops petitioned the Holy See to let people of their dioceses satisfy their Sunday obligation at Mass on Saturday evenings. They argued from conditions such as a shortage of priests, population spread, and people's travel on weekends.[7]

In granting approval for these individual cases, the Holy See upheld two principles. First, the Mass on Saturday evening had to be the one for Sunday. Apparently, some people had assumed that a Saturday weekday Mass could account for Sunday.

Second, the Mass was not to omit the homily or prayer of the faithful. The Sacred Congregation of Rites had already required the homily on Sundays. The same document gave instructions for the prayer of the faithful, but now the Congregation was explicitly requiring a homily on Sundays—and on Saturday evenings.[8]

The Congregation reasserted this permission in 1967. To comply with the indult a Saturday evening Mass was to use

7. Sacred Congregation of the Council, "Rescript (Germany), allowing the Sunday Mass on Saturday evening," 19 October 1965, DOL 445 (3830), p. 1171.

8. Sacred Congregation of Rites, "Letter *Impetrata prius* to Cardinal P. Ciriaci, Prefect of the Congregation of the Council, regarding Sunday Mass on Saturday evening," 25 September 1965, DOL 444 (3829), pp. 1170–71.

the Sunday liturgical texts, include a homily, and offer the prayer of the faithful. Special Masses pertained to the Vigils of Christmas and Pentecost. The local ordinary could determine what time on Saturday would satisfy the Sunday obligation. However, the Easter Vigil, because of its special nature, had to begin after dusk.[9]

This permission eventually entered the church's Code of Canon Law. People may fulfill their obligation to participate at Mass on a Sunday or holy day on the day itself or the preceding evening (canon 1248 §1).

Consecutive Solemnities

In 1974 the Sacred Congregation for Divine Worship addressed a practical question concerning anticipated Masses: What happens when a solemnity falls on a Saturday or a Monday? How are the consecutive days to be observed, especially since one Evening Prayer has to replace another?

A principle had already been established for the Liturgy of the Hours. If Evening Prayer II of one day conflicts with Evening Prayer I for the following day, the day that ranks higher in the Table of Liturgical Days takes precedence (UNLYC 61).

Some weekday solemnities have their own Vigil Mass: the Nativity of John the Baptist, Saints Peter and Paul, and the Assumption, for example. If those were to fall on a Monday, the Congregation said in 1974, then a Sunday night Mass would be the Vigil of the solemnity, even if people came to satisfy their Sunday obligation. The local bishop might depart from those norms.[10]

9. Sacred Congregation of Rites, "Instruction *Eucharisticum mysterium*, on worship of the eucharist," 28, 25 May 1967, DOL 179 (1257), p. 407.

10. Sacred Congregation for Divine Worship, "Note: *Instructio 'Eucharisticum mysterium*,'" on the Mass of a Sunday or holy day anticipated on the preceding evening," May 1974, DOL 448 (3837–41), pp. 1177–78.

Ten years later, the Congregation changed its mind. Several conflicts arose for the liturgical year of 1984–1985, and additional factors had emerged. Not all solemnities are days of obligation, so they do not carry the same weight, at least regarding Mass. The Congregation for Divine Worship received this inquiry:

> Some editors of the "Ordo for Celebrating Mass and Fulfilling the Divine Office" proposed questions about the liturgical calendar of the Year of Our Lord 1984–1985 that concern the formularies to be applied for Mass and Evening Prayer of those Saturday or Sunday evenings when a certain solemnity, whether or not it is kept as a day of obligation, occurs on Saturday or Monday.
>
> For on the evening of the first festival day (Saturday or Sunday), a conflict appears in these cases between two liturgical days because the celebration of Sunday and of solemnities "begins already on the evening of the previous day" (see UNLYC 3).[11]

The current rules did not account for those faithful wanting to participate in a Sunday night Mass in Ordinary Time. This pastoral situation prompted these premises:

> 1. As to the celebration of Mass: In the indicated cases, attentive to the general prescript of canon 1248 §1 of the Code of Canon Law, on the possibility of satisfying one's obligation already on "the evening of the preceding day," precedence always must be given to the celebration that must be observed as an obligation, independent of the liturgical rank of the two concurrent celebrations.
>
> 2. As to the celebration of the Divine Office: The arrangement of number 61 in the Universal Norms on the Liturgical Year and Calendar must be kept: "Should on the other hand,

11. Acta Congregationis, "De Calendario Liturgico Exarando Pro Anno 1984–1985," *Notitiae* 219, vol. 20, no. 10 (October 1984): 603.

Vespers (Evening Prayer) of the current day's Office and First Vespers (Evening Prayer I) of the following day be assigned for celebration on the same day, then Vespers (Evening Prayer) of the celebration with the higher rank in the Table of Liturgical Days takes precedence; in cases of equal rank, Vespers (Evening Prayer) of the current day takes precedence."

Nonetheless, in a celebration taking place with the people a departure from the norm will be possible, so that the celebration of Evening Prayer I of the following day will be replaced, when, having taken the law into account, the Mass of the current day may be celebrated.[12]

The Congregation applied these principles to several celebrations occurring that year: the Immaculate Conception, the Presentation of the Lord, the Nativity of John the Baptist, Peter and Paul, the Exaltation of the Holy Cross, All Souls, and the Dedication of the Lateran Basilica. It added these pastoral notes:

The indications presented above cannot consider all individual cases because pastoral needs and different local customs will be found.

Concerning that, the Conferences of Bishops or individual diocesan Bishops, attentive to additional concerns of a pastoral nature, may indicate in individual cases at the beginning of the year in the particular liturgical calendar the praxis to be followed.[13]

Therefore, several factors come into play in determining which liturgies to observe on the evening when Evening Prayer II of one feast conflicts with Evening Prayer I of the next. Is one of these a day of obligation? Is the liturgy in question Evening Prayer or Mass? Will a congregation be present? Do

12. "De Calendario Liturgico Exarando," p. 603.
13. "De Calendario Liturgico Exarando," p. 605.

local customs apply? Has the local bishop made a particular determination? These are weighed each time these concurrences arise in the calendar.

No Fixed Date for Easter

In the Roman Catholic Church, Easter falls on the first Sunday after the first full moon of the northern hemisphere's spring. Among the Eastern Orthodox Churches, the formula changes to the Sunday after the first full moon of Passover. This generally separates the two observances of Easter by one or more weeks. The disagreement lingers as a sorrowful sign of division among Christians, even on a matter as important as when to celebrate the central tenet of faith: the resurrection of Christ.

At the Second Vatican Council, the suggestion to unify the date of Easter appeared as an appendix to the Constitution on the Sacred Liturgy. The bishops were open to it if other Christians were. There would be no point in changing the date of Easter if it did not achieve a unified celebration.

In the same appendix, the bishops considered a perpetual calendar developed for civil society. This would place the dates of the months on the same days each year. The bishops were open to this if the week remained seven days, beginning on Sunday.

For a while, the revisers naively thought that Easter would land on a fixed date. One report from 1965 prepared for it. Writing just after the close of the council, the group drafted a liturgical calendar with dramatic ideas:

> In assigning days of celebration, we kept in mind the possibility that the feast of Easter in the near future could be celebrated on the Second Sunday of the month of April. Therefore the saints that fall during Lent or in the Easter octave have been transferred to another day, as follows:

a) The saints of the month of March, to the same day of the month of February

b) The saints of the month of April to the same day in the month of May.[14]

Several pages outlined the changes. Overall, these observe the pattern already under exploration—reducing the number of saints and introducing a few new ones. However, February included several saints traditionally observed in March. In May, one finds several saints traditionally assigned to April.

The idea went nowhere. The revision intended to more properly assign saints' days with the dates of their deaths. To move some of these traditional observances exactly one month forward or backward now seems wildly arbitrary. Still, the exercise showed that a fixed date of Easter would pose challenges.

In 1966 Pope Paul sent an Epistle to the Patriarch of Alexandria, expressing the Holy Father's eagerness to receive from the Orthodox a proposal on a common date for Easter. He noted that even the Council of Nicaea urged uniformity in the early fourth century.[15] Further study occurred in ensuing years. In 1969 a European Ecumenical Symposium took up the question, generating considerable excitement among participants.[16]

In 1975 Cardinal Johannes Willebrands of the Secretariat for Christian Unity sent a letter to the presidents of the conferences of bishops recommending a specific date for Easter.

14. Consilium ad Exsequendam Constitutionem de Sacra Liturgia, Schemata, n. 138, De Calendario, 8, 30 December 1965, p. 1.

15. Paul VI, "Epistle *Nous nous apprêtons* to His Beatitude Christophoros, Pope and Patriarch of Alexandria, on a common date for Easter," 31 March 1966 (excerpt), DOL 146 (961–62), pp. 318–19.

16. Athénagoras I de Constantinople, "Pour one Commune célébration de la fête de Pâques," *Notitiae* 48, vol. 5, nos. 9–10 (September–October 1969): 391–97.

He observed that very soon, in 1977, the calendars aligned: All Christians would celebrate Easter on the same day, April 10, the Sunday after the second Saturday of April. Willebrands proposed that all Christian bodies adopt that formula going forward.[17]

Two years later, Cardinal Willebrands shared the disappointing results of the consultations. In the West there was considerable agreement to the proposal; however, the Orthodox churches could not reach a consensus and asked for more time. Pope Paul saw the imprudence of changing the date in the West if it did not achieve unification with the East.[18] Variations in the calendar persist. In fact, some parts of the Eastern Orthodox Church follow the Julian calendar, which calculates its days almost two weeks apart from the Gregorian calendar throughout the year.

Rogation and Ember Days

The norms for the calendar explain that Rogation and Ember Days are occasions on which the church "is accustomed to entreat the Lord for the various needs of humanity, especially for the fruits of the earth and for human labor, and to give thanks to him publicly" (UNLYC 45). These underwent considerable change.

In the past, April 25 was the major Rogation Day, and the three weekdays preceding Ascension Thursday were the minor days. Processions, litanies, and fasting characterized these

17. Secretariat for Christian Unity, "Letter *Le deuxième Concile du Vatican* of Cardinal J. Willebrands to presidents of the conferences of bishops, on a common date for Easter," 18 May 1975, DOL 160 (1070–71), pp. 348–50.

18. Secretariat for Christian Unity, "Letter *Dans ma lettre* of Cardinal J. Willebrands, President, to presidents of the conferences of bishops, on a common celebration of Easter," 16 March 1977, DOL 164 (1078–79), pp. 352–53.

days. Ember Days fell during Lent, after Pentecost, in September and within Advent. Each set required special Masses and fasting on Wednesday, Friday, and Saturday. Because these four times of the year had become associated with agricultural harvests, they unified the church in prayer for abundant produce and related needs.

As the church expanded to lands beyond its Mediterranean origins, the universal association of these days with crops weakened. Consequently, the council allowed conferences of bishops to determine days of prayer and purposes for observing them.

The Constitution on the Sacred Liturgy approved the calendar's "pious practices for soul and body, by instruction, prayer, and works of penance and mercy" (SC 105),[19] surely an allusion to Rogation and Ember Days. Therefore, the revisers addressed the issue from the start, and always at the end of questions pertaining to times of the year. The norms imitate the same pattern, putting instructions concerning Rogation and Ember Days at the end. In the earliest extant report, for example, one finds these questions:

> Is it agreed that the major and minor Litanies [the Rogation Days] be celebrated as an option?
> Is it agreed that the Four Seasons [Ember Days] be so arranged that they are celebrated at the beginning of the four seasons of the year (or about the twenty-first of the months of March, June, September and December)?[20]

A month later, Van Doren favored letting the local ordinary make the major and minor litanies optional. He cautioned that the major litanies could conflict with important days in Easter Time and noted that the Rogation Days were celebrated only at Mass, not in the office. Martimort found anomalous observ-

19. *Vatican II*, p. 150.
20. Consilium ad Exsequendam Constitutionem de Sacra Liturgia, Schemata, n. 61, De Calendario, 1, 12 February 1965, p. 3.

ing penitential days during Easter Time. Nocent wanted the litanies placed in the Roman Ritual and the Mass among the Votive Masses of the Missal. Overall, the group favored having particular calendars determine these observances.[21]

Regarding the placement of the Ember Days on the twenty-first of four different months, Martimort objected:

> The question is not agreeable as proposed, nor the declaration raised up on this matter by our most esteemed friend P. Jounel. The matter is far more complicated, and it requires a deeper study, with the collaboration of A. Chavasse. For concerning the nature and method of celebrating the Seasons, it will first have to be determined if they are to be celebrated only in the liturgy, or also through a penitential discipline? And what indeed are the Seasons? Should four be kept? Or should they be reduced to three (because Lent supplies the first month, as it stands from a primeval tradition)?
>
> After these questions there will have to be an answer, and then a discussion of the days could be begun.
>
> Certainly inconvenient would be celebrating them after December 21, as much because of the liturgy as of the holidays and civic vacations in the northern hemisphere.[22]

Later the revisers reinforced these thoughts. They favored moving these days from universal to particular observances:

> 1. Litanies. The "major litanies," invariably fixed on April 25, are suppressed because the reason that could justify their assignment to the feast of St. Mark is completely lacking in our times. If in fact the establishment of April 25 works well for Rome and the West (speaking of a *local* "Roman" Feast), it has no concrete value in other countries where the course of the seasons is completely different.

21. Consilium ad Exsequendam Constitutionem de Sacra Liturgia, Schemata, n. 65, De Calendario, 2, 15 March 1965, p. 14.

22. Schemata, n. 65, p. 15.

The Rogation Days, however, are preserved, but every Episcopal Conference will have to establish what time and what manner may be more fitting to celebrate them appropriately in the territory of their jurisdiction. It is evident that, given the immense geographical extension of the Latin-Roman Rite and the days assigned to the Rogations (Monday to Wednesday preceding the feast of the Ascension), are no longer fitting to many regions of other latitudes.

2. Ember Days. A widespread desire throughout nearly all the Church asks that the celebration of the Ember Days be regulated by the Episcopal Conferences so that they may be established according to the clime and the seasons in a more opportune time. Therefore, adhering to this desire, there has been adopted the principle that the Ember Day Masses be votive, without a particular connection with the unfolding of the seasonal cycle.[23]

These Masses are taken from those for "Various Needs and Occasions" (UNLYC 47). The days, formerly fixed on the universal calendar, are now observed in a variety of ways on a variety of days. In 1971, Pope Paul hoped that the conferences would include among them prayers for vocations in the church.[24] These days opened to new potential intentions.

In the United States, the bishops publish a list of special days of prayer that may affect the choice of Mass, intentions in the universal prayer, and customs in homes, schools and churches. They include some universal days, such as the World Day of Peace on January 1.[25] These descend from Rogation and Ember Days.

23. Consilium ad Exsequendam Constitutionem de Sacra Liturgia, Schemata, n. 260, De Calendario, 16, 30 November 1967, pp. 6–7.

24. Bugnini, p. 321.

25. USCCB Divine Worship, "Days of Prayer and Special Observances," https://www.usccb.org/committees/divine-worship/special-observances.

Chapter Three

Revising the Proper of Saints

Mary

Towering above all other saints is Mary, the mother of Jesus. She is the "most excellent fruit of the redemption," an image of the goal that the faithful seek (SC 103).[1]

The previous calendar teemed with observances of the life of Mary and devotion to her. The revisers maintained five feasts associated with her life: The Immaculate Conception, Nativity, the Visitation, her Assumption, and her role as the Mother of God. The Presentation and the Annunciation would convert into feasts of the Lord.[2]

The calendar would retain certain days of devotion: Our Lady of Lourdes, Our Lady of Mount Carmel, Our Lady of Sorrows, Our Lady of the Rosary. The revisers intended to suppress several other days: The Seven Sorrows, Queen of Heaven, Our Lady of the Snows, the Immaculate Heart of Mary, the Holy Name of Mary, Our Lady of Mercy, and the Presentation of the Blessed Virgin Mary.

---

1. *Vatican II*, p. 149.

2. Consilium ad Exsequendam Constitutionem de Sacra Liturgia, Schemata, n. 188, De Calendario, 11, 22 September 1966, p. 29.

The previous Missal assigned open Saturdays as devotional observances for Mary, with prayers and readings reflecting the times of the year. The revisers put no Votive Masses on certain days but allowed local communities to select them on permitted days. In 1967, Jounel explained,

> It is better to group the office of the Blessed Virgin Mary on Saturday into a votive office, rather than an optional memorial. That is first of all the proper nature of this office. Even more, one does not inscribe a votive office into the calendar. Now, lest it go unmentioned, in the calendar of 1969 to celebrate all the offices of the Blessed Virgin on Saturday would require doing them thirty-two times. This simple enumeration would give Marian devotion a materially excessive importance, contrary to the spirit that has presided over the reform of the Proper of Saints.[3]

The Missal today recommends but does not require the Saturday commemoration of the Blessed Virgin Mary (GIRM 378).

The Ranking of Saints' Days

The church honors the saints, especially the martyrs, who provide a model for Christian life, whose entry into heaven embodies the paschal mystery, and who intercede with God (SC 104). The calendar ranks certain days as solemnities, feasts, and memorials, some of which are optional. All Sundays are solemnities. Days without such ranks are called weekdays.

The revisers considered several options before finalizing the system. Previously the days were ranked by "class." This probably seemed too blandly juridic for a faith-based calendar.

---

3. Consilium ad Exsequendam Constitutionem de Sacra Liturgia, Schemata, n. 237, De Calendario, 15, 14 August 1967, p. 1.

The new categories reveal the value of each day. The revisers explained in 1967,

> Feasts are celebrated according to three ranks: solemnity, (which corresponds to the first class today), feast, (which corresponds to the second class), memorial, (which corresponds to the third class).
>
> A feast that is celebrated as an option is called an optional memorial.[4]

These ranks remain in force. In some instances, days first ranked in one category have moved upward to another. Saints' days holding lesser categories are impeded when they fall on a Sunday.

In English, some people use the word "feast" more broadly. They may speak of the "feast of All Saints" or one's "patronal feast." Such colloquial usage differs from the official designation.

During the last week of Advent, the octave of Christmas, and Lent, another rank appears in the Liturgy of the Hours: commemoration. Because those weekdays rank high, most saints honored on them are optional and receive a limited treatment.

Celebrating Solemnities at Mass

The manner of celebration distinguishes these ranks. At Mass, solemnities have three Scripture readings, as do Sundays (GIRM 357; ILM 66). The Gloria is sung on all solemnities (GIRM 53), and the Creed is recited (GIRM 68), except for the weekday solemnities during the octave of Easter. A bishop may not authorize a Mass for Various Needs and Occasions on a solemnity (GIRM 371, 374). Funeral Masses may be celebrated on most solemnities. Other rules apply on solemnities of obligation, as noted below.

---

4. Consilium ad Exsequendam Constitutionem de Sacra Liturgia, Schemata, n. 213, De Calendario, 12, 1 March 1967, p. 4.

Ritual Masses are permitted on Sundays of Ordinary Time (GIRM 372), but prohibited on solemnities (371, 374), whether or not they are days of obligation. A wedding, for example, may take place during a Mass on November 1, but the congregation is supposed to hear the readings and prayers of All Saints' Day. The same applies to ordinations. Similar instructions apply to the rites of initiation, anointing of the sick and viaticum, and to certain ceremonies pertaining to those in religious orders. However, when anointing of the sick takes place during a solemnity that is not a holy day of obligation, one of the readings may come from those recommended for the Ritual Mass (PCS 134, OUI 81).

The dedication of a new church may take place on most solemnities. Certain ones are excluded because of their centrality to the Christian year: Christmas, Epiphany, Easter, Ascension, and Pentecost.[5]

Celebrating Solemnities at the Liturgy of the Hours

In the Liturgy of the Hours, solemnities outrank all other observances. A votive celebration from the Commons or for the dead cannot take place on a solemnity (GILH 245).

Solemnities begin with Evening Prayer I (GILH 225). The hymn, antiphons, reading, responsory, and concluding prayer are all proper. If a proper text is missing, it comes from the Commons (154, 226). Worshipers may not change these formularies (247).

The psalms are proper, as are their antiphons (GILH 62, 117). These generally repeat psalms for Sundays or that relate to the celebration. At Evening Prayer I, the choices come from the "Laudate Psalms" (Psalms 113, 117, 135, 146, 147A, and 147B). The intercessions may be proper or come from the Common (GILH 134, 226).

---

5. Roman Missal: Ritual Masses, X. For the Dedication of a Church and an Altar.

Morning Prayer on a solemnity repeats the psalms from Sunday of the first week. These appear as old friends inviting worshipers to recall the freshness of the resurrection and the joy of remembering it in the morning. The hymn, antiphons, and reading are proper. Some elements may come from the Commons, such as the intercessions (GILH 134, 226–27).

For Daytime Prayer, the psalms break from the usual cycle and return to "complementary psalmody," drawn from the "Gradual Psalms" (Psalms 120–28) and traditionally prayed during the middle hours of the day. Proper antiphons frame each of these to color the day. On solemnities the weekday hymn is generally used (GILH 82, 229).

The Office of Readings on solemnities has a proper hymn, antiphons, psalms, readings, and responsories. The second reading may introduce the saint of the day or present a passage written by the saint. On solemnities this office includes the *Te Deum* and the prayer of the day (GILH 68, 228).

As on Sundays, the Office of Readings may expand into Vigils (GILH 71, 73). Whereas the gospel for Vigils on Ordinary Time Sundays recalls the resurrection of Christ, the one for a solemnity comes from a designated place in the Lectionary for Mass. For example, for the solemnity of the Sacred Heart, which always falls on a Friday when a reading about the resurrection would not so naturally connect, those praying Vigils draw the gospel from one of those offered at Mass in other years of the cycle. A homily may follow.

On solemnities, the concluding prayer for Morning Prayer, Daytime Prayer, and Evening Prayer is the same as the collect for Mass (GILH 199). The one concluding Night Prayer still pertains to that hour (198).

The two Night Prayers on solemnities match those following Evening Prayer I and II of Sunday. However, each concludes with a prayer that does not refer to celebrating the resurrection that day (GILH 230).

Celebrating Solemnities of Obligation

Certain solemnities are set aside as days of precept when the faithful are obliged to participate at Mass. A conference of bishops chooses from the following list: Christmas, Epiphany, Ascension, the Most Holy Body and Blood of Christ, Mary the Mother of God, the Immaculate Conception, the Assumption, St. Joseph, the apostles Peter and Paul, and All Saints (canon 1246, §2).

In the revision, four days are to be observed by all the faithful: Christmas, Epiphany, Ascension, and the Most Holy Body and Blood of Christ. However, only the first of these had to remain on its traditional day; conferences of bishops could transfer the other three to another day, but only to a Sunday, so that the whole church celebrates these mysteries every year. The revisers did not recommend transferring other days to Sunday (such as the Assumption or All Saints) because of the priority given the paschal mystery of Christ over other observances (SC 102 and 106). Local churches desiring to move a day such as All Saints to align with a day on the secular calendar may request it from the Holy See.[6] Although nothing came of it, the revisers also considered moving holy days to Saturdays in Israel and to Fridays in Islamic countries.[7]

The United States observes several days of obligation, though with some exceptions.[8] Three of them lose their obligatory status if they fall on a Monday or a Saturday: Mary the Mother of God, the Assumption of the Blessed Virgin Mary, and All Saints. This relieves clergy and laity of excessive duties on weekends. Two of these days are always obligatory: The Immaculate Conception of the Blessed Virgin Mary, because

---

6. *Calendaria particularia* 36, DOL 481 (4031), p. 1253.

7. Bugnini, pp. 322–24.

8. USCCB Canonical Affairs & Church Governance: Complementary Norms, "Canon 1246, §2—Holy Days of Obligation," https://www.usccb.org /committees/canonical-affairs-church-governance/complementary-norms #tab--canon-1246-§2-holy-days-of-obligation.

she is patroness of the country under that title, and Christmas. Even when these dates fall on a Monday or a Saturday, the obligation remains.

The conference of bishops could not reach a national agreement relative to the Ascension of the Lord, traditionally observed on the fortieth day after Easter. Consequently, throughout most of the country, the Ascension replaces the Seventh Sunday of Easter. More of the faithful will therefore celebrate this important event in the life of Christ. However, in some dioceses, the faithful are accustomed to the traditional day, and their bishops have kept Ascension on Thursday. These are the archdioceses and dioceses within the Ecclesiastical Provinces of Boston, Hartford, New York, Omaha, and Philadelphia.[9]

In England and Wales, the following days are holy days that, if they fall on a Saturday or a Monday, transfer to the adjacent Sunday: Epiphany, Peter and Paul, Assumption, and All Saints.[10] Scotland does the same for Peter and Paul and the Assumption. If November 1 falls on a Saturday in England and Wales, All Souls moves to Monday, November 3, but in Scotland All Saints moves to Sunday, and when falling on a Monday, it remains a holy day of obligation.[11]

As on Sundays, there is to be a homily at Mass celebrated with the people (GIRM 66). Originally, two days of obligation allowed the faithful to receive communion a second time: Christmas and Easter, as both of them have a Vigil Mass.[12]

9. USCCB, Committee on Divine Worship, "The Liturgical Celebration of Consecutive Feast Days (and Nights)," *Newsletter* LII (May–June 2016): 19. Office of Divine Worship, Archdiocese of Newark: "Transfer of the Solemnity of the Ascension of the Lord," https://rcan.org/transfer-of-the-solemnity-of-the-ascension-of-the-lord/.

10. "Liturgical Calendar: Frequently Asked Questions," https://www.liturgyoffice.org.uk/Calendar/FAQ.shtml.

11. Archdiocese of Glasgow, "Holy Days of Obligation," http://www.cathedralgl.org/uploads/3/8/7/2/3872483/holy_day_of_obligation.pdf.

12. *Inter Oecumenici*, no. 60, DOL 23 (352), p. 103.

Later the Code of Canon Law permitted the faithful to receive communion at a second eucharistic celebration, regardless of the day (canon 917).

As noted above, certain rules apply to consecutive solemnities. In the United States, these concern only the Immaculate Conception and Christmas, because Ascension never falls on Saturday or Monday, and because the obligation is lifted from the other three solemnities when they do.

Funerals may not be celebrated on solemnities of obligation (GIRM 380). In the United States, when the obligation is lifted on a Monday or a Saturday, a funeral Mass may take place.

Celebrating Days without Rank

Neither Ash Wednesday nor All Souls' Day is ranked as a solemnity. However, they are listed respectively in the second and third tiers in the table of liturgical days. At Mass, each has three readings during the Liturgy of the Word, but neither includes the Gloria.

Celebrating Feasts

Feast days rank just below solemnities. At Mass, the Gloria is said or sung, even if the feast falls during Advent or Lent (GIRM 53). Instead of two readings, only one precedes the proclamation of the gospel (GIRM 357). The antiphons and prayers of the Missal are proper to a feast.

In the Liturgy of the Hours, feasts have no Evening Prayer I. An exception is made for feasts of the Lord that fall on Sunday (GILH 231). Many other features resemble those for solemnities (231). In the Office of Readings the psalms are proper, as are their antiphons (62). The second reading pertains to the feast (67, 154), and the *Te Deum* precedes the prayer (69). This office may be expanded into Vigils, with a pertinent gospel from the Lectionary. For example, those extending the Office of Readings on the Conversion of St. Paul use canticles from the Common of Apostles and a gospel from various options, such as Mark 3:13-19, from Friday of the Second Week in Ordinary Time.

The hymns at the principal hours may pertain to the feast (GILH 173). Antiphons for the psalms at Morning and Evening Prayer are proper (117, 134). The Canticles of Zechariah and of Mary use proper antiphons, or, if needed, from the Common. At Daytime Prayer, the psalms come from the current weekday (134, 232). The readings at Morning and Evening Prayer are proper for feasts (157). Some feasts have specially composed intercessions (183). The prayer that concludes Morning, Daytime, and Evening Prayer is the collect of the feast day Mass (199–200). No changes happen to Night Prayer (233).

Celebrating Feasts of the Lord

Although there is no rank between "solemnities" and "feasts," certain days are "feasts of the Lord" and receive special treatment. Unlike other feasts, when they fall on a Sunday, they replace the liturgy of the day. The feasts of the Lord are the Baptism of the Lord, the Presentation of the Lord, the Transfiguration of the Lord, the Exaltation of the Holy Cross, the Dedication of the Lateran Basilica, and the Holy Family of Jesus, Mary and Joseph.

An early draft added others to this list: The Octave of the Nativity, the Name of Jesus, the Epiphany, the Annunciation of the Lord, the Most Precious Blood, Christ the King, the Dedication of the Basilicas of Peter and Paul, and the Nativity of the Lord.[13]

---

13. Consilium ad Exsequendam Constitutionem de Sacra Liturgia, Schemata, n. 132, De Calendario, 7, 3 December 1965, p. 8.

When a feast of the Lord falls on a Sunday, Evening Prayer I is celebrated on Saturday (GILH 205, 231). Its Sunday Mass includes a second reading after the responsorial psalm before the gospel, and all recite the Creed—but not when the feast of the Lord is a weekday. When combining an office with Mass, Evening Prayer I may be included only in the Saturday evening Mass, not earlier (96). In general, many of the rules for solemnities apply (217). Formularies assigned to feasts of the Lord may not be changed (247).

When a feast of the Lord falls on a weekday, only one reading precedes the gospel in most countries, but not in the United States. All three readings are still proclaimed on a weekday, according to the spoken preference of the Bishops' Committee on Divine Worship.

Celebrating Memorials

Most saints' days are memorials. These have a minimal impact on the day. Most importantly, the collect of the saint from Mass is repeated at Morning and Evening Prayer. These are commonly called "obligatory memorials" although the Missal's Proper of Time simply calls them "memorials." Nonetheless, the term "obligatory memorial" appears elsewhere in the Missal and in the Liturgy of the Hours.

At Mass, the antiphons and prayers are proper to the day or drawn from the pertinent Common of Saints. Even the preface of the eucharistic prayer follows the category of the saint (martyr, pastor, or member of a religious community, for example). The Lectionary provides alternative Scripture readings, but those of the weekday are preferred: "For Memorials of Saints, unless proper readings are given, the readings assigned for the weekday are normally used. In certain cases, particularized readings are provided, that is to say, readings which highlight some particular aspect of the spiritual life or activity of the Saint. The use of such readings is not to be insisted upon, unless a pastoral reason truly suggests it" (GIRM 357).

This principle gained support in the earliest days of the reform. In 1965 Dirks wrote, "Lest the celebration of Mass in honor of the Saints become excessively boring, and in order to avoid monotony, a continuous reading from the course of Scripture may be retained for weekday Masses, applying even to the Masses of the Saints, unless they enjoy a proper formula."[14]

The Lectionary makes an exception if the saint appears within a biblical passage; then, that proper reading becomes obligatory. For example, on the memorial of Saints Timothy and Titus, the first reading must come from either the Second Letter to Timothy or the Letter to Titus, but the gospel usually comes from the weekday. This principle applies to Barnabas; Martha, Mary, and Lazarus; the passion of John the Baptist; and the Holy Guardian Angels.

The priest and deacon wear vestments of a color appropriate to the saint of the day; for example, red for martyrs or white for holy women. These Masses do not include the Gloria or the Creed. At weekday Mass in Lent, an obligatory memorial becomes optional and may be observed only with its collect (GIRM 355a).

The Missal offers no restrictions for the celebration of Ritual Masses on memorials. For example, a wedding Mass may be celebrated with all appropriate readings and prayers in place of an assigned memorial of a saint.

In the Liturgy of the Hours, memorials have a small though important impact. The concluding oration at Morning and Evening Prayer is the collect from Mass (GILH 199). A memorial usually does not affect the psalms, which come from the current day (62) Some exceptions are Agnes, the passion of John the Baptist, Our Lady of Sorrows, the Holy Guardian Angels, Our Lady of the Rosary, and Martin of Tours, all of whom at Morning and Evening Prayer have special psalms and

---

14. Ansgar Dirks, "Principia seu criteria generalia ad calendarium liturgicum instaurandum," *Notitiae* 6, vol. 1, no. 6 (June 1965): 151.

antiphons, readings, responsories, and antiphons for the gospel canticles. The Holy Guardian Angels have special intercessions at Morning and Evening Prayer. Together with Barnabas, the Angels have special readings at Daytime Prayer. Barnabas's day has no special psalms and antiphons, but his Morning and Evening Prayer use special readings, responsories, and antiphons for the gospel canticle and intercessions.

A memorial has no impact on Daytime Prayer and Night Prayer. The sole exceptions are for Barnabas and the Guardian Angels.

Some memorials have proper antiphons to the psalms, but more have them for the canticles of Zechariah and Mary (GILH 118–19). If these gospel canticles have no proper antiphons, then worshipers choose one either from the Commons or from the current weekday (119).

Celebrating Optional Memorials

Optional memorials may be completely omitted. If they are observed, their celebration looks no different from a regular memorial, except during Lent.

Optional memorials came into being with the revisions. Formerly, if more than one memorial occupied the same day, all of them were observed. The new rules allow one memorial a day (GIRM 54, GILH 221). When two occur on the same day, both become optional, as may happen, for example, with a movable observance such as the Immaculate Heart of Mary.

In reviewing the proposed calendar in 1967 and 1968, the Congregation for the Doctrine of the Faith hesitated to approve many optional memorials. They feared that permitting the omission of certain saints' days would diminish their devotion among the faithful.[15] However, the concept proved practical and popular. It allowed various regions to adopt or omit additional saints.

---

15. Bugnini, p. 311. Future references to the Congregation and Paul VI at this time refer to Bugnini, pp. 311–13.

When a memorial has been inscribed into a particular calendar, such as that of a diocese or a religious order, and when it conflicts with another memorial on the general calendar, both become optional. However, the observance of the particular one is preferred (GIRM 355).

Votive Masses of the mysteries of Jesus Christ, the Blessed Virgin Mary, and of any saint in the Martyrology (see below) may replace an optional memorial on a weekday (GIRM 375; GILH 244). Any Mass for Various Needs and Occasions or any Ritual Mass may do the same (GIRM 377).

In practice, the decision to celebrate an optional memorial at Mass usually falls to the priest. However, he is to make this decision while thinking of the people. "Hence in arranging the celebration of Mass, the Priest should be attentive rather to the common spiritual good of the People of God than to his own inclinations. He should also remember that choices of this kind are to be made in harmony with those who exercise some part in the celebration, including the faithful, as regards the parts that more directly pertain to them" (GIRM 352).

In celebrating the Liturgy of the Hours, a similar point applies: "In deciding whether to celebrate an optional memorial in an Office celebrated with the people or in common, account should be taken of the common good or the genuine devotion of the congregation, not simply that of the person presiding" (GILH 220).

On Saturdays when no higher observance impedes it, the Mass and the Liturgy of the Hours may come from the Commons of Mary (GIRM 378; GILH 240). The revisers wanted to keep this traditional practice without making it obligatory.

Celebrating Commemorations

When an obligatory or optional memorial falls during one of the privileged times of the calendar, the Liturgy of the Hours treats it as a commemoration (GILH 234, 238). This applies to saints' days during the last week of Advent, the octave of Christmas, and the weekdays of Lent.

During these privileged times, if the saint is to be observed, special rules apply:

> a. in the Office of Readings, after the patristic reading (with its responsory) from the Proper of Seasons, a proper reading about the saint (with its responsory) may follow, with the concluding prayer of the saint;
>
> b. at Morning and Evening Prayer, the ending of the concluding prayer may be omitted and the saint's antiphon (from the Proper or Common) and prayer added. (GILH 239)

Thus on these occasions a third reading is permitted at the Office of Readings. When that office is celebrated independent of others such as Morning Prayer, the prayer of the saint may conclude it.

To conclude Morning Prayer on St. Patrick's Day, for example, the leader recites the prayer of the Lent weekday, omits "Through our Lord Jesus Christ . . . ," adds the antiphon assigned to March 17 ("Go, and teach all nations, baptizing them in the name of the Father, and of the Son, and of the Holy Spirit."), and then continues with the complete prayer of the saint, "God our Father, you sent Saint Patrick to preach your glory to the people of Ireland . . . ," concluding with "Grant this through our Lord Jesus Christ . . . "

Celebrating Weekdays

On weekdays without any memorials, feasts, or solemnities, the liturgy assumes a simplified pace. During Advent, Christmas, Lent, and Easter, the readings and prayers at Mass and the other texts of the Liturgy of the Hours all explore the nature of these times and provide entry points into the events of the life of Jesus.

On Ordinary Time weekdays, the prayers at Mass and the Liturgy of the Hours are more generic. For example, the proper prayers from the third week in Ordinary Time do nothing to prepare the faithful for the fourth week. In fact, on weekdays, the presidential prayers may come from any Ordinary Time Sunday. A random series of themes meanders through the largest part of the year. The readings at Mass, however, follow a plan.

Occasionally a day requiring its own readings interrupts the semicontinuous weekday readings. On these occasions, worshipers may hear the omitted reading on the following day, creating a more extended passage that continues the flow of the week's readings (GIRM 358). This option may aid daily homilies and prayer.

Celebrating Ritual Masses on Weekdays

Ritual Masses may replace most other celebrations. These include sacraments such as confirmation and marriage, as well as other rituals, such as the Rite of Election, the scrutinies, and Viaticum (communion for the dying).

The Lectionary provides special readings for all Ritual Masses. This feature, unknown in the previous Missal, has enriched these celebrations.

The priest and deacon wear vestments of an appropriate color. The scrutinies call for violet, and confirmation calls for red. However, the Missal allows white or a festive color for any Ritual Mass (GIRM 347).

The Missal prohibits Ritual Masses on certain days: Sundays of Advent, Lent, and Easter, solemnities, Ash Wednesday, Holy Week, the Octave of Easter, and All Souls' Day (GIRM 372). Other restrictions apply to individual Masses.

Ritual Masses are by their nature connected to a particular celebration (GIRM 372). Their prayers and readings may not otherwise substitute for those assigned to a weekday (377).

For example, on an Ordinary Time weekday, the priest may not offer the Mass of Confirmation if no one is being confirmed.

Celebrating Masses for Various Needs and Occasions on Weekdays

The Missal contains a section of Masses and Prayers for Various Needs and Occasions. This rich collection addresses a range of circumstances. These fall into three divisions: For Holy Church, For Civil Needs, and For Various Occasions. Christian unity, political leaders, weather events, and spiritual welfare arise among the many themes of this section. The collects are useful even outside Mass when someone seeks words to pray about some timely concern.

These Masses are allowed on weekdays of Ordinary Time (GIRM 355c). The diocesan bishop may direct or permit them on Sundays in Ordinary Time, but not on solemnities, Ash Wednesday, Holy Week, the Octave of Easter or All Souls' Day (GIRM 374). A priest may use these Masses even on obligatory memorials, weekdays of Advent before December 17, weekdays of Christmas after January 2, and weekdays of Easter after its octave if in his judgment there is a grave pastoral need (376).

A special eucharistic prayer may be used. It appears in the Missal near the end of the Order of Mass. Tabs protrude from most missals by the eucharistic prayers so that the priest may easily locate them. This is generally considered one eucharistic prayer with four variations, entitled The Church on the Path of Unity; God Guides His Church along the Way of Salvation; Jesus, the Way to the Father; and Jesus, Who Went About Doing Good. Headings recommend Masses appropriate for each variation, which has its own preface and unique middle section. This prayer is not expressly forbidden on Sundays, but it was composed for these weekday celebrations.

If the Mass has a penitential theme, the priest and deacon may wear violet. Otherwise, they may wear white. However, they may wear the color appropriate to the day or time of year (GIRM 347). During Ordinary Time, for example, they may wear green even while celebrating a Mass such as the one "For the Family."

The readings are ordinarily taken from the weekday so that those at daily Mass hear the prepared sequence of passages (GIRM 355). This fulfills the church's wish that people become familiar with a wider portion of Sacred Scripture (SC 51).

Celebrating Votive Masses on Weekdays

Votive Masses nourish devotion to the mysteries of the Lord, or they honor the Blessed Virgin Mary, the angels, or the saints (GIRM 375). Mysteries of the Lord include the Mercy of God, the Mystery of the Holy Cross, the Most Holy Eucharist, the Most Precious Blood of Our Lord Jesus Christ, and the Most Sacred Heart of Jesus. Votive Masses pertaining to Mary regard a variety of her titles. Votive Masses for various saints include Joseph and the apostles.

Votive Masses may be celebrated on weekdays in Ordinary Time, even on an optional memorial (GIRM 355c, 375). For pastoral advantage, the priest may celebrate one of these in place of an obligatory memorial, on weekdays of Advent before December 17, weekdays of Christmas after January 2, and weekdays of Easter after the octave (376). The ordinary may direct or permit these on other days except solemnities; the Sundays of Advent, Lent, and Easter; Ash Wednesday; Holy Week; the Easter octave, and All Souls.

The priest and deacon wear a suitable color, usually white, though the Missal designates red for honoring the apostles. Ministers may always wear the color of the day (GIRM 347). During Ordinary Time, for example, if the priest opts for a Votive Mass of the Blessed Virgin Mary, he may still wear green, especially when the readings remain those of the Ordinary Time weekday.

External Solemnities

In the Liturgy of the Hours, on an open weekday, a votive office for some saint could be celebrated, drawing from the Commons. Such an office may be celebrated in whole or in part on an "external solemnity" (GILH 245).

The previous Missal used this term for special Masses in two different circumstances: an important day impeded by one of greater rank, or an important weekday inconvenient for the faithful to gather. In the first instance, in addition to the Mass of greater rank, an impeded Mass—or two of them—could be added. In the second instance, the Mass could transfer to Sunday or another convenient day. Permission for such an external solemnity did not apply to the office.[16]

GILH 245 permits celebrating the office in addition to the Mass on an external solemnity. However, in the revised calendar, the first instance no longer applies. An impeded celebration cannot take place on its normal day. Instead, it may become a Votive Mass on a nearby unimpeded day. In the second instance, an important weekday such as the parish patronal solemnity or anniversary of the dedication of its church may transfer to a more convenient Sunday in Ordinary Time, and the transfer may apply to all the Masses at which the people participate (UNLYC 58). In that case, GILH 245 implies transferring also the office of the solemnity. The term "external solemnity" appears nowhere in the Missal.

Celebrating Masses for the Dead on Weekdays

Masses for the Dead also aid those who are alive. The living receive comforting hope as they implore divine aid for the dead (GIRM 379).

---

16. *General Rubrics of the Roman Missal* 356, https://www.divinum officium.com/www/horas/Help/Rubrics/Missal1960%20rubrics.html.

Prior to the liturgical reforms, a priest frequently offered a Mass for the Dead on open weekdays. The Missal now requests that Masses for the Dead be used in moderation because every Mass benefits the living and the dead, and every eucharistic prayer commemorates the dead (GIRM 355).

First among Masses for the Dead are funerals. Funeral Masses may be celebrated on any day except solemnities of obligation; Sundays of Advent, Lent, and Easter; Holy Thursday and the Paschal Triduum (GIRM 380). Other Masses follow the news of someone's death or supply prayers on the day of burial or on the anniversary of someone's death. These may be used on any weekday, on an obligatory memorial, but not on Ash Wednesday or during Holy Week (GIRM 381).

The readings for a funeral Mass are usually taken from those recommended in the Lectionary. Nonetheless, a priest may choose readings for a special group, as long as these come from somewhere in the Lectionary (GIRM 358). Readings at a funeral depart from the daily Mass readings. In other Masses for the Dead, the readings of the day would fittingly remain.

In Masses for the Dead, the priest may use the special formulas to Eucharistic Prayers II and III. These are permitted in a Mass "for a particular deceased person" and for "Masses for the Dead" respectively (GIRM 365b, c), and the Order of Mass permits them for "Masses for the Dead" in general, but they are most commonly heard at funerals.

In the United States the priest and deacon may wear violet, white, or black. The options also pertain to funerals (GIRM 346d). White vesture probably became widespread in resonance with the paschal mystery.

Reducing the Number of Saints on Weekdays

The revisers reduced the large number of saints on the calendar. The council had praised the traditional honor accorded the saints, yet it advised that "the celebration of many of them should be consigned to particular churches, nations, or religious families. Only those should be extended to the universal church which commemorate saints of truly universal importance" (SC 111).[17]

From the beginning the revisers followed norms: the saints should represent the universality of the church, duplications of devotional days should be diminished, saints sharing the same day should become alternates, and the categories of saints should be revised, including both clergy and laity.[18]

The revisers offered reasons for omitting certain saints:

> a) either nothing is known of them except their name alone
> b) or if the *passions* [biographies] exist, these writings in the judgment of experts were merely invented or abound in fables
> c) devotion to them is found nowhere, and only those who are more learned know about them from literary sources (hagiographic or historical).[19]

A later draft established five conditions for removing saints from the calendar: Saints who carry grave hagiographic difficulties, founders of "titles" (local churches) in Rome, saints of local interest, pope saints, and Roman martyrs. These criteria eliminated nearly 150 saints from the Missal.[20]

Devotional Days on Weekdays

The revisers took a negative view toward some devotional days. Early on they asked, "Should the so-called 'devotional'

17. *Vatican II*, p. 152.
18. Dirks, pp. 151–52.
19. [Consilium ad Exsequendam Constitutionem de Sacra Liturgia,] Schemata, n. 109, De Calendario, 6, "De Calendario ecclesiae universalis: Proprium de Sanctis" [25 September 1965], p. 2.
20. Schemata, n. 260, pp. 51–61.

feasts be generally suppressed, especially if they establish duplications of other feasts?"[21]

The revisers explained, "The feasts of devotion do not commemorate an event in the mystery of salvation but celebrate either an aspect of this mystery or a title under which the Lord, the Madonna, or the saints may be invoked. . . . Their popularity varies according to regions."[22]

They offered examples of double observances in the previous missal: two feasts of the Most Precious Blood, one of the Most Pure Heart of Mary and another of the Purity of Mary, and one of the Sorrowful Mother and another of the Seven Sorrows of the Blessed Virgin Mary.

They recommended that several remain unchanged: the Most Holy Trinity, the Body of the Christ, and the Sacred Heart of Jesus. They moved the feasts of the Holy Family and of Christ the King of the Universe. "The Holy Name of Jesus would be commemorated in the gospel of January 1. The feast of the Most Precious Blood would be suppressed, and its formulary would transfer into the Votive Masses."[23]

They listed the feasts of Mary added to the calendar after Pope Pius V: The Most Holy Name of Mary (1683), the Blessed Virgin Mary of Mercy (1696), the Most Holy Rosary of the Blessed Virgin Mary (1716), the Blessed Virgin Mary of Mount Carmel (1725), the Sorrowful Mother (1727), the Seven Sorrows of the Blessed Virgin Mary (1814), the Apparition of the Immaculate Blessed Virgin (1907), the Motherhood of the Blessed Virgin Mary (1931), and Blessed Mary the Virgin Queen (1954). Numerous other days were celebrated

---

21. Consilium ad Exsequendam Constitutionem de Sacra Liturgia, Schemata, n. 71, De Calendario, 3, 30 March 1965, p. 2.

22. Schemata, n. 260, p. 45.

23. Schemata, n. 260, p. 46.

extensively. The group recommended these become optional Votive Masses.[24]

Adding Saints

To complement the diminished number of saints, the revisers recommended additional ones for diversity, making it more representative of faithful around the word and in every age. From the beginning, revisers sought to avoid the exclusionary appearance that the "universal" calendar was actually "a Roman calendar or a Mediterranean calendar."[25]

The revisers proposed martyrs of the primitive church with reliable biographies: Fructuosus and companions of Spain; Pothinus, Blandina, and companions of France; Roman protomartyrs; and Speratus and companions of Africa. Of these, only the Romans survived the reductions.[26]

Modern martyrs were all retained: Paul Miki and companions of Japan, Peter Chanel of Oceania, Charles Lwanga and companions of Uganda, John Fisher and Thomas More of England, Maria Goretti of Italy, and Isaac Jogues and companions of Canada and the United States. Four non-martyr saints were also recommended and accepted: Ansgar of Sweden and Denmark, Columban of Ireland, Toribius of Peru, and Martin de Porres of Peru.

The revisers diversified saints by geographic origins and centuries. They enumerated twenty-five days honoring saints from Rome, six from Great Britain, one from Czechoslovakia, seventeen from France, eight from Germany, two from Greece and the Slavic regions, two from Ireland, thirteen from Spain, one from the Netherlands, two from Hungary, thirty-eight from Italy, one from Yugoslavia, three from Portugal, four

24. Schemata, n. 260, pp. 49–50.
25. Dirks, p. 152.
26. Schemata, n. 260, p. 62.

from Poland, one from Russia, two from Scandinavia, four from Egypt, six from North Africa, one from Uganda, four from Palestine, three from Syria, six from Turkey, one from China, one from Japan, one from Canada and the United States, three from Peru, and one from Oceania.

In the chronological list, they tallied two from the first century, five from the second, twelve from the third, twenty-six from the fourth, eight from the fifth, four from the sixth, five from the seventh, three from the eighth, two from the ninth, one from the tenth, eight from the eleventh, five from the twelfth, twelve from the thirteenth, four from the fourteenth, seven from the fifteenth, seventeen from the sixteenth, seventeen from the seventeenth, three from the eighteenth, six from the nineteenth, and two from the twentieth.

Only a few recently canonized saints have been added to the general calendar since the revision. New saints more regularly populate regional calendars.

Commons of Saints by Category

Many saints fit into categories. The previous Missal grouped the Commons of Saints as follows: one or more popes; a martyr outside Easter Time: a pope martyr, a non-pope martyr; several martyrs outside Easter Time; one or more martyrs during Easter Time; a confessor pope; a doctor (both bishop and non-bishop); a non-pope confessor; an abbot; a virgin and martyr; several virgin martyrs; a simple virgin; a non-virgin martyr; and a non-virgin non-martyr.

After these came two more Commons: for the Dedication of a Church and for the Blessed Virgin Mary. The anniversary of a church's dedication, the Missal noted, is a feast of the Lord.

The revisers desired new categories and made these recommendations:

a) The apostles, who are the foundation of the Church, and the Evangelists are all to be retained in the calendar of the universal Church.

b) Of the more ancient martyrs are to be retained or inserted 1) those who have a universal devotion or have a universal importance for the life of the Church; 2) those chosen from the various groups of clergy and lay faithful.

c) The greater doctors are to be retained; of the lesser ones there will be a conversation about each.

d) All the saints who carry universal importance for the universal Church because of their unique form of spirituality or apostolate, started by them and spread throughout the whole Church, are to be retained.[27]

The current Missal regroups the Commons of the Saints. It begins with the Anniversary of the Dedication of a Church, putting this feast of the Lord at the head. Then come the Commons of the Blessed Virgin Mary, the most highly honored of all saints. The revisers justified this "total innovation" of sequence because "the theological logical reason seems to imply a new order, as does our contemporary piety in which we honor the Blessed Virgin Mary the Mother of God, and by which we celebrate the feasts of the Church with a certain new love."[28]

The other Commons resemble the order of the previous Missal, often subdivided by prayers for individuals and for several saints: martyrs outside Easter Time or during Easter Time, missionary martyrs, a virgin martyr, a holy woman martyr; pastors who were a pope or a bishop, a bishop, a pastor; founders of churches; missionaries; doctors; and virgins. Finally there is a grouping of holy men and women (all categories); monks and religious (an abbot, a monk, a nun, a religious); those who practiced works of mercy; educators; and holy women.

27. Dirks, p. 152.
28. Schemata, 153, p. 5.

These categories are not restrictive. In particular calendars, dioceses and religious orders may supply other titles for the saints to suggest their state in life, such as "king," "father" or "mother."[29]

Determining a Saint's Day

The revisers shifted the days for observing certain saints. They favored the *dies natalis*, the saint's "birthday" into heaven. Sometimes this raised a conflict. For example, they wanted to minimize the number of saints during Lent, to highlight that season and to celebrate the saint outside a time of penitence. They researched alternative dates. They wrote, "The *dies natalis* of the saints in general must be *strictly* retained. Some exceptions have been made if the *dies natalis* is unknown (in which case another day has been selected having some relation with the same saint), but *especially* in *the time of Lent*."[30]

In local calendars the same principles apply. The exact date of death is preferred. If that date is unknown, then another date associated with the saint may be assigned, "for example, the date of the discovery, exhumation, or transfer of the body, or the date of canonization."[31] A traditional date may be retained because of devotions, traditions, or civil custom.

The Roman Martyrology

The Roman Martyrology is the complete list of saints. Although the title suggests only martyrs, it includes them all. The book lists up to more than dozens of names per day.

---

29. *Calendaria particularia* 27, DOL 481 (4022), p. 1252.
30. Schemata, n. 109, p. 1.
31. *Calendaria particularia* 21, DOL 481 (4016), p. 1250.

Since the council, the Martyrology has been revised twice.[32] Work on an English translation has required countless hours. A book of such detail raises questions: Are the dates correct? How should place names be listed, especially when, over time, different countries governed the same city? How can the book be updated when the Dicastery for the Causes of Saints adds saints each year?

Those researching the day to celebrate a saint will find a listing in the Martyrology. Any of its saints may be honored on their day at Mass and in the Liturgy of the Hours when no day of higher rank impedes it (GIRM 355 b, c; GILH 244).

The Anniversary of Dedication

The anniversary of the dedication of a church is a solemnity in that place. Each parish, therefore, has a unique solemnity associated with the dedication day of its church.

The parish has several options according to the Sacred Congregation for Divine Worship. It may choose the anniversary date or the day when the people keep the festival. In Ordinary Time it may choose "the Sunday closer to this anniversary day." Or the parish may choose "the Sunday before the solemnity of All Saints," to show the connection between the earthly and heavenly church.[33] This aids churches whose dedication date is unknown.

In the cathedral, the same applies. Additionally, the anniversary of the dedication of the cathedral is a feast in the parishes of the diocese. The Congregation explained,

> The anniversary celebration of the dedication of the cathedral church must be carried out in a degree of a solemnity

---

32. The edition in force is *Martyrologium Romanum, Editio altera* (Vatican City: Typis Vaticanis, 2004).

33. "Documentorum explanatio: De Celebratio annuali dedicationis ecclesiae," *Notitiae* 71, vol. 8, no. 3 (March 1972): 103.

in the cathedral church itself, but in the degree of a feast in the other churches of the diocese on the annual day on which the church was consecrated. When this day is perpetually impeded, then the celebration is assigned to a nearby day that is open.

Nonetheless, it is appropriate that on the day of celebration the faithful of the entire diocese gather to celebrate the Eucharist together with the bishop.[34]

The practice shows the significance of another day: the Dedication of the Lateran Basilica, the cathedral of Rome and mother of all churches in the world. Thus, every parish celebrates three dedication anniversaries: its own as a solemnity, its cathedral's as a feast, and the Lateran's as a feast of the Lord.

Co-cathedrals do not merit the same celebration. When they exist in a diocese,

the anniversary of their dedication is carried out *only* in the dedicated church itself, but not throughout the diocese. For the title of co-cathedral is generally given to churches because of a special importance kept in the life of the diocese. And the cathedral church, a sign of the unity of the local church, is unique, and only its anniversary of dedication ought to be celebrated in the entire diocese.[35]

The Title and Patrons of Churches

In addition to the dedication anniversary, the title is also a solemnity. For example, a church dedicated to St. Aloysius observes June 21 as a solemnity. In the case of parish consolidations, the community may receive a new patronage, but if they assemble in a previously consecrated church, the

34. "De Celebratio," p. 103.
35. "Documentorum explanatio: De dedicatione ecclesiae," *Notitiae* 82, vol. 9, no. 4 (April 1973): 152.

original patronal day continues to be observed as a solemnity (canon 1218).

A patron is a saint or a blessed "who because of an ancient tradition or lawful custom is celebrated as a protector, that is, as an advocate before God."[36] Ordinarily there is only one patron, unless the calendar has grouped several saints.

The Table of Liturgical Days includes the observance of Proper Solemnities and Proper Feasts. It also notes that secondary patrons are observed as an obligatory memorial.

When choosing a title or patron saint for a particular calendar, the diocese or religious order chooses the date from the Martyrology or from their own research showing the *dies natalis* or other important date. Only saints are patrons; to choose a blessed requires an apostolic indult, a permission from the Apostolic See.[37] If the community has Mary as its patron under a title not on the liturgical calendar, the patronal day may become August 15, as noted below.

Images of Saints in Churches

Catholic churches customarily enshrine images of various saints, including their title or patron. These inspire the faithful, but the Missal requests "that their number not be increased indiscriminately, and moreover that they be arranged in proper order so as not to draw the attention of the faithful to themselves and away from the celebration itself" (GIRM 318). This preference flows from the council, which feared that the number and position of certain images could confuse Christians or "foster devotion of doubtful orthodoxy" (SC

---

36. Sacred Congregation for Divine Worship, "Norms: *Patronus, liturgica acceptione*, on patron saints," 1 and 5, 19 March 1973, DOL 477 (3971), p. 1239.

37. *Calendaria particularia* 28, DOL 481 (4023), p. 1252.

125).[38] The statement confronts those who may think that Catholics worship false images.

"There should usually be only one image of any given Saint" (GIRM 318). This aligns with the preference that saints have only one annual day. Furthermore, feasts of the saints are not to take precedence over feasts commemorating the mysteries of salvation (SC 111).

Even so, the Consilium cautioned against the extreme of removing all images. The mysteries of redemption and the eucharistic celebration are to remain at the center of worship, but "there is a consonant and perfectly subordinate place for the veneration of the Virgin Mary, Mother of God, and of the saints."[39]

The Litany of the Saints

Certain occasions call for a litany of supplication invoking many saints. Revisers also scrutinized the litany. A longer form for public intercessions and processions was first published together with a shorter form for use among rites taking place during Mass.[40]

The revised Litany of the Saints for Use in Solemn Supplications from the *Ordo Cantus Misæ* unfolds in several parts: supplication to God, invocation of the saints, invocation to Christ, supplication for various needs, and conclusion. Some of these have alternative formulas. The listing of saints begins with Mary under various titles, and then continues with archangels and angels. The remaining saints are patriarchs

38. *Vatican II*, p. 157.

39. Consilium, "Letter *Le renouveau liturgique* of Cardinal G. Lercaro to presidents of the conferences of bishops, on furthering liturgical reform," 30 June 1965, DOL 31 (408): 117.

40. Sacred Congregation of Rites, "Decree *Anni liturgici ordinatione*, promulgating the *editio typica* of the General Roman Calendar," 21 March 1969, DOL 441 (3765), p. 1155.

and prophets, apostles and disciples, martyrs, bishops and doctors, priests and religious, and laity. Within these groups men precede women, and each subgroup lists its saints in chronological order.[41]

The introduction states, "In a list of Saints, some names may be inserted in their proper places (for example, patrons, titles of churches, founders, etc.) Similarly to the supplications for various needs may be added other invocations appropriate to the additions of circumstances and places."[42]

Some changes occurred in 1970. John the Baptist, apparently missing, was inserted after Elijah and before Joseph. Stanislaus, bishop and martyr, was added after Boniface and before Thomas Becket, but only in the litany for solemn supplications.[43]

Ritual books often call this a "litany of supplication" instead of a "Litany of the Saints." After invoking the names of saints, the faithful make pertinent petitions to Christ.

In the baptism of adults the litany may include the title and patrons of the church, along with the patrons of those to be baptized. The names are fewer than those in the *Ordo Cantus Missæ* (OCIA 221).

The baptism of children names only Mary, John the Baptist, Joseph, Peter, and Paul (OBC 48). It allows adding patrons. In the United States, the standard litany from the baptism of adults may be used instead (OBC 220A).

In the dedication of a new church, the standard litany appears, subtly connecting the building to baptized people. The names of patrons and of saints whose relics are deposited there may be added.

For a deacon's ordination, the standard litany has three changes. The deacons Vincent and Ephrem are added, and

41. *Ordo Cantus Missæ, Editio Typica Altera* (Vatican City: Libreria Editrice Vaticana, 1987), pp. 197–202.

42. *Ordo Cantus Missæ*, p. 197.

43. Sacred Congregation for Divine Worship, "Acta Congregationis: Litaniae Sanctorum," *Notitiae* 58, vol. 6, no. 9 (November 1970): 375.

Francis and Dominic, usually invoked together, are separated because Francis served as a deacon. Patrons of candidates may be added. In the ordination of priests, Vincent and Ephrem are removed from the list, and Francis and Dominic are rejoined.

In the ordination of a bishop, Peter and Paul are invoked separately, which stresses Peter's role as bishop of Rome. The nine other faithful apostles are named individually, as is Matthias, who replaced Judas. Most of these appear in the same order as in the first eucharistic prayer, the sequence of their feast days on the preconciliar calendar. Patron saints may be added.

A litany of supplication also takes place during the rite of perpetual profession.[44] Andrew, Ignatius of Antioch, Perpetua and Felicity, Gregory the Great, and Athanasius are all omitted. In the profession of men, Bernard the abbot is added, as are Ignatius of Loyola, Vincent de Paul, and John Bosco, who founded male religious communities. Saints venerated by the particular religious family or by the people may be added.

The litany for the religious profession of women makes adjustments. Added are Macrina, an early consecrated virgin and sister of Basil and Gregory of Nyssa, but not a saint on the general calendar; Scholastica; Clare of Assisi; Rose of Lima; Jane Francis de Chantal; and Louise de Marillac, who with St. Vincent de Paul founded the Daughters of Charity, but who has no date on the general calendar.

In the Consecration of Virgins, the litany resembles the one for the profession of religious women, but with a few changes.[45] At the very beginning, the invocation to Holy Mary, Mother of God becomes two, one to Holy Mary and the other to the Holy Mother of God, followed by an insertion, Holy Virgin of virgins. This teases out Mary's role as a model of virgins. Perpetua and Felicity remain, though neither was a

44. *Ordo Professionis Religiosae* (Vatican City: Libreria Editrice Vaticana, 1975), 62.

45. *Ordo de Consecratione Virginum, editio typica* (Vatican City: Libreria Editrice Vaticana, 1970), 20.

virgin. Maria Goretti, a virgin martyr canonized in the mid-twentieth century, has been added. Basil is missing, perhaps in deference to his sister Macrina. Athanasius and Ambrose are added before Augustine, and Jerome follows him; all four of them wrote about the vocation of virginity, though the work attributed to Athanasius is probably pseudonymous. Dominic and Francis appear together, but in reverse order, possibly to give Dominic deference, in accordance with the tradition that the Virgin Mary revealed the rosary to him. Jane Frances de Chantal is missing, probably because she was a widow, and Margaret Mary Alacoque (the Visitation sister who promoted devotion to the Sacred Heart) is included.

The commendation of the dying includes a litany of saints (PCS 219, OUI 145). The list omits Michael, but then adds Abraham and David as examples of all holy patriarchs and prophets—David a prophet because of the book of Psalms. Although the litany in the *Ordo Cantus Missæ* opens with this category, it appears only here among the rites. The rest of the saints are identical to the standard list. An alternative, brief litany is provided. It copies the one from the Order of Baptism of Children, though it adds the holy angels of God.

In the United States the *Book of Blessings* has a litany in its Order for Visiting a Cemetery on All Souls' Day (November 2), Memorial Day, or on the Anniversary of Death or Burial.[46] The list is considerably shorter, removing names from virtually every category, and separating Peter and Paul. It perhaps mistakenly reversed the order of Catherine and Teresa while adding other women saints to balance the list: Ann, the mother of Mary, and two Americans: Frances Cabrini and Elizabeth Seton.

---

46. *Book of Blessings* (Collegeville, MN: Liturgical Press, 1989), no. 1746.

Chapter Four

Proper of Time

Advent

Advent opens the year and prepares for the Nativity of Jesus Christ. It begins on the fourth Sunday before December 25, and it ends before Evening Prayer I or the first evening Mass of Christmas Eve. The revisers first extended it from first Vespers of the First Sunday of Advent through Nones of Christmas Eve, the last of the middle hours before Evening Prayer.

Advent now begins on the Sunday on or nearest to November 30 and ends before Evening Prayer I of Christmas (UNLYC 40). The earliest Advent can begin, therefore, is November 27, and the latest is December 3.

Starting the liturgical year with Advent may seem obvious, but the revisers questioned it. They wondered "whether the time of Advent must be kept as the beginning of the liturgical year so that it is a preparation for the feast of the Nativity of the Lord, or whether it should be considered the conclusion of the liturgical year so that its eschatological meaning may be restored."[1]

The group traced the origins of Advent to the sixth century and reiterated its longstanding dual purpose—preparation for Christmas and preparing for the Second Coming of Christ.

1. Schemata, n. 65, p. 11.

The revisers felt that starting the year with Christmas would be too abrupt and devalue the importance of Old Testament passages foreshadowing the Messiah. They also noted the pastoral difficulty of scheduling a liturgical time anticipating the Second Coming when the faithful were engaged in preparations to honor the First Coming at Christmas. The revisers even endowed the weeks that end the church year with a sense of awaiting the Second Coming of Christ.[2]

The Meaning of Advent

Some aspects of Advent appear penitential: The priest and deacon wear violet vesture as in Lent (GIRM 346d), with an optional modification to rose vesture for the Third Sunday (346f). Flowers are to be used in moderation (305), as is the organ (313), both penitential attributes of Lent.

However, the revisers wanted Advent to exude more joy than repentance. "The Time of Advent is not a penitential time, but rather of joyful expectation."[3] "It is not a time of penance but of delightful expectation."[4] "The time of Advent offers itself as a time of devout and joyful expectation, in which the encouragement of the Apostle [Paul] reechoes: Rejoice in the Lord (Phil 4:4)."[5]

As early as 1964 the church recommended the preservation of customs associated with the calendar.[6] One thinks of household and parochial traditions like the Advent wreath and decorations that maintain a joyful spirit.

2. Schemata, n. 65, pp. 11–12.
3. Schemata, n. 188, p. 1; and n. 260, p. 6.
4. Schemata, n. 213, p. 3; Consilium ad Exsequendam Constitutionem de Sacra Liturgia, Schemata, n. 225, 18 April 1967, p. 4.
5. Consilium ad Exsequendam Constitutionem de Sacra Liturgia, Schemata, n. 328, 27 November 1968, p. 7.
6. *Inter Oecumenici*, no. 14, 17, DOL 23 (306, 309), pp. 91–92.

Advent Sundays

In addition to the restraint given flowers and the organ, and the penitential color of the vestments, Advent Sundays exclude the singing of the Gloria (GIRM 53). The Third Sunday opens with an antiphon urging people to rejoice. Its first word in Latin gives this Sunday its title, *Gaudete*. The collect prays to attain the joys of salvation and to celebrate them with glad rejoicing.

The gospels are heard in reverse chronological order: on the First Sunday, the Lord's coming at the end of time; on the Second and Third Sundays, John the Baptist; and on the Fourth Sunday the events leading to the birth of Jesus. The Old Testament readings prophesy the Messiah, featuring the book of Isaiah. The second readings contain exhortations and proclamations consonant with Advent (ILM 93).

The eucharistic prayer opens with one of two prefaces composed for Advent. Because these Masses have their own preface, Eucharistic Prayer IV, which has its own invariable preface, may not be used (GIRM 365d).

In the Table of Liturgical Days, the Sundays of Advent rank in the second tier, just after the Paschal Triduum. They lead a chronological group of Sundays (Advent, Lent, and Easter) that follow the principal solemnities of Christmas, Epiphany, Ascension, and Pentecost.

Ritual Masses may not be celebrated on Advent Sundays (GIRM 372). If a wedding takes place during one of those Masses, it uses the readings, prayers and vestment color of Advent. An ordination would follow the same rules. The Ritual Mass for Anointing the Sick is forbidden on Advent Sundays, but one of its readings and its solemn blessing may replace those of Advent (PCS 134, OUI 81).

One exception concerns the dedication of a church. The Mass for the dedication, complete with its readings, the Gloria, prayers, and vestment color, replaces the same on a Sunday in Advent. If, however, only a new altar is being dedicated, the

Advent Sunday Mass takes precedence except for the prayer over the offerings and the preface, which are unique to the dedication of an altar.

Masses for Various Needs and Occasions are not permitted on Advent Sundays. Not even a diocesan bishop may authorize one (GIRM 374). Funeral Masses are not allowed (380), but funeral without Mass may take place.

Occasionally, December 24 falls on a Sunday. The Sacred Congregation of Rites dealt with this in 1967 before the final versions of the Lectionary and Missal. They permitted the Fourth Sunday of Advent Mass on Saturday evening for those with the permission to celebrate the night before, and the Vigil Mass of Christmas on Sunday.[7] Today many parishes offer morning Masses of the Advent Sunday, and afternoon and evening Masses the same day for Christmas Eve. Some reduce the usual schedule, encouraging the faithful to gather in greater numbers at fewer Masses.

Advent Weekdays through December 16

Each Advent weekday has a unique set of antiphons, readings, and prayers, a feature the previous Missal had not adopted. "Each day of this time is adorned with its proper prayer [collect]."[8] That oration reappears at the end of Morning, Daytime, and Evening Prayer each day of Advent in the Liturgy of the Hours (GILH 199–200).

At Mass the weekday readings favor Isaiah, who supplies a semicontinuous series through Wednesday of the Second Week of Advent. The gospels answer the theme of the first reading (ILM 94). Thursday of the Second Week begins gospels pertaining to John the Baptist, and the first readings

7. Declaration *Cum Dominica IV Adventus*, on the evening Mass for 23 December 1967, 12 December 1967, DOL 447 (3836), pp. 1174–75.
8. Schemata, n. 225, p. 4.

match their themes through December 16 (74). These readings repeat each year (69 §3).

A homily is recommended at Mass on Advent weekdays (GIRM 66). Indeed, it is "strongly" recommended (ILM 25). The eucharistic prayer opens with the first of Advent's two prefaces.

Up until December 16, the community may celebrate any optional memorial in place of the Advent weekday, or the memorial of another saint from the Martyrology (GIRM 355b). On obligatory memorials, the saint's collect replaces the one for Advent (354a).

During these weekdays there are no Votive Masses or a Mass for Various Needs and Occasions. However, in case of a "some real necessity or pastoral advantage," the priest or the rector of the place may authorize the use of one (GIRM 376).

In the Liturgy of the Hours, the Advent weekdays introduce the historical Psalms 78, 105 and 106. Omitted during Ordinary Time, they help establish the character of Advent (GILH 130).

Advent Weekdays from December 17–24

The final week forms the immediate preparation for Christmas. In the Lectionary, the gospels relate events leading up to the birth of Christ, and the first readings complement their themes (ILM 94). These readings also repeat each year (69 §3).

The prayers for these days are privileged. The second option for the Advent preface begins the eucharistic prayer. If a memorial occurs, only its collect may be used (GIRM 355a); the other components come from the weekday Mass. Even in particular calendars, communities should avoid assigning memorials and feasts to these weekdays (UNLYC 56f).

The priest does not have the authority to celebrate a Mass for Various Needs and Occasions. However, a bishop may authorize one in the case of "a graver need or of pastoral advantage" (GIRM 374). The Missal's introduction to its collection of Votive Masses gives the same permission to the bishop "if some serious pastoral benefit is to be gained."

In the Liturgy of the Hours, proper antiphons accompany each psalm at Morning and Evening Prayer (GILH 116). The formularies of these antiphons, as well as the hymns, readings, responsories, and prayers, may not be changed (247).

In the Liturgy of the Hours, "obligatory memorials are not celebrated" on these days (GILH 238). Memorials of saints are treated as commemorations, as explained above (239).

Christmas Time

Christmas Time celebrates the birth of the Lord and manifestations of his divinity (UNLYC 32). These are especially evident on Epiphany and the Baptism of the Lord. Christmas Time begins with Evening Prayer I on December 24, though the Vigil Mass may begin it even before (34). Christmas Time continues through the Baptism of the Lord (33, 38).

Vestment color during this time is white (GIRM 346). An exception occurs when the celebration of martyrs calls for red.

Christmas Day

In the Table of Liturgical Days, the topmost level belongs exclusively to the Paschal Triduum. Several important days share the second rank. First among these is the Nativity of the Lord (Christmas), followed by Epiphany.

The church has long offered one Mass for the Vigil of Christmas and three Masses on Christmas Day. The first of these is during the night, traditionally begun at midnight. The others are at dawn and during the day. The revised calendar kept all these celebrations (UNLYC 34). Participation at the Vigil Mass on the afternoon or evening of December 24 satisfies one's obligation; however, the liturgical texts presume that the real celebration of Christmas is the next day. For example, the entrance antiphon says "in the morning you will see his glory"; the collect says, "as we wait in hope for our redemption"; and the prayer over the offerings says, "As we look forward, O Lord, to the coming festivities." These texts presume that those who gathered for the Vigil Mass would gladly return the following day to celebrate a Christmas Mass. In practice, most people come on Christmas Eve to celebrate their Christmas Day.

The Missal offers a Mass during the day for December 24, usually celebrated in the morning, and even more clearly anticipating the arrival of Christmas. This Mass completes Advent, bringing the readings and prayers to a climax. In 1969 the Sacred Congregation for Divine Worship clarified that the Mass in the morning of December 24 may not be celebrated as the Vigil of the Nativity:

> It is called a weekday Mass. The idea of vigils has completely changed. Vigils are no longer held as they were formerly understood. Now the evening of the preceding day of certain solemnities is called the proper Mass of the Vigil, which pertains to the solemnity. Therefore it is the Mass of the feast.[9]

A priest may celebrate or concelebrate three Masses on Christmas Day if he uses the separate formulas (GIRM 204). This challenges parishes with only one priest. People usually participate in only one Christmas Mass, even though the priest may be celebrating several. The readings come from examples in the tradition (ILM 95).

When reciting the Creed even at the Vigil the faithful genuflect at the words of the incarnation (OM 18). The only other day with this practice is March 25, the solemnity of the Annunciation (GIRM 137).

Eucharistic Prayer I carries a special insert for Christmas Day and its octave. The priest is not obliged to use Prayer I, but

---

9. Sacred Congregation for Divine Worship, "Documentorum explanatio: Ad Calendarium," *Notitiae* 48, vol. 5, nos. 9–10 (September–October, 1969): 405.

if he does, he proclaims that the community is celebrating the night "on which blessed Mary the immaculate Virgin brought forth the Savior for this world" (OM 86).

The introduction to the Liturgy of the Hours names Christmas as a day especially appropriate for expanding the Office of Readings into Vigils (GILH 71). The Office of Readings is normally not joined to Mass. If it is, the office ends after the responsory following the second reading, and Mass begins with the Gloria—or with the collect if there is no Gloria. One opportunity for this rare combination is Christmas Eve (98). When a solemn vigil is celebrated before Mass on Christmas Eve, the participants do not celebrate Night Prayer (215).

On Christmas Day, Morning Prayer is usually offered before the Mass at Dawn (GILH 216). Otherwise, it appears that the Mass at Dawn pertains to the vigil, rather than to the day.

Ritual Masses are excluded on solemnities (GIRM 372). Even the dedication of a new church building is forbidden on Christmas. A new altar may be dedicated, in which case the Christmas Mass is said, but the ritual's prayer over the offerings and preface replace those of Christmas.

As explained above, special rules apply to consecutive solemnities. When Christmas falls on a Monday, the Fourth Sunday of Advent takes place on Saturday night and Sunday morning. By Sunday afternoon, Masses for Christmas begin. Those praying the Liturgy of the Hours celebrate Evening Prayer I of Christmas in place of Evening Prayer II of the Fourth Sunday of Advent, and ideally before the first Mass on Christmas Eve. The faithful are obliged to participate in both Masses. A bishop may establish local practice.

When Christmas falls on a Saturday, Evening Prayer II replaces Evening Prayer I for Holy Family, which will be observed on Sunday, December 26. A Mass on Saturday afternoon or evening remains that of Christmas, but those who participated in a Christmas Mass earlier could satisfy their obligation for Sunday Mass with such a celebration. Many parishes cancel

Saturday afternoon and evening Masses so that ministers may celebrate Christmas with their families, retaining only the Sunday Masses for Holy Family on December 26.

Anastasia is among the martyrs whose name may be read aloud in Eucharistic Prayer I. The Martyrology lists her among saints honored on December 25. In the past, the pope celebrated the Christmas Mass at Dawn at St. Anastasia Church in Rome, and the preconciliar Missal preserved a remembrance of her in that Mass. The revised calendar removed saints such as Anastasia if their following was more local than universal. December 25 is now uniquely the celebration of the Nativity of the Lord, though Anastasia may be remembered in the first eucharistic prayer.

The Christmas Octave

The eight days from December 25 through January 1 prolongs the joy of Christmas. The revisers enriched each weekday of Christmas Time with its own collect at Mass. This prayer is repeated at Morning, Daytime, and Evening Prayer in the Liturgy of the Hours (GILH 199–200). On memorials, the collect of the saint may replace the one for the weekday (GIRM 355a). The other prayers remain those of the octave. However, in developing particular calendars, memorials and feasts are to be avoided if possible (UNLYC 56f).

At Mass the first reading comes from the First Letter of John (ILM 74), beginning on the feast of the same apostle. The gospels relate manifestations of the Lord, especially events from the infancy of Jesus, as well as the first chapter of John's gospel (96).

If the priest offers the first eucharistic prayer, he continues using the special insert of Christmas Day. Apart from funerals, a Mass for the Dead does not replace other Masses during this octave; however, it may for a special reason, such as receiving the news of a death, conducting the final burial, or honoring the first anniversary (GIRM 381).

In the Liturgy of the Hours, proper psalms adorn the Office of Readings, and Morning and Evening Prayer repeat the psalms of Christmas Day (GILH 62, 116, 134). As with Advent, Christmas Time includes the historical Psalms 78, 105, 106, which set a context for the mystery of redemption. The formularies proper to the Liturgy of the Hours during this octave cannot be changed (247).

The Holy Family of Jesus, Mary, and Joseph

The revisers questioned retaining Holy Family Sunday. It entered the calendar rather late, only in 1893 during the papacy of Leo XIII. Featuring the gospel of finding of the child Jesus in the temple, the feast fell on the first Sunday after the Epiphany to maintain the chronology of events.

The revisers thought that this devotional celebration dimmed the focus on the three traditional manifestations of the Lord: the coming of the magi, the baptism in the Jordan, and the miracle at Cana. They considered moving Holy Family into Votive Masses, among regional celebrations, or even suppressing it, but "Pastoral reasons are convincing that the feast be retained especially because in our times the holiness of the family is most tragically falling apart!"[10] After considering other options, such as the Sunday between January 1 and Epiphany, the group settled on the day formerly known as the Sunday within the Octave of Christmas. The Lectionary offers additional gospels that tie the feast more closely to Christmas. The day is a feast of the Lord.

After announcing the revisions, the Congregation for Divine Worship addressed the years when no Sunday fell between Christmas and January 1. In those instances, it assigned Holy Family to December 30.[11]

---

10. Schemata, n. 65, p. 9.
11. Bugnini, pp. 315–16.

Mary the Mother of God, January 1

On the octave day of Christmas the church observes a solemnity in honor of Mary as the Mother of God. In a single verse of his gospel (2:21), Luke notes that the child was circumcised and given his name on the eighth day. Previously this feast had been called the Circumcision of Jesus, and the Sunday between January 2 and 5 became that of the Most Holy Name of Jesus. If no Sunday fell on those days, Holy Name moved to January 2.

Early on, the revisers wondered whether the octave of Christmas should be dedicated to Mary the Mother of God, "or to the celebration of the Name of Jesus, so that the civil year may begin in the name of the Lord."[12] Van Doren noted the antiquity of assigning this day to the motherhood of Mary; indeed, it was the first Marian feast in the Roman liturgy. Martimort had strong words:

> A feast of the name of Jesus serves no purpose, not even in devotion. And the formulas are flavored with a kind of sensibility that is completely anachronistic! It should be completely abolished.
>
> Besides, also in the modern feast of the Octave of the Lord, both in the Mass and in the office, there remain most beautiful elements of the memorial of the Mother of God. It would be best if these elements were embellished, after investigating the tradition, as illustrated by B. Botte, B. Capelle, A. Chavasse, and G. Frénaud. The circumcision is in no way a "feast."[13]

At the same meeting, Nocent offered a wider reflection in support of renaming the day:

> The Feast of the Name of Jesus seems like an abstract celebration to me, not immediately aligned with the paschal mystery

12. Schemata, n. 65, p. 8.
13. Schemata, n. 65, p. 8.

and leading to "religious feelings" more than to the truth and dogmatic reality of the mystery of Christ.

The memorial of the Mother of God, though, brings many good things to the pastoral field, both to the paschal mystery and to the Virgin Mary of God as obeying and collaborating with the will of God. In the modern world the Virgin Mary would rejoice in this festival of a true understanding on the part of the faithful. Evidently the feast of the "Maternity" [October 11] remains an abstract feast, while the feast of Mary the Mother of God acquires an objective reality in the Octave of Christmas. Therefore the Feast of the Maternity should be abolished or reduced to a third class feast with the possibility of a more solemn celebration in some places.[14]

At first the revisers proposed, "The eighth day of the Nativity becomes the commemoration of the Mother of God (or of the Most Holy Name of Jesus.)"[15] Later, the group noted, "Because the Name of Jesus was imposed on the eighth day, and in many regions the civil year begins on the first day of January, petitions may be added to the prayer of the faithful for the happy beginning of the year under the protection of the Name of Jesus."[16]

Scholars had collected information about other traditions. An eighth-century antiphonary called this day "The Birth of Holy Mary."[17] In the seventh century the Roman Church wanted to christianize the pagan feast of January 1 with its licentious gift-giving, so the church instituted a fast and a Mass for the prohibition of idols. Some regions fixed January 1 as the memorial of the Theotokos, the God-bearer, celebrated in the Eastern Rites a day after Christmas with various parts of

14. Schemata, n. 65, p. 9.

15. Schemata, n. 71, p. 1.

16. Consilium ad Exsequendam Constitutionem de Sacra Liturgia, Schemata, n. 75, De Calendario recognoscendo, 4, 10 April 1965, p. 1.

17. Schemata, n. 188, p. 9.

the Mass and the office under the title "The Birth of Mary."
Frankish countries celebrated the Octave of the Lord with the
gospel about Jesus receiving his name. These countries had
circulated the title "The Circumcision of the Lord," which
the church suppressed in 1961. Calling it "The Octave of
Christmas" seemed too colorless for a holy day of obligation,
and in many regions the day began the civil year.[18] All of this
demonstrated inconsistency in celebrations across the ages.

As a result, the revisers completely removed the observance
of the Holy Name of Jesus from the calendar, as well as the
October observance of the Maternity of Mary. They removed
references to acknowledging the new civil year in the universal
prayer, though it remains a good practice. The Lectionary assigns the blessing of Aaron as the first reading, which perhaps
orients the start of the civil year.

This is the last day of the octave. The special insert to Eucharistic Prayer I still applies.

Pope Paul established January 1 as the World Day of Peace,
beginning in 1969. He invited all people of good will to
observe it on the day "that marks and measures the passage
of human life through time," which he dedicated "to reflection and resolve about peace."[19] That year the pope insisted
that the liturgical texts be those of Mary the Mother of
God and the Holy Name of Jesus; however, the Consilium
issued helpful texts usable outside Mass, such as greetings,
readings, intentions for the Universal Prayer, presidential
prayers and concluding blessings. Then, with the local ordinary's permission, the Consilium allowed a Votive Mass "For
Peace" wherever there was a special celebration for peace on

18. Schemata, n. 260, pp. 46–47.
19. Paul VI, "Message (written) to all people 'of good will,' urging their
observance on 1 January of a World Day of Peace," 8 December 1967, DOL
497 (4097), p. 1282.

January 1.[20] The permission reappeared for 1978,[21] but it is no longer in force; the Missal's Mass "For the Preservation for Justice and Peace" carries a heading excluding it from January 1. The intention for world peace remains. It heads the USCCB's list of special days of prayer.

In the United States, this is a holy day of obligation, but not when it falls on a Monday or a Saturday. In those cases, the liturgical texts of Sunday take precedence at Evening Prayer I and II, and the evening Masses on Saturday and Sunday are those of Sunday.

The Litany of the Saints traditionally begins with an invocation to Mary. She is called "Holy Mary, Mother of God," the title under which she is honored on the octave day of Christmas.

The Second Sunday of Christmas

In countries like the United States, Epiphany is observed on the second Sunday following Christmas. Other countries observe it on January 6 as a holy day of obligation. In those places, the Second Sunday of Christmas has its own liturgy. The readings repeat each year: Sirach 24:1-2, 8-12; Psalm 147:12-13, 14-15, 19-20 with John 1:4 or Alleluia as the refrain; Ephesians 1:3-6, 15-18; 1 Timothy 3:16 as the inspiration for the Alleluia verse; and John 1:1-18 for the gospel. The Missal presents thematic antiphons and prayers.

Occasionally one finds that the Sundays of Christmas enjoy equal rank with those of Ordinary Time (UNLYC 13). A bishop could authorize a Mass for Various Needs and Occasions in case of grave need or pastoral advantage (GIRM 374).

---

20. The Consilium for Implementing the Constitution on the Sacred Liturgy, "Acta Consilii: Textus Liturgici pro Celebratione Diei Pacis," *Notitiae* 43, vol. 4, nos. 11–12 (November–December 1968): 366–79, especially 377.

21. The Sacred Congregation for Sacraments and Divine Worship, "Celebrationes particulares: Normae de Celebratione Missae 'Pro Pace,'" *Notitiae* 137, vol. 13, no. 12 (December 1977): 609.

January 2–5

The remaining weekdays of Christmas Time do not hold the same weight as the octave. A memorial may be observed, and a priest may celebrate a Mass for Various Needs and Occasions if he judges it in the interests of his people (GIRM 376).

Unfortunately, the first English translation of the Liturgy of the Hours in the United States gave some incoherent instructions for these days. The heading reads, for example, "from January 2 to Epiphany: Monday," but it should simply read "January 2." The same applies to the next several days. Perhaps the translators tried to mimic the Missal, which organizes these days by weekdays instead of dates. The Lectionary uses dates instead of days. It is a confusing week in that regard because the principal liturgical books use different systems to locate the proper prayers and readings.

The Epiphany of the Lord

Each year Christians commemorate the coming of the magi to the Christ child on a day called "Epiphany," meaning "manifestation." These representatives of Gentile nations came to adore the Word made flesh. The star that led them still inspires art and song. On the Table of Liturgical Days, the Epiphany shares the second tier with days like Christmas.

The traditional date for the celebration, January 6, marks the twelfth day of Christmas, usually landing on a weekday. Although many Catholics associate that date with Epiphany, few had participated in its Mass, especially where January 6 was not a civic holiday. The revisers asked at an early meeting whether the observance should move to a Sunday, such as the one on or after January 6. According to Jounel, in 1802 France and Belgium received an indult to remove Epiphany from the days of obligation, celebrate it in choir on January 6, and make it an external solemnity at one Mass the following Sunday. Some priests and faithful therefore celebrated Epiphany twice. In a city like Paris a church may have had ten Masses for Holy Family that day and one for Epiphany. Many conferences wanted to transfer Epiphany to a Sunday. Jounel projected that moving it to the following Sunday would endanger celebrating the Baptism of the Lord, which the group wanted on or before the traditional date, January 13. Conferences therefore received permission to move Epiphany to the Sunday after January 1 unless it remained a holy day on January 6.

At Mass, if the priest offers Eucharistic Prayer I, he uses a special insert for Epiphany, calling it the day on which the only-begotten Son, eternal with the Father in glory, "appeared in a human body, truly sharing our flesh" (OM 86). The word "appeared" expresses the meaning of "Epiphany."

At Evening Prayer in the Liturgy of the Hours, the New Testament canticle is based on 1 Timothy 3:16, appearing only here and on the Transfiguration. It praises Christ, manifested in the flesh.

The dedication of a new church building is forbidden on Epiphany. An altar may be dedicated, and the prayer over the offerings and the preface replace those assigned for Epiphany.

Weekdays from Epiphany to the Baptism of the Lord

A full week may separate Epiphany and the Baptism of the Lord. The intervening weekdays continue the theme of manifestation in the Scripture readings, prayers, and antiphons. For example, the gospels at Mass feature miracles that manifest the power of Christ, and first readings prophesy them. The Missal's weekdays for Christmas Time offer alternative collects for the days following Epiphany.

The Baptism of the Lord

All four gospels and the Acts of the Apostles testify to the baptism of Jesus. This event, so important to the apostolic church, had been celebrated in the previous calendar on a weekday, January 13. When January 13 fell on a Sunday, the priest celebrated the Mass of the Holy Family. The revision signifies the importance of the Baptism of the Lord.

From the beginning, the revisers asked whether the Baptism should move to a Sunday; most agreed. Nocent writes,

> I prefer that the Commemoration of the Baptism of the Lord be assigned to the first Sunday after Epiphany. This Baptism of Jesus is seen of the greatest importance in the economy of salvation and for the theology of the Holy Spirit and for understanding the sacrament of confirmation. During the week many faithful cannot celebrate this commemoration. Nevertheless, the celebration may be kept on the first Sunday after Epiphany; that is, it may be entitled: "The First Sunday after the Epiphany, the Commemoration of the Baptism of the Lord." A new composition of a Mass is demanded, in which the chants and some texts of the Mass of the First Sunday may be retained; some texts and above all the gospel from the Baptism of the Lord may be included.[22]

The Baptism of the Lord closes Christmas Time, but even this was not clear to the revisers. Some thought that Christmas should close with Epiphany or on the second Sunday after Epiphany, with its gospel of the wedding at Cana. They even considered moving the Transfiguration of Jesus from August 6 into the Epiphany cycle.[23]

In the end, the Baptism of the Lord moved to the Sunday after Epiphany except in those years when Epiphany falls on January 7 or 8. The group preferred not to add another week to Christmas Time, displacing the Baptism beyond January 13, and moved it instead to the Monday after Epiphany. It therefore occasionally remains on a weekday, as it had in the past.

In the Table of Liturgical Days, the Baptism of the Lord is part of number 5, a feast of the Lord. The Missal says that Ordinary Time begins on the following day. The Lectionary

---

22. Schemata, n. 65, p. 10.

23. Consilium ad Exsequendam Constitutionem de Sacra Liturgia, Schemata, n. 93, De Calendario, 5, 10 May 1965, p. 2.

co-entitles the Baptism of the Lord as the First Sunday in Ordinary Time. However, at the end of the readings for this day, it states that the readings for the Sundays in Ordinary Time begin the following week. The liturgical books show some discrepancy over the proper placement of the Baptism of the Lord. It concludes Christmas Time, but it also launches Ordinary Time.

Ritual Masses may be celebrated on this day. A wedding, for example, may use the ritual's readings, prayers, and antiphons.

Whenever the Baptism falls on a Monday, the full Liturgy of the Hours for Epiphany is celebrated on Sunday. Sunday evening calls for Evening Prayer II of the Epiphany, not Evening Prayer I of the Baptism of the Lord.

Lent

Lent has a twofold purpose: "the recalling of Baptism or the preparation for it, and Penance" (SC 109).[24] Catholics across many generations have practiced repentance during Lent through prayer, fasting, and almsgiving. Since the Second Vatican Council, the rites for the Christian initiation of adults have received renewed attention. With many people coming to know Christ for the first time in places previously untouched by evangelization, these rites have proven expressive around the world. They underscore Lent's purpose by recalling a Christian's baptism and preparing for the baptism of new followers of Christ.

During Lent the word "Alleluia" is removed from important places in the liturgy. At Mass, the acclamation before the gospel uses a different refrain. GIRM 62 explains this as though the verse alone remains, which the renewal had initially envisioned.

24. *Vatican II*, p. 151.

Eucharistic Prayer IV has its own invariable preface. It may not be used during Lent because each Mass has its own preface (GIRM 365d).

In the Liturgy of the Hours, the introductory verse for the offices concludes without its usual "Alleluia" (GILH 41, 60, 79, 85). On Sundays, the New Testament canticle from the book of Revelation featuring Alleluias is replaced with a more sober canticle from the First Letter of Peter (137).

The norms state more broadly, "From the beginning of Lent until the Paschal Vigil, the Alleluia is not said" (UNLYC 28). This seems to apply to all parts of the liturgy, including congregational hymns and choral music. The best practice is to suppress the word throughout Lent.

Priests and deacons wear violet (GIRM 346d). Exceptions pertain to celebrations such as Ritual Masses, solemnities, feasts, or the Fourth Sunday.

Laws of fasting and abstinence are in force (canons 1251–52). The prayers and readings for the liturgy assume that the faithful are marking this time with such signs of repentance.

This restraint applies even to flowers and music. Whereas floral decoration around the altar during Advent is to be moderate, it is forbidden during Lent. Exceptions pertain to the Fourth Sunday, solemnities and feasts (GIRM 305). Similarly, the playing of the organ and other musical instruments is restricted to support singing. The same exceptions apply (313).

Ash Wednesday

"On Ash Wednesday, the beginning of Lent, which is observed everywhere as a fast day, ashes are distributed" (UNLYC 29). This day ranks within the second tier of the Table of Liturgical Days. It replaces any other solemnities or feasts that may coincide. The date is computed six and a half weeks back from Easter.

Lent begins on Ash Wednesday, but the revisers considered a historic change. Some wanted Lent to begin on the

First Sunday, with the distribution of ashes on a different day. Amore believed that the forty days of fast excluded Sundays, requiring Lent to begin on Wednesday. However, Nocent cited Pope Leo the Great's expectation that "fasting from vices and sins, and fostering charity toward one's neighbor" was to continue on Sundays.[25] The revisers of special ceremonies in the liturgical year preferred to have Lent begin with the First Sunday, counting forty days forward from then.

The proposal prompted questions on when to distribute ashes. Van Doren suggested Saturday evening before the First Sunday or even on the Monday following, because such a penitential act should not take place on a Sunday. Martimort concurred that "the imposition of ashes may never be permitted on a Sunday when fasting is wrong."[26] He proposed the weekdays preceding the First Sunday. Jounel agreed that Sunday and ashes were contradictory, and for that reason he also opposed ashes on Saturday evening, preferring Monday of the first week. Dirks suggested letting the various regions choose the day. Schmidt preferred widening the window for imposing ashes from Ash Wednesday until the Second Sunday of Lent. Nocent also saw the difficulty of imposing the sign of "sad and sorrowful repentance" on a day that signifies the resurrection; he preferred Saturday after Evening Prayer I or Monday.[27]

Almost all the principal consultors from two key study groups wanted Lent to begin on the First Sunday. The revisers explained,

> And indeed not because of vain archeologism, but because of the typology of forty days: Jesus fasted forty days and forty nights in the desert; Moses was forty days and forty nights on

25. Schemata, n. 65, p. 6.
26. Schemata, n. 65, p. 7.
27. Schemata, n. 65, pp. 7–8.

Mount Sinai; Elijah walked forty days and forty nights up to
Mount Horeb (readings of the first week of Lent).

Computing from the First Sunday of Lent up to Holy
Thursday inclusive, not excluding Sundays, there remain forty
penitential days before the sacred Triduum.[28]

The group noted that the Ambrosian Rite began Lent on
the First Sunday, so this would bring some coherence. They
pointed to the first words of the prayer over the offerings on
the First Sunday of Lent, "As we solemnly offer the annual
sacrifice for the beginning of Lent," as evidence of a tradition
that Lent began on that day. Additionally, the Roman Breviary
put Ash Wednesday and the three days following within its
volume of weeks after Epiphany, and began its volume con-
taining Lent with the First Sunday.

As late as August 1967, the proposed Table of Liturgical
Days listed major weekdays in one group. These included
the first part of Holy Week, the Easter octave, December 24,
All Souls' Day, and "the Day of Ashes"—without specifying
when it would be, "because of the movable character of this
day."[29] The same source projected it would be celebrated on
the first Monday of Lent, February 24, in 1969.

When the Congregation for the Doctrine of the Faith
reviewed the plans in 1968, it preferred to preserve Ash
Wednesday. Pope Paul himself settled the matter. As the
former archbishop of Milan, he knew that the Ambrosian
Rite began Lent on a Sunday. However, he was now bishop
of Rome:

It would admittedly be difficult, and even questionable, to
introduce [the first four days of Lent] for the first time in our
day; but now that they have been accepted by all the peoples
who follow the Roman Rite, it is not a good idea to suppress

28. Schemata, n. 75, p. 3.
29. Schemata, n. 237, pp. 2–3.

them, especially if the rite of the imposition of ashes is to be observed on the Wednesday before the first Sunday, as is now the case.[30]

The Roman Rite came very close to losing Ash Wednesday. The beloved tradition has been preserved.

The day is so sacred that no other Mass may replace it. No optional memorial is permitted—not even its collect, as would be the case on other weekdays (GIRM 355). No Ritual Mass may take place, such as one for a wedding or confirmation (372). No new church or altar may be dedicated. If anointing of the sick takes place during an Ash Wednesday Mass, one of the readings may come from its Ritual Mass (PCS 134, OUI 81). Although permitted, the inclusion of this sacrament in this day's Mass is pastorally inadvisable, given the prominence of other themes.

Not even a bishop may authorize a Mass for Various Needs and Occasions (GIRM 374). A Mass for the Dead may not be celebrated (381).

The blessing and distribution of ashes may take place apart from Mass. The *Book of Blessings* provides an order of service (1656–78). It includes a Liturgy of the Word and intercessions. There is no short form in which, for example, people in cars may drive up, roll down the window, extrude their head, receive ashes, and drive away. All are expected to make time to pray, to hear the Word of God, and to embrace the sign of repentance.

Ash Wednesday is a day of fasting and abstinence (canons 1251–52). Even outside the liturgy, this day affects daily life.

In the Liturgy of the Hours, the psalms come from Wednesday of the fourth and last week of the cycle because the First Sunday of Lent inaugurates the first week of the psalter. Morning Prayer, however, uses the psalms of the third Friday. This brings into the office of Ash Wednesday the most emblematic

---

30. Bugnini, pp. 310–11.

of penitential psalms, Psalm 51, which is prayed every Friday, but stepping back to the third week of the cycle at this one office. As a result, the faithful do not pray all the same psalms for Morning Prayer two days apart.

The Sundays of Lent

In the Table of Liturgical Days, the Sundays of Lent rank with those of Advent and Easter. They come below the Triduum but equate with major celebrations that would never conflict: Christmas, Epiphany, Ascension, and Pentecost.

Sunday Mass omits the Gloria (GIRM 53) and adds an obligatory Prayer over the People before the final blessing. Ritual Masses are forbidden (372). If a wedding takes place during Mass on a Sunday during Lent, the priest and deacon wear the color of the day (violet, rose, or red), and the readings and prayers come from the Sunday, which also blocks the Gloria. The same applies to an ordination. The Ritual Mass for Anointing the Sick is forbidden, but one of its readings and its solemn blessing may be used (PCS 134, OUI 81).

The Ritual Mass for the dedication of a new church may replace the Lent Sunday. However, if only a new altar is dedicated, the Sunday Mass of Lent is celebrated, but the prayer over the offerings and the preface come from the Ritual Mass.

Certain Ritual Masses pertain to the initiation of adults. On the First Sunday, following an ancient tradition probably related to beginning Lent on a Sunday, the bishop may preside for the Rite of Election: Unbaptized adults and children of catechetical age are named among the elect, chosen for baptism at the Easter Vigil, and they enroll their names. The Missal provides a special set of antiphons and prayers for this Mass. However, in many dioceses, this takes place apart from Mass.

Those who were named elect are to celebrate the three scrutinies on the Third, Fourth, and Fifth Sundays of Lent. These Masses have special antiphons, prayers, and readings that replace the usual ones on the respective Sunday.

A bishop may not authorize a Mass for Various Needs and Occasions on Sundays during Lent (GIRM 374). A funeral Mass may not take place (380).

The readings for Mass have a special shape. The gospels for the first two Sundays maintain the accounts of the temptation and the transfiguration of Christ from the previous Missal, though now on a three-year cycle featuring the accounts of Matthew, Mark, and Luke. In Year A, the next Sundays offer the gospels about the Samaritan woman, the man born blind, and the raising of Lazarus—all from John. These are also used in Years B and C at Masses with the scrutinies. Otherwise, in Year B the gospels from John on these three Sundays tell of the events leading to the passion and resurrection of Christ, and in Year C they present passages from Luke about conversion. The Old Testament readings catalogue events in salvation history, generally unrelated to the day's gospel. The second readings relate either to the first or to the gospel (ILM 97). The psalms echo a theme from the first reading or gospel.

The visual and aural restraint receives a reprieve on the Fourth Sunday. Named *Laetare* after the first word of the entrance antiphon, the day alerts the faithful that their time of penitence is happily half past. Consequently, flowers and instrumental music may be used in moderation (GIRM 305, 313). The priest and deacon may wear rose, though violet is permitted (346f). Although the antiphons and prayers of the Missal echo this theme of rejoicing, the readings follow their own pattern, nearly oblivious to the day's otherwise joyful tone.

In the Liturgy of the Hours, the *Te Deum* is omitted from the Office of Readings (GILH 68). At Morning and Evening Prayer, Sundays in Lent have proper antiphons for the psalms (116). The concluding prayer for Morning, Daytime, and Evening Prayer is proper (199–200), matching the collect from the day's Mass.

The Weekdays of Lent

In the Table of Liturgical Days, the weekdays of Lent rank ninth, along with the final weekdays of Advent and the octave of Christmas. Solemnities and feasts may replace them, but not memorials. For this reason, late in 1965, the revisers tested the following extreme idea:

> All the feasts of the Saints that occur during the time of Lent are transferred to another time. Nevertheless:
> a) March 19 becomes an external solemnity of St. Joseph where a pastoral reason demands it because of the devotion of the people.
> b) March 25 becomes the day of the Annunciation of the Lord.[31]

In the end, some but not all of the saints' days were transferred, such as that of Benedict. The two featured dates of March became solemnities.

Particular calendars are to avoid adding celebrations to Lent. Imitating the general calendar, these are best moved to other times of year. Exceptions include the proper feasts from 8a through 8d in the Table of Liturgical Days.[32]

All memorials become optional. The Mass for the Lent weekday is to be used, but the priest may offer the collect of the saint (GIRM 355). Particular calendars may include optional memorials.

The readings follow a one-year cycle. The first part of Lent accounts for its baptismal and penitential character (ILM 69 §2). The second part features the gospel of John and events leading to the passion of Christ (74, 98). On a weekday of the third, fourth, and fifth weeks, readings relating to the woman

---

31. Schemata, n. 132, p. 3.
32. *Calendaria Particularia* 2b, DOL 481 (3997), p. 1245.

at the well, the man born blind, and the raising of Lazarus may be used. Especially in years when they go unheard on Sundays, these important readings may replace another set (98).

In many parishes each daily Mass features a homily. GIRM 66 recommends one on these weekdays, and ILM 25 "strongly" recommends it. A Prayer over the People is supplied each day, but it is optional.

A Ritual Mass may be offered (GIRM 372). Therefore, a Saturday wedding Mass in Lent may draw from all the antiphons, readings, and prayers appropriate to a wedding. Such a Mass in Lent does include the Gloria because it replaces the Lent weekday Mass. However, the Alleluia remains silenced. Some people mistakenly believe that weddings may not take place during Lent, but the Missal makes provision for it. The wedding ritual even offers a Lenten gospel acclamation (OCM 56).

Two weekday Ritual Masses apply to adult initiation: the Handing On of the Creed and of the Lord's Prayer (OCIA 157–63 and 178–84). In these rituals, those preparing for baptism (or those already baptized who have had little catechetical formation) receive these two pillars of the faith. The celebrations take place on weekdays during the third and fifth weeks of Lent, respectively, preferably at Mass, with their special readings and prayers.

Among the Masses for the Dead, a funeral Mass may be celebrated (GIRM 380). The same is true for a Mass on receiving the news of a death, for the final burial, or the first anniversary (381). Other Masses for the Dead are not celebrated on Lent weekdays.

In the Liturgy of the Hours, Psalms 78, 105, and 106 appear as they had in Advent and Christmas Time (GILH 130). The oration that concludes Morning, Daytime, and Evening Prayer is the same as the collect from that day's Mass (199–200).

When obligatory memorials occur, the Liturgy of the Hours treats these as commemorations, as explained above (GILH 238, 239b). The formularies proper to the celebration of Lenten weekdays may not be changed (247).

Catholics abstain from meat on the Fridays of Lent. The readings and prayers of the liturgy especially note the penitential character of that weekday.

The Final Two Weeks of Lent

In the previous calendar, the final two weeks of Lent were called Passiontide. These opened with the First Passion Sunday and continued with the Second Passion Sunday, better known as Palm Sunday. Images of saints and crosses were kept veiled.

The revision saw Lent differently—as a single, flowing time. The readings on the Third, Fourth, and Fifth Sundays form a unit. The Fourth Sunday retains a sense of rejoicing. Semicontinuous readings from John's gospel begin in the fourth week. The last two Sundays have been renamed the Fifth Sunday of Lent and Palm Sunday of the Lord's Passion. The revisers reshaped these last two weeks by integrating them into the arc of Lent.

They held a low view of veiling images: "The veiling of the cross will not have to be done except in the celebration of Friday of the Passion of the Lord (for this veiling for fourteen days offers no pastoral sense today)."[33] "Passiontide, as it is now enforced, is abolished, so that a series of six Sundays of Lent may be kept, the sixth of which is called 'Of the Passion or of the Palms.' The veiling of images at Passiontide now in force is suppressed."[34]

However, veiling images is allowed in the United States. On the Fifth Sunday of Lent, the Missal notes, "In the Dioceses of the United States, the practice of covering crosses and images throughout the church from this Sunday may be observed." Crosses are to be uncovered after the celebration of the Passion of the Lord on Good Friday, and images of saints

---

33. Consilium ad Exsequendam Constitutionem de Sacra Liturgia, Schemata, n. 104, De Anno Lit., 3, 10 September 1965, p. 4.

34. Schemata, n. 132, p. 3. Also, Schemata, n. 188, p. 3.

are uncovered before the Easter Vigil. Some churches continue the custom; others do not. Although veiling is permitted, the designation "Passiontide" remains abolished.

The revisers removed the feast of the Compassion of the Blessed Virgin Mary from Friday of the first week of Passiontide because it doubled the theme of Our Lady of Sorrows on September 15. However, the third edition of the Missal added an alternative collect to that day, recalling the previous observance.

In the Liturgy of the Hours, the psalms all end with the short Christian prayer offering glory to the Trinity. Prior to the revision, this prayer was removed during the two weeks before Easter. Now it remains.

One remnant of Passiontide persists in the Liturgy of the Hours. During the fifth week of Lent, one may use the hymns assigned to Holy Week for the Office of Readings, Morning Prayer, and Evening Prayer.

Palm Sunday of the Passion of the Lord

Holy Week opens with Palm Sunday. The priest and deacon wear red (GIRM 346b), a color associated with martyrs, who shared in the suffering and death of Christ.

The Missal provides three formulas to open the celebration. In one Mass people gather outside the church for the blessing of palms. At other Masses, the branches are blessed inside. The third formula contains no blessing of branches but opens more simply with an antiphon that must be sung or recited. It makes the only reference to palms in that entire liturgy. If branches were blessed at a previous Mass, people take home some of what remains.

Branches may not be blessed outside Mass. In 1974 the Congregation addressed the question, "Whether the blessing and imposition of ashes (on Ash Wednesday), the blessing and distribution of palms (on Palm Sunday) and of candles (on the Presentation of the Lord) may be carried out without Mass." The members responded, "The blessing and imposition of ashes, for pastoral reasons, may also take place without Mass (see the Roman Missal, p. 180 [Ash Wednesday]). The other blessings are strictly connected to the celebration of Mass in the manner of a procession or of a solemn entrance."[35]

The passion accounts of Matthew, Mark, and Luke used to be proclaimed annually during Holy Week on Sunday and two of its weekdays. Now they rotate on Palm Sunday across the three years.

The Weekdays of Holy Week

The Table of Liturgical Days lists the early weekdays of Holy Week higher than the other weekdays of Lent. They share the second rank with other days of great importance, such as Christmas and Pentecost. When the solemnities of St. Joseph or of the Annunciation of the Lord fall during Holy Week, they move to another date. Because the octave of Easter also shares the second rank, those solemnities move to the second week of Easter.

Other celebrations that may fall during Holy Week are not observed. Feasts, memorials, and optional memorials are not rescheduled (GIRM 355a). Ritual Masses may not take place (372), not even the dedication of a church. There could be a wedding during Mass, but it would use the readings and prayers of the weekday, preparing for the passion of Christ. Anointing of the sick may take place, and a reading from its Ritual Mass may be heard (PCS 134, OUI 81), though this seems ill advised. The local bishop may not authorize a special Mass for Various Needs and Occasions (374). Masses for the Dead are not allowed (381)— except for a funeral (380). Only a funeral without Mass may take place on Holy Thursday morning (380), even though the Triduum has not yet begun.

---

35. Sacred Congregation for Divine Worship, "Documentorum explanatio: Ad Missale Romanum et Ordinem Missae," *Notitiae* 90, vol. 10, no. 2 (February 1974): 80.

The Chrism Mass

Once a year the bishop consecrates chrism and blesses the other oils for administering sacraments. Priests in attendance renew their promises. All are welcome, and the ceremony may especially appeal to those who will be anointed in the coming year, such as catechumens and candidates for confirmation.

Traditionally, this ceremony takes place at the cathedral on Holy Thursday morning. Priests would then return to their parishes for the evening Mass of the Lord's Supper. However, many dioceses take advantage of a permission in the Roman Missal. When it is difficult for the clergy and the faithful to gather for the Chrism Mass on Holy Thursday, the bishop may anticipate its celebration on another day, but still close to Easter.

Even when the Chrism Mass takes place on Holy Thursday, the celebration occurs during Lent. Early on, Van Doren remarked,

> The Mass of Chrism must not be considered as an ending but as a preparation and a beginning. In it, namely, are confected the holy chrism and the holy oil of the catechumens, which in the following night of the Sunday of the resurrection are administered to the new Christians.
>
> The solemn conclusion of Lent stands rather as the Mass of the reconciliation of penitents. But there is no present reason why this ancient practice should be taken up again.[36]

Schmidt summarized another verdict about the timing of the Chrism Mass: "The consecration of chrism per se has no relationship with Thursday of the Lord's Supper. It was moved from the paschal vigil to this day in the Roman liturgy only because of practical reasons!!"[37]

36. Schemata, n. 65, p. 2.
37. Schemata, n. 65, p. 2.

As the COVID-19 pandemic spread in early 2020, it limited public gatherings, and many dioceses canceled or postponed the Chrism Mass. The Vatican permitted conferences of bishops to delay it, probably the first time in history that a Chrism Mass could follow Easter instead of precede it.[38] At St. Peter's Basilica, in his Holy Thursday homily for the Mass of the Lord's Supper with only a few people in attendance, Pope Francis remarked, "There is no Chrism Mass today—I hope we can have it before Pentecost, otherwise it will have to be postponed to next year."[39] The pope never celebrated the Chrism Mass in 2020, though there was no other indication beyond this homily that the Chrism Mass must precede Pentecost.

The Sacred Paschal Triduum

In the Table of Liturgical Days the topmost entry is the Paschal Triduum of the passion and resurrection of the Lord. Although many believers enjoy Christmas more, Easter outranks even the birth of Christ. The resurrection is not celebrated in isolation. Its meaning inseparably connects to the passion of the Lord.

The revisers explained, "In order that the faithful may understand that the Paschal Triduum does not pertain to preparing the solemnity of Easter, but is itself truly the most sacred Triduum of the crucified, buried and risen One (St. Augustine), it takes its beginning at the Evening Mass of the Lord's Supper."[40] The Triduum includes the entire mystery of the death and resurrection of Christ, foreshadowed in

38. Robert Cardinal Sarah, "Decree: In Time of Covid-19 (II)," https://www.vatican.va/roman_curia/congregations/ccdds/documents/rc_con_ccdds_doc_20200325_decreto-intempodicovid_en.html.

39. Pope Francis, Homily, Mass of the Lord's Supper, 9 April 2020, https://www.vatican.va/content/francesco/en/homilies/2020/documents/papa-francesco_20200409_omelia-coenadomini.html.

40. Schemata, n. 213, p. [1].

the institution of the Eucharist. "The Supper *is* the paschal mystery."[41] The revision even expanded the proclaimed accounts of the passion to include the Lord's Supper.

The Missal echoes the words of Augustine. Its introduction to the Triduum says that the church keeps "by means of special celebrations the memorial of her Lord, crucified, buried, and risen" (1).

No other celebrations may replace these. All ritual Masses are excluded. Funeral Masses are forbidden (GIRM 380), as is any Mass for the Dead (381). A funeral may be celebrated without Mass.

In the Liturgy of the Hours, the psalms and antiphons for the Triduum are proper (GILH 62, 116, 134). Daytime Prayer uses the complementary psalms with proper antiphons (82).

Holy Thursday

The Mass of the Lord's Supper commemorates the institution of the Eucharist and of the priesthood. It may include the washing of the feet and ends with a procession and adoration of the Blessed Sacrament. The Missal requests "the full participation of the whole local community and with all the Priests and ministers exercising their office" (1). A priest may not celebrate a Mass individually on this day (GIRM 199). He is to celebrate or concelebrate in the presence of the people.

The local ordinary may permit a second Mass—for example, in the morning, if people are unable to gather in the evening, or in the evening in cases of genuine necessity. Some bilingual communities request permission for a Mass in each language.

The tabernacle is to be completely empty before the Mass begins. At any Mass the faithful preferably receive communion from the bread and wine consecrated at the same Mass, rather than from previously consecrated bread in the tabernacle (GIRM 85). On Holy Thursday, the church takes extra care

41. Bugnini, p. 307, summarizing the thought of several of the revisers.

to ensure this practice. All receive communion from the sacrifice that they have come to offer. A sufficient amount of bread is to be consecrated for communion on Good Friday as well.

Although flowers are not permitted during Lent, the Missal says that they may adorn the area around the altar "with a moderation that accords with the character of this day" (5). Bells are rung during the Gloria, but then they remain silent until the Gloria of the Easter Vigil. Likewise, the organ and other musical instruments may only be used to support singing during the same interval (7).

Before Morning Prayer, the people are encouraged to gather for the Office of Readings (GILH 209). This replaces the former custom of *Tenebrae* services, which featured increasing darkness.

Those taking part in the evening Mass do not pray Evening Prayer (GILH 209). This goes unexplained, but it probably relates to the depth of the celebration of the Mass on this night. Those who pray Evening Prayer use special antiphons for the usual Thursday psalms. After the reading comes a special responsory, which proclaims that Christ in obedience accepted death for the sake of the faithful. The responsory recurs during Night Prayer.

The readings for this Mass feature the remembrance of the meal that the ancient Israelites ate before the Exodus, the institution of the Eucharist, and the example of Christ washing his disciples' feet (ILM 99). These passages show the origins of the Eucharist and its implications for service.

Parishes may not distribute communion outside Mass on Holy Thursday. However, communion may be given to the sick at any hour (4). Even so, the Missal makes a recommendation for this Mass: "At an appropriate moment during Communion, the Priest entrusts the Eucharist from the table of the altar to Deacons or acolytes or other extraordinary ministers, so that afterwards it may be brought to the sick who are to receive Holy Communion at home" (33). Ideally, the sick receive communion from the bread and wine consecrated at this Mass.

Catholics believe in the real presence of Christ in the Eucharistic species. This belief leads them "to worship this wondrous Sacrament through adoration in a special way on Thursday of the Lord's Supper in Holy Week" (GIRM 3). The Missal says that the faithful may stay after the Mass for a period of adoration, "but after midnight the adoration should take place without solemnity" (43).

Good Friday

Catholics practice fasting and abstinence on Good Friday, as on Ash Wednesday (canons 1251–52). These acts of penance prepare one for worship.

In a similar spirit, the Missal's introduction for Good Friday states that the church does not celebrate sacraments on this day except for penance and the anointing of the sick (1). For this reason no weddings may take place, and any funerals are celebrated without Mass. The Order of Baptism of Children does not restrict the days for an emergency baptism (OBC 21).

Holy Communion will be distributed to the faithful only during the celebration of the Passion of the Lord. Only the sick may receive communion apart from this celebration (2).

As on Holy Thursday, those who participate in the main service do not pray Evening Prayer (GILH 209). Those who do pray this office use special psalms and antiphons, as well as a reading longer than usual, Philippians 2:6-11. The responsory repeats the one from the previous evening, but adds a few words indicating how Christ died: death on a cross. The same responsory recurs at Night Prayer. The intercessions that conclude Evening Prayer may come from the Missal's celebration of the Passion of the Lord or be replaced with silent prayer.

The priest and deacon vest in red (GIRM 346b). As on Palm Sunday, the color commemorates the sacrificial death of Christ, imitated by martyrs in subsequent centuries.

The Missal says that the altar is completely bare: no cross, candles, or cloths adorn it (3). The main celebration offers readings, solemn intercessions, adoration of the cross, and Holy Communion. In the United States, the bishop may permit a community to repeat the celebration. This may happen, for example, if the number of worshipers is large, or if celebrations in separate languages are preferred.

The liturgy opens dramatically. The clergy prostrate themselves before the altar and pray in silence (5).

The readings feature the passion according to John. To prepare for it, the people hear one of Isaiah's songs of the Suffering Servant and a passage from Hebrews about Christ the high priest (ILM 99).

For communion, the altar is prepared with cloth and candles, and a minister brings the Blessed Sacrament to the altar (22). The faithful receive the Body of Christ consecrated the previous day. At the conclusion, the ministers genuflect to the cross, which receives adoration only on this day.

Holy Saturday

Having celebrated the passion of the Lord, the church observes Holy Saturday. The Missal sums it up well: "On Holy Saturday the Church waits at the Lord's tomb in prayer and fasting, meditating on his Passion and Death and on his Descent into Hell, and awaiting his Resurrection" (1).

The altar is bare. There is no celebration of the Eucharist during the day (2). Holy Communion may be given only as viaticum to the dying (3). Those who are otherwise sick must await Easter to receive communion. As noted on Good Friday (1), no other sacraments are celebrated, except for penance and anointing of the sick. No weddings may take place on Holy Saturday. In an emergency, baptism may always be celebrated (OBC 21).

The faithful are not under a canonical obligation to fast on Holy Saturday, but the practice is encouraged. The council recommended extending the paschal fast of Good Friday into Holy Saturday, to clear the mind and lift up the spirit to celebrate the resurrection (SC 110).

If the cross remains on display during the day on Holy Saturday, it receives a special reverence. Those entering the church or passing by the cross genuflect as they would before a tabernacle (GIRM 274).

Before Morning Prayer, the people are encouraged to gather for the Office of Readings (GILH 209). This replaces the former custom of *Tenebrae* services.

Those preparing to be baptized celebrate the Preparation Rites sometime during the day (OCIA 185–205). These feature the recitation of the Creed. As the elect received the Creed from the faithful, so now, having meditated on and memorized it, they recite it back to the community. This demonstrates their readiness to make their baptismal promises during the Easter Vigil.

The Liturgy of the Hours features Evening Prayer—the only Saturday of the year with its own, instead of Evening Prayer I for Sunday. Similarly, Easter is the only Sunday without Evening Prayer I. This office has special antiphons and psalms. After the reading, the responsory further extends the one begun on Holy Thursday, which recalls the obedience of Christ accepting death on a cross. Here are added the words that God raised him on high and gave him a name above every other name. Night Prayer is said only by those not participating in the Vigil. They repeat this responsory in its fullness.

The Easter Vigil

The church observes many vigils throughout the year, but, as Augustine noted, the Easter Vigil is the mother of all holy vigils (UNLYC 21). The church gathers to greet the news of the resurrection in the dark of night. No priest may celebrate Mass by himself on this day; its nature requires the gathering of believers (GIRM 199). Furthermore, the Missal states that only one celebration may take place in each church (2). Even bilingual communities gather for a single celebration. The Mass is an Easter Mass, even if it concludes before midnight, and those who receive communion may receive again on Easter Day (4–5).

Seven Old Testament readings recall the works of God in salvation history. From the New Testament, Paul shows how Christian baptism is the sacrament of Christ's resurrection, and the gospel proclaims the good news of the resurrection (ILM 99).

During the Easter Vigil, it is most fitting to celebrate the baptism of adults and children. If the priest recites the first eucharistic prayer, he uses special inserts proclaiming that the community celebrates the most sacred night "of the Resurrection of our Lord Jesus Christ in the flesh" (OM 86). The dismissal dialogue concludes with a double Alleluia.

Those who participate in the Easter Vigil omit the Office of Readings (GILH 212). Others draw readings from the Easter Vigil into their prayer. Similarly, those participating in the Vigil do not pray Night Prayer on Holy Saturday (211).

Easter Sunday

The liturgical calendar hinges on Easter Sunday, the celebration of the resurrection. As Sunday celebrates the resurrection weekly, so Easter celebrates it annually (UNLYC 1).

A priest who has celebrated or concelebrated the Easter Vigil may celebrate again on Easter Day (GIRM 204b). This would even be appropriate for the faithful.

At Mass the Easter sequence follows the second reading and precedes the gospel acclamation. In the United States the Missal states that the renewal of baptismal promises may replace the Creed as at the Easter Vigil (72). In practice, many priests add a sprinkling of the congregation with blessed water.

The special inserts to Eucharistic Prayer I pertains to Easter Day as to the Vigil. The dismissal formula at Mass concludes with a double Alleluia.

In the Liturgy of the Hours, the antiphons and psalms are proper (GILH 116). Even though there was no Evening Prayer

I, and those who participate in the Vigil omit the Office of Readings and Night Prayer, all offer Morning Prayer of Easter Sunday. A solemn celebration of Evening Prayer is recommended to end this sacred day, and "to commemorate the occasions when the Lord showed himself to his disciples" (213). This may include a procession to the baptismal font during the psalms.

Easter Time

Citing an expression of Athanasius, the Missal declares that "The fifty days from the Sunday of the Resurrection to Pentecost Sunday are celebrated in joy and exultation as one feast day, indeed as one 'great Sunday'" (UNLYC 22). Basil used the same image, seven weeks celebrated as a single day.[42]

Prior to the reforms, Easter Time extended through the octave of Pentecost. The revisers proposed suppressing that octave to restore Easter to fifty days. Van Doren objected:

> Don't let the Pentecost octave be suppressed! If a reason from antiquity may be brought forth, the Pentecost octave already existed in Rome by the end of the sixth century. . . .
>
> The liturgy of this week is deservedly judged among the pearls of the sacred year. For it is the best exposition of the action of the Spirit Paraclete, both in the universal Church, the Body of Christ, and in the soul of each of the baptized. A judgment based on pastoral usefulness and of the value of liturgical teaching must be preferred there instead of the arithmetic argument about the number fifty. It must be added, if the octave is suppressed, must the Mass of the preceding Sunday, the Spirit of the Lord [Pentecost], be repeated on the weekdays of this week?[43]

42. Schemata, n. 260, p. 2, citing *"Liber de Spiritu Sancto*, cap. XXVII, n. 66: PG 32, 192."

43. Schemata, n. 65, p. 3.

At the time, it was customary to repeat the Sunday anti-phons, prayers, and readings on succeeding weekdays. Van Doren wondered if the Masses of the octave would be re-placed with a disappointing repetition of Pentecost. Schmidt proposed an idea that eventually influenced the design:

> I agree if the days between Ascension and Pentecost still more closely celebrate the mission of the Holy Spirit.
> This must be said:
> 1) that the most ancient unity between the Ascension and Pentecost be restored;
> 2) that the members of the Consilium see that we are not destroying Pentecost but instead are making it more precise.[44]

At Mass, the priest and deacon wear white throughout Easter Time. Exceptions occur on days such as those of apostles and martyrs, when they wear red (GIRM 346a).

The readings at Mass favor the gospel of John, Acts of the Apostles, the First Letter of John, and Revelation (ILM 66, 74, 84, 99, 101, and 107). For fifty days, all readings come from the New Testament. This is to include Ritual Masses as well, whether of confirmations, weddings, or ordinations. Funeral Masses are also to exclude readings from the Old Testament.

Eucharistic Prayer IV is not used during Easter Time be-cause it has its own invariable preface (GIRM 365d). The prefaces of Easter begin Eucharistic Prayers I, II, and III.

The Alleluia is heard not only in the gospel acclamation, but also at the end of the entrance and communion antiphons at Mass. When celebrating a Mass for Various Needs and Oc-casions, the Alleluia is added to the same antiphons unless it would clash with their meaning. For example, the Mass for the Sick opens with an antiphon drawn from Psalm 6: "Have

---

44. Schemata, n. 65, p. 4.

mercy on me, Lord, for I languish; Lord, heal me; my bones are trembling, and my soul is greatly shaken." It would not be fitting to add "Alleluia." At Masses for the Dead, the Alleluia may be left off any antiphon.

In the Liturgy of the Hours, an Alleluia is added to the antiphons unless it would clash with the meaning (GILH 120, 214). For example, at the Office of Readings on Wednesday of the second week, the two antiphons of Psalm 39 express the anguish of a sick person; on Friday of the third week, the second antiphon of Psalm 69 laments receiving vinegar to slake one's thirst. In Latin, the Alleluia is not sung after those antiphons even during Easter Time, though in English the Alleluia mistakenly and incongruously appears.

As in Advent, Christmas, and Lent, Psalms 78, 105, and 106 enter the four-week psalter. The oration that concludes Morning, Daytime, and Evening Prayer matches the collect from Mass (GILH 199–200). This helps unify the liturgies and underscores the special nature of each of these days.

The Sundays of Easter

In the Table of Liturgical Days, the Sundays of Easter stand in the second tier, just after major solemnities such as Christmas and Pentecost, and equal in rank to the Sundays of Advent and Lent. This corrects a situation in the previous Missal, where the Sundays of Advent ranked higher than those of Easter. Nocent remarked,

> The faithful in our times, who are exceedingly "distracted" by different threads of devotions in the Christian life, need a liturgy that clearly indicates the essential Christian faith, namely the death and resurrection of Christ, the paschal mystery. This Easter Time cannot be celebrated too much.[45]

---

45. Schemata, n. 65, p. 5.

As the group revised the Table of Liturgical Days, Jounel offered a commentary on the proposed new arrangement:

> Solemn Sundays correspond to the former Sundays of the first class. There have been added here the Sundays of Easter Time, from now on called Sundays of Easter. It would be unacceptable that these Sundays be less important than those of Advent.[46]

Formerly called Sundays "after Easter," they were now to be known as Sundays "of Easter." The subtle shift shows that they participate in the joy of the fifty days.

At Mass, the sprinkling of blessed water may replace the penitential act on any Sunday, but many parishes favor this change during these weeks. The Missal offers the option "from time to time on Sundays, especially in Easter Time" (OM 4).

The gospels for the first three Sundays recount appearances of Christ after the resurrection. The Fourth Sunday has a gospel about the Good Shepherd. The last Sundays draw excerpts from Jesus' final discourse and prayer at the Last Supper. First readings all come from Acts of the Apostles: Each year narrates the start of the early church, its witness and its growth. The second readings in Year A come from the First Letter of Peter with its baptismal catechesis. The First Letter of John supplies readings for Year B, and Year C presents excerpts from Revelation with its vision of the full glory of the risen Christ (ILM 100).

Ritual Masses are forbidden (GIRM 372). If a bishop offers the sacrament of confirmation on a Sunday in Easter Time, he uses the readings and prayers of the day, rather than those of the Ritual Mass. The same applies to an ordination. However, if a priest anoints the sick, one reading from the Ritual Mass may replace one from Sunday (PCS 134, OUI 81). This used

46. Schemata, n. 237, p. 3.

to be permitted at weddings, as noted in the 1969 *Rite of Marriage* (11).[47] However, the edition in force calls for all the readings of the Sunday Mass if a wedding takes place on that day in Easter Time (OCM 54).

The Ritual Mass for the Dedication of a Church may be celebrated in full. This marks a rare exception when a first reading during Easter Time comes from the Old Testament. At a dedication, even in Easter Time, even on a Sunday, the first reading must be Nehemiah 8:1-4a, 5-6, 8-10, about the people of Jerusalem gathering to hear the proclamation of the Law of God (ODCA II:12). If an altar is to be dedicated, the Mass of the Sunday is used, except for the prayer over the offerings and the preface.

A Mass for Various Needs and Occasions may not replace the Sunday Mass of Easter Time (GIRM 374). Nor may a funeral Mass (380).

Specific Sundays of Easter

The Second Sunday of Easter has had various titles. Historically, it was the Sunday *in albis* because those who had been baptized on Easter Sunday returned after a week of mystagogy wearing their white baptismal garments. It was also called Low Sunday, as it demanded less detailed attention than Easter Day. Josef Jungmann had requested of the revisers that this Sunday restore the character of the octave of Easter.[48] The early editions of the revised Missal called it the Second Sunday of Easter, but the third edition added a subtitle: Divine Mercy Sunday.

St. Faustina Kowalska († 1938), a Polish mystic, popularized the devotion of Divine Mercy, having reported a vision that

47. "Rite of Marriage," *The Rites of the Catholic Church*, vol. I (Collegeville, MN: Liturgical Press, 1990), p. 722.
48. Schemata, n. 93, p. 3.

Jesus had requested observances on the Sunday after Easter. When Pope John Paul II, himself a Pole, canonized Faustina on the Sunday after Easter in 2000, he declared that the Second Sunday of Easter throughout the church be henceforth known as Divine Mercy Sunday.[49] A rubric heading the missal's Votive Mass of the Mercy of God specifies that its prayers and antiphons may not replace those of the Mass for the Second Sunday of Easter.

Because the Second Sunday closes the octave, the sequence of Easter is optional. If the priest offers Eucharistic Prayer I, he affirms that the community is celebrating the resurrection, as on Easter Day. It is also the last day until Pentecost that the dismissal formula concludes with the double Alleluia.

The Fourth Sunday is commonly called Good Shepherd Sunday because the gospel each year draws from the tenth chapter of John, where Jesus applies that title to himself. The Holy See designates it as a World Day of Prayer for Vocations. Paul VI had inaugurated this day of prayer in 1964 when, under the previous calendar, Good Shepherd Sunday was the Third Sunday of Easter.[50] The USCCB lists it among its Days of Prayer and Special Observances.

The USCCB has World Communications Day on the Seventh Sunday of Easter. In 1967, Paul VI established this to inspire the use of "modern means of social communication, such as the press, motion pictures, radio and television" to

49. Pope John Paul II, "Homily of the Holy Father: Mass in St. Peter's Square for the Canonization of Sr. Mary Faustina Kowalska," Sunday, 30 April 2000, 4, https://www.vatican.va/content/john-paul-ii/en/homilies/2000/documents/hf_jp-ii_hom_20000430_faustina.html.

50. "Radiomessaggio del Papa Paolo VI per la I Giornata Mondiale delle Vocazioni," 11 April 1964, https://www.vatican.va/content/paul-vi/it/messages/vocations/documents/hf_p-vi_mes_19640411_i-word-day-for-vocations.html.

help spread the gospel.[51] Even where the Ascension of the Lord replaces the Seventh Sunday of Easter, World Communications Day is observed. The pope publishes his annual message on the memorial of Francis de Sales, the patron of journalists.

The Octave of Easter

An octave follows the two greatest celebrations of the year, Christmas and Easter, and each has its own rules (UNLYC 12). In Easter, the days are all celebrated as solemnities (24). They rank in the second tier on the Table of Liturgical Days, a level shared with major solemnities, Ash Wednesday, and the weekdays of Holy Week. The days even displace other solemnities that may fall during this week. Those making particular calendars are discouraged from choosing dates that may fall within this octave (56f).

The weekdays receive several features: The Gloria is sung. The sequence may be repeated. The gospels proclaim appearances of the risen Christ (ILM 101). When using Eucharistic Prayer I, the priest adds the special lines about the community celebrating the resurrection. The dismissal formula concludes with the double Alleluia. It feels like Easter Day every day for eight days.

Ritual Masses are forbidden during the octave (GIRM 372). If a bishop administers confirmation at any Mass this week, he uses the readings and prayers of the day. The same applies to an ordination. For anointing the sick at Mass this week, one reading from the Ritual Mass may replace a weekday reading (PCS 134, OUI 81). A wedding at Mass on the first Saturday after Easter takes the prayers and readings of the weekday in order to proclaim the resurrection. An evening wedding Mass

51. Paul VI, "Message of the Holy Father for the World Social Communications Day," https://www.vatican.va/content/paul-vi/en/messages/communications/documents/hf_p-vi_mes_19670507_i-com-day.html.

that day uses these or the prayers and readings of the Second Sunday of Easter.

If a church is dedicated during the octave, the Ritual Mass may replace the one for the weekday, including its first reading from the Old Testament. If an altar is to be dedicated during the octave, the Mass of the weekday is used, except for the prayer over the offerings and the preface.

The Masses for Various Needs and Occasions may not replace these weekdays, even if a bishop were so inclined (GIRM 374). A funeral Mass may replace the prayers and readings of the octave (380), but other Masses for the Dead are not celebrated. Those on receiving the news of a death, for the final burial, or for the first anniversary are permitted on "weekdays," but the Latin word *feria* would exclude the solemnities of this octave (381).

In the Liturgy of the Hours, the octave has proper antiphons for the psalms at Morning and Evening Prayer (GILH 116), and special psalms, antiphons and readings at the Office of Readings (62, 134), when the *Te Deum* is sung each day (68). At Daytime Prayer the complementary psalms are offered with proper antiphons (82, 134). Memorials that fall during this week are disregarded (237). The proper antiphons, hymns, readings, responsories, prayers, and often the psalms for these days cannot be changed (247). Votive offices, such as those of a local saint or while on pilgrimage, may not replace those of this octave (245).

The Other Weekdays of Easter

After the octave, the other weekdays of Easter drop to the thirteenth tier on the Table of Liturgical Days. The weekdays of Advent and Lent rank higher than those of Easter Time. Still, each has its own proper liturgy, including a unique collect at Mass, whereas the prayers over the offerings, prefaces, and prayers after communion are used more than once.

The readings at Mass all come from the New Testament. The first reading is semicontinuous from the Acts of the Apostles (GIRM 357; ILM 74, 101). The gospels come from John, with the last weeks turning to the final discourse and prayer of Jesus at the Last Supper (ILM 101). These readings remain the same every year (ILM 69 §3).

At solemnities of saints, three readings are offered, and the first is to come from Acts or the book of Revelation (ILM 84 §2). On feasts and memorials, the first reading comes from one of the apostles, and the gospel, as far as possible, from John (84 §3). In setting up particular calendars, the readings during Easter Time are to avoid the Old Testament.[52]

A daily homily is recommended on these days (GIRM 66). The Lectionary "strongly" recommends one (ILM 25).

The memorials of saints may be celebrated in full (GIRM 355a). The same applies to any saint listed in the Martyrology.

Ritual Masses may be celebrated in full (GIRM 372). For a good cause the rector or presider may choose one of the Masses for Various Needs and Occasions or a Votive Mass; otherwise, these are in principle forbidden (376). A funeral may be celebrated (380). A daily Mass for the dead is not permitted, except on receiving the news of a death, for the final burial, or on the first anniversary (381).

As noted above, the former calendar observed three minor Rogation Days just before Ascension Thursday. The norms now allow conferences to distribute these differently (UNLYC 45–47). The days before the Ascension simply flow with the other weekdays in the sixth week of Easter Time.

The Ascension of the Lord
On the Table of Liturgical Days, the Ascension of the Lord shares space in the second tier along with other key solemnities: Christmas, Epiphany, and Pentecost. Traditionally ob-

---

52. *Calendaria particularia* 42, DOL 481 (4037), p. 1254.

served on a Thursday, it marks the day when, according to Acts 1:3, the risen Jesus ascended into heaven after forty days with his apostles (UNLYC 25). As noted above under solemnities of obligation, the observance may transfer to Sunday (UNLYC 7b).

Perhaps the most important reading is the first, taken from the Acts of the Apostles, which recounts the ascension of the Lord. The second reading presents the exaltation of Christ at the right hand of the Father. The gospel comes from Matthew, Mark, or Luke, according to the year of the cycle (ILM 102).

If the priest offers Eucharistic Prayer I, he uses a special insert, proclaiming the significance of the day: When the Son of God made flesh ascended, he amazingly placed weak human nature at the right hand of the Father (OM 86).

Ritual Masses are forbidden, so a wedding at Mass uses the prayers and readings of the solemnity. A new church may not be dedicated on this day. A new altar may be dedicated, using the Mass of the solemnity, except for the prayer over the offerings and the preface. Masses for Various Needs and Occasions, Votive Masses, and Masses for the Dead are forbidden (GIRM 372, 374, 381). Not even a funeral Mass may be offered on this day (GIRM 380).

Weekdays Between the Ascension and Pentecost

The weekdays following the Ascension prepare for the coming of the Holy Spirit at Pentecost (UNLYC 26). Because the octave of Pentecost is discontinued, its theme, focused on the Holy Spirit, was moved to this period. As the revisers explain, "all the texts of the octave are being reused, and in a worthy manner, during Easter Time, especially in the days between the Ascension and Pentecost, which will become a kind of liturgical 'novena' in preparation for the descent of the Holy Spirit."[53] For example, the prayer after communion

---

53. Schemata, n. 260, p. 2.

on Tuesday after the Ascension is a slightly modified version of the one from Friday after Pentecost in the previous Missal.

Permission to celebrate Ascension on a Sunday preceded the revised liturgical books. In 1968, the Sacred Congregation of Rites had to explain where to find the texts for each day. If Ascension moved to a Sunday, the prayers assigned to Friday, Saturday, and Sunday in the Roman Breviary moved to Wednesday, Thursday, and Friday, so that the Ascension and its vigil could move to the weekend.[54]

The Missal in the United States accounts for both possibilities because of the different approved practices. On Wednesday of the Sixth Week, the texts for Mass are restricted to the morning in those places where the Ascension remains a holy day of obligation. There, the Mass for the Vigil of the Ascension is to be used on Wednesday night. Texts for a Thursday weekday Mass pertain to those places where Ascension has been transferred to Sunday. On Friday and Saturday the Missal offers two options for the collect, depending on whether or not the community has already celebrated the Ascension.

In the Lectionary, the responsorial psalms during these weekdays all carry themes of the Ascension. These include the psalms on Friday and Saturday of the sixth week of Easter, even where the Ascension has not yet been celebrated.

Pentecost

The Table of Liturgical Days lists Pentecost at the top of the second tier, together with Christmas, Epiphany, and the Ascension. Pentecost is the terminus of "the whole mystery of Christ," which the church celebrates over the course of the liturgical year (UNLYC 17). Easter Time concludes with Pentecost Sunday (23).

The revisers eliminated the octave to help people interpret the meaning of Pentecost. Early on they proposed "that the

---

54. Benno Cardinal Gut and Fernandus Antonelli, "Declaratio," *Notitiae* 42, vol. 4, nos. 9–10 (September–October 1968): 279.

octave of Pentecost be suppressed (two consultors feeling otherwise), and Pentecost be held as the seal of Easter Time. Because the day of Pentecost has no longer been understood above all as the fiftieth day of Easter Time, but as the anniversary feast of the descent of the Holy Spirit, an octave had been added."[55]

At Mass the priest and deacon wear red (GIRM 346b), a color associated with the Holy Spirit. The Lectionary has separate readings for the Vigil Mass. These anticipate the coming of the Holy Spirit, celebrated in full on Pentecost Day. The *Supplement* to the Lectionary in the United States provides the set of four Old Testament readings and psalms for an extended vigil (62),[56] and the Missal has prayers that follow these, imitating the practice at the Easter Vigil.

The readings from Paul this weekend show the working of the Holy Spirit throughout the church and also within the individual (ILM 102). The primary account for Pentecost comes from the Acts of the Apostles, so the first reading has unusual presence. The gospels tell of Jesus' promise of the Spirit (at the Vigil) or bestowing the Spirit on the day of his resurrection (during the day).

The sequence is obligatory on Pentecost Day (GIRM 64). It is not part of the Vigil. However, in the United States for pastoral reasons the readings and prayers of Pentecost Day may be used on Saturday evening instead of the Pentecost Mass.[57] In that case, the sequence should be sung. Pastoral reasons may include, for example, a mission church where

55. Schemata, n. 75, p. 4.

56. Committee on Divine Worship, USCCB, *Lectionary for Mass: Supplement for Use in the Dioceses of the United States of America, Second Typical Edition* (New York: Catholic Book Publishing, 2017).

57. *Ordo: Order of Prayer in the Liturgy of the Hours and Celebration of the Eucharist 2024*, Book 18, compiled by Peter D. Rocca, CSC (Mahwah, NJ: Paulist Press, 2023). In private correspondence, Rocca told this author that the permission appears in the Vatican Ordo, and the USCCB approves him including it in the Ordos of the United States.

the only weekend Mass takes place on a Saturday afternoon or evening.

The Mass for Pentecost has its own preface. A priest using Eucharistic Prayer I adds a special insert. His words proclaim that the community is celebrating the day when the Holy Spirit appeared to the apostles in tongues of fire (OM 86).

Ritual Masses are forbidden, including the one for the dedication of a church. The dedication of an altar may take place, and the prayer over the offerings and preface become those of the dedication Mass. An ordination or a wedding at Mass requires the use of the Pentecost prayers and readings.

In its presentation on the office of Vigils, the Liturgy of the Hours notes that Pentecost is among the days when a vigil is most appropriate, as on Christmas and Easter (GILH 71). The Mass offers one way to extend the Pentecost Vigil, and the Liturgy of the Hours offers another. The double Alleluia returns for the conclusion of Mass and of Evening Prayer II.

Ordinary Time

"Besides the times of year that have their own distinctive character, there remain in the yearly cycle thirty-three or thirty-four weeks in which no particular aspect of the mystery of Christ is celebrated, but rather the mystery of Christ itself is honored in its fullness, especially on Sundays. This period is known as Ordinary Time" (UNLYC 43).

The weeks of Ordinary Time are split by Lent and Easter Time. Ordinary Time begins the day following the Baptism of the Lord. It continues through the Tuesday that precedes Ash Wednesday. It resumes on the Monday after Pentecost and concludes on Saturday before Evening Prayer I of the First Sunday of Advent (UNLYC 44).

Some years do not have time for all thirty-four weeks. After Pentecost, Ordinary Time resumes with the week that puts the thirty-fourth week on the days preceding the next Advent.

One week may be omitted, affecting both the Liturgy of the Hours and the Mass.

The former calendar used different terms for these two halves: Sundays after Epiphany and Sundays after Pentecost. Those expressions made it appear as if Epiphany and Pentecost were extended for many weeks and months. The more neutral designation honors the complete mystery of Christ.

The former calendar designated several days to prepare for Lent. Septuagesima, Sexagesima, and Quinquagesima Sundays signified approximately seventy, sixty, and fifty days before Easter. The titles had more meaning in language groups that called Lent "the time of forty," as does Spanish with the word *Cuaresma*. This time before Lent had its own penitential quality, and the revisers thought that this detracted from a proper appreciation of Lent:

> The time of Septuagesima offered nothing characteristic of itself, and the divine office took its parts into Ordinary Time. It was a most difficult task to speak about it to the people, and it especially diminished the note of the newness of the penitential liturgy of Lent before it could begin. The texts of all of this time are placed elsewhere in the Roman Missal.[58]

These weeks featured penitential aspects, such as removing the Gloria and the Alleluia, and wearing violet vesture. The revisers perceived confusion: "The external signs of a time of penance were already in use, as in Lent, but [the people] were not held to particular penance as in Lent."[59] The Constitution on the Sacred Liturgy called for greater clarity in the liturgical year, so the revisers favored suppressing these weeks. They offered a word of caution, though, motivated by ecumenical concerns: "As to what pertains to the names Septuagesima,

---

58. Schemata, n. 225, p. 3. See also Schemata, n. 260, p. 4.
59. Schemata, n. 75, p. 2.

Sexagesima, and Quinquagesima, because these names have also been used by some of our separated brothers and sisters, we must advance cautiously in this matter, and we must promote conversation about this matter, as in other things."[60]

The decision was not easy. Pope Paul once referred to Septuagesima as the first of the bells calling people to Sunday Mass. But the revisers believed that Lent would better regain its force by removing its preliminary extension.[61] They pointed out the absurdity of the titles of these days, again with a concern for ecumenical uniformity:

> For many, the essence of this time holds to the names of Septuagesima, Sexagesima, and Quinquagesima. Even though the names are traditional, it is difficult to grasp their meaning because the Sundays represent respectively the forty-seventh, the fifty-fourth, and the sixty-first days before the sacred Triduum. If a certain number of Christian churches of the West have kept this appellation, many have already abandoned it, and some others foresee changing it in the "updating" of their respective liturgies.[62]

The vestment color for Ordinary Time is green (GIRM 346c). This lengthy period provides a break from the intense celebrations of Advent, Christmas, Lent, and Easter.

Ordinary Time Sundays

In the Table of Liturgical Days, Sundays in Ordinary Time rank sixth. The readings for Mass spotlight a semicontinuous presentation of one of the gospels: Matthew in Year A, Mark in Year B, and Luke in Year C of the three-year cycle. Portions

60. Schemata, n. 75, p. 2.
61. Bugnini, p. 307.
62. Consilium ad Exsequendam Constitutionem de Sacra Liturgia, Schemata, n. 188 addenda, De Calendario 11, 22 September 1966, p. 5.

of John's gospel are heard on the Second Sunday of Ordinary Time each year, and on certain Sundays of Year B (ILM 105).

At the head of Ordinary Time, the missal states that the Baptism of the Lord is the first Sunday in Ordinary Time, with a lower case "f." The presidential prayers that follow are for the First Week in Ordinary Time.

The Old Testament supplies the first readings, which correspond to the gospel of the day (ILM 106). The number of passages has greatly increased in the revision, giving worshipers an extensive encounter with the Old Testament.

The second readings are semicontinuous passages from the letters of Paul and James. First Corinthians is long and important, so it spreads over all three years on the first Sundays of Ordinary Time. The Letter to the Hebrews spans Years B and C (ILM 107).

Ritual Masses may replace those for these Sundays (GIRM 372). A bishop offering the sacrament of confirmation may use the complete Ritual Mass with its readings. The same applies to a priest celebrating a wedding Mass. If, however, the wedding takes place during a regularly scheduled parish Sunday Mass, the Mass in Ordinary Time takes precedence, though one reading may be exchanged for one from those recommended for weddings (OCM 34).

Ordinarily, a Mass for Various Needs and Occasions may not take place on a Sunday in Ordinary Time. However, the diocesan bishop may authorize one for a serious need or pastoral advantage (GIRM 374).

Funeral Masses are permitted on these Sundays (GIRM 380), though not all cemeteries can accommodate a Sunday interment. Other Masses for the Dead are not allowed (GIRM 381).

In the Liturgy of the Hours, the hymns for the Office of Readings has options for the extended celebration of Vigils (GILH 73). The same office includes the singing of the *Te Deum*.

Holy Trinity Sunday

The Sunday after Pentecost is the Solemnity of the Most Holy Trinity. It held this position in the previous calendar as well, but the revisers considered moving it or eliminating it. In early meetings they proposed reassigning it to the Monday after Pentecost or even Thanksgiving Day, when the Votive Mass of the Trinity could be used. Nocent favored "the abolition of this celebration, whose texts are poor," and thought that "the celebration itself is an abstract celebration."[63]

Others concurred that the feast was unnecessary because "the whole liturgy is trinitarian, especially the baptismal liturgy."[64] Still others argued against suppressing it for ecumenical reasons: "because of some separated brethren who celebrate this feast, or who at least call this Sunday Trinity Sunday."[65] In the end, no change was made.

The readings correspond to the principal themes (ILM 108). Unfortunately, the collect in the Missal has a mistranslation in English, asking that the faithful adore the Unity of God the Father, instead of the Unity of the Trinity.

The Most Holy Body and Blood of Christ (Corpus Christi)

Although people commonly refer to this solemnity by its former title in Latin, Corpus Christi, its full title is significant. This day celebrates belief in the real presence of Christ in the Eucharist, his Body and Blood under the forms of bread and wine. The day joined the calendar in the thirteenth century, and it sustains popular devotion. Eucharistic processions enter public streets in many countries. Traditionally it is celebrated on the Thursday after Trinity Sunday, probably to resonate with the events of Holy Thursday. However, conferences of

63. Schemata, n. 65, p. 14.
64. Schemata, n. 75, p. 4.
65. Schemata, n. 75, p. 4.

bishops move it unless they make Thursday a holy day of obligation. In the United States, it falls on the Sunday after Trinity Sunday.

The former calendar had two feasts of the Precious Blood. The older one was among a group of seven offices of the Passion of the Lord celebrated each week from Septuagesima into Lent. It was composed at Sarzana, Italy, about the year 1750, in honor of a relic of the Most Precious Blood. Observed on Friday of the fourth week of Lent, it was removed from the calendar in 1961.[66] The second day, celebrated on July 1 every year,

> was instituted by Pope Pius VII in 1822 for the Congregation of the Most Precious Blood, on the request of St. Gaspar del Bufalo. It was extended to the entire Church in 1849, following a promise made by Pius IX during his exile in Gaeta on the advice of his confessor, the superior general of the Congregation of the Most Precious Blood. The date chosen, (the first Sunday of July in 1849, July 1 in 1913), is that on which French troops put down the Roman revolution.

Pope Pius XI elevated this feast to the grade of first class, to commemorate the jubilee of the nineteenth centenary of the redemption in 1935.[67]

The revisers planned to eliminate this devotional feast altogether, leaving the observance of Corpus Christi unchanged. They argued that the devotion came late to the church's calendar, that every day honors the passion, death, and resurrection of the Lord, and that many other feasts invite the faithful to venerate the redeeming Blood. Besides, Corpus Christi already included references to the Blood of Christ in the collect, epistle, Alleluia, sequence, gospel, communion antiphon,

---

66. Sacred Congregation of Rites, "*De calendarii particularibus,*" 33, http://www.introibo.fr/instruction-de-calendariis.

67. Schemata, n. 260, p. 48.

and prayer after communion. Furthermore, the feast of the Sacred Heart of Jesus mentions water and blood flowing from the heart of Christ in the gospel and communion antiphon. "But above all, the feast of the Exaltation of the Holy Cross 'adorned with royal purple,' is an act of faith in redemption by means of the Blood of Christ."[68]

> For this reason it seems preferable to suppress this feast, which, after all, cannot be celebrated by the faithful with all appropriate solemnity because it ordinarily falls during the week. Rather than propose to the devotion of the faithful one specific feast of the mystery of the redemption detached from the paschal solemnity, it is better to accent how it is carried in the catechesis on the Mass (especially on the eucharistic prayer) and in communion under both kinds, permitted now to all the faithful on certain occasions of their life.[69]

Allowed to move Corpus Christi to a Sunday, some conferences wanted broader permission to choose a different day altogether. "In reality, in the southern hemisphere, the first weeks after Pentecost fall in winter, and the faithful would like a eucharistic procession to take shape in the season of flowers—in spring or summer—as in Europe."[70]

Not everyone agreed. In 1968 the Congregation of the Doctrine of the Faith resisted the elimination or reduction in class of numerous feasts of devotion that recent popes had established. This seemed "a danger to religious practice."[71] After the new calendar was announced in 1969, the elimination of the feast of the Most Precious Blood faced the strongest objection. The Congregation for Divine Worship received 367 petitions from eleven countries asking that it be restored. The revisers

68. Schemata, n. 260, pp. 46, 48.
69. Schemata, n. 260, p. 49.
70. Schemata, n. 260, p. 77.
71. Bugnini, p. 310.

held their ground. References to the Precious Blood were still in the Missal, such as the entrance antiphon on many Fridays of Easter Time.[72] That was not enough. Already in 1969 the Congregation corrected an error in the first publication of the General Roman Calendar, which had renamed Corpus Christi as "The Most Holy Eucharist." The title changed back to "Corpus Christi."[73] In 1970 the Holy See announced not so much a change, but additional words to entitle the former Corpus Christi as "The Most Holy Body and Blood of Christ."[74] A commentary on the change appeared shortly afterward, stating, "In the revised Roman Calendar the solemnity of 'Corpus Christi' is called the solemnity 'of the Body and Blood' of the Lord."[75] The article revealed that Pope Paul had announced the change on February 4, 1970, to a visiting group of Sisters of the Most Precious Blood.

The readings at Mass correspond to the principal themes of the celebration (ILM 108). Several selections adorn the three-year cycle.

The Missal promotes adoration of the Blessed Sacrament on this day (GIRM 3) and encourages conducting a eucharistic procession after this Mass, in keeping with an earlier instruction by the Sacred Congregation of Rites.[76] A host consecrated at the Mass is to be carried in procession afterwards. The local ordinary decides on the advisability, place, and plan of such a procession, so that decorum may be observed.

The Liturgy of the Hours preserves many of the eucharistic hymns composed for this day and attributed to Thomas

72. Bugnini, p. 315.

73. Sacred Congregation for Divine Worship, "Corrigenda," *Notitiae* 47, vol. 5, nos. 7–8 (July–August 1969): 303.

74. Sacred Congregation for Divine Worship, "Variationes in 'Calendarium Romanum' Inductae," *Notitiae* 54, vol. 6, no. 5 (May 1970): 192.

75. "Santissimo Corpo e Sangue di Cristo," *Notitiae* 56, vol. 6, no. 7 (July–August 1970): 275.

76. "Instruction *Eucharisticum mysterium*," DOL 179 (1288), p. 417.

Aquinas. Many are well known by their Latin titles: *Pange, lingua*, with its final verses *Tantum ergo*; *Sacris sollemniis*, with its final verses *Panis angelicus*; and *Verbum supernum*, with its final verses, O *salutaris hostia*.

In countries moving the solemnity to a Sunday, it fell on June 24 in 1973. With two solemnities on the same day, the Sacred Congregation for Divine Worship moved the observance of the Nativity of John the Baptist to Saturday, June 23 that year.[77] When the convergence occurred again in 1984, the USCCB transferred the Nativity of John the Baptist to Monday, June 25.[78] This will happen again in 2057.

Our Lord Jesus Christ, King of the Universe

The Sundays of the liturgical year close with the solemnity of Our Lord Jesus Christ, King of the Universe, commonly called "Christ the King." In 1925 Pope Pius XI established the feast of Our Lord Jesus Christ the King on the last Sunday in October—that is, the Sunday immediately preceding All Saints. In an increasingly secularized society, he wanted to underscore that Christ was king over all places and times.[79]

The revised calendar expanded its title and moved it to the end of the liturgical year to anticipate the Second Coming of Christ at the end of time. Inside the Missal, the day also moved out of the Proper of Saints, preceding All Saints' Day, and into the Proper of Time. It now bridges the end of one

77. Sacred Congregation for Divine Worship, "Notification *Instructione de Constitutione*, on the Roman Missal, the book of the Liturgy of the Hours, and the Calendar," 14 June 1971, DOL 216 (1777), p. 546.

78. "Calendar Change in 1984," USCCB, Bishops' Committee on the Liturgy, *Thirty-Five Years of the BCL Newsletter: 1965–2000*, XVII (August–September 1981): 784.

79. Pius XI, "*Quas primas*," 11 December 1925, https://www.vatican.va/content/pius-xi/en/encyclicals/documents/hf_p-xi_enc_11121925_quas-primas.html.

liturgical year with the First Sunday of the next Advent, when the gospel recounts Jesus' promise to come again.

The selected readings at Mass cohere with the solemnity. They show how David prefigured the coming of Christ, and how Jesus ruled as king even from the cross (ILM 108).

The Dicastery for the Laity, the Family and Life in consultation with the pope establishes themes for World Youth Day, observed on Christ the King.[80] The day is observed throughout the world, and every few years an international event is held over several days. The USCCB encourages participation[81] and presents a guidebook for this celebration of youth and young adults.[82]

Ordinary Time Weekdays

On the Table of Liturgical Days, weekdays in Ordinary Time occupy the lowest rank of the lowest tier. They give way to solemnities and feasts, and are "combined with" memorials (UNLYC 16c), meaning some aspects of the weekday remain.

At Mass, the Missal offers no specific presidential prayers for each weekday. It permits the previous custom of repeating the antiphons and prayers from the preceding Sunday, while also allowing antiphons and prayers of any Ordinary Time Sunday. Masses for Various Needs and Occasions, or just their collect, may also be offered (GIRM 363). The gathered community may celebrate any saint in the Martyrology of the day,

80. "Statement of the Dicastery for the Laity, Family and Life," 26 September 2023, https://press.vatican.va/content/salastampa/en/bollettino/pubblico/2023/09/26/230926c.html.

81. USCCB Topics: World Youth Day, "Welcome, Read about the Feast of Christ the King and World Youth Day Below," https://www.usccb.org/topics/world-youth-day.

82. USCCB Secretariat of Laity, Marriage, Family Life and Youth, *National Pastoral Guidebook for the Global Celebration of Young People* (Washington DC: USCCB, 2021), https://www.usccb.org/resources/usccb-christ-the-king-guidebook.pdf.

or a Votive Mass. Masses for the Dead may be celebrated in moderation (355c). This deters the previous custom when the priest celebrated a Mass for the Dead on almost every available weekday. It may now be celebrated if the Mass is actually applied for the dead (381), and not just as a devotional exercise. All Masses offer prayers for the living and the dead.

The prayers from a Ritual Mass may not be used unless the ritual takes place within it (GIRM 377). Masses of the Blessed Virgin Mary on Saturday are especially commended "because it is to the Mother of the Redeemer that in the Liturgy of the Church firstly and before all the Saints veneration is given" (378).

The readings change every day, offering the faithful a full exploration of the principal passages of the Bible. The gospels come from the synoptics, form a one-year cycle, and are proclaimed in the order of their composition: Mark opens the year, Matthew takes over in the weeks after Pentecost, and Luke concludes the year, beginning in early September (ILM 109).

The first readings and responsorial psalms span a two-year cycle. These alternate a series of weeks of semicontinuous passages from the Old and New Testaments. The year concludes with excerpts from Daniel and Revelation, their eschatological themes resonating with the conclusion of Luke's gospel, the solemnity of Christ the King, and the turning of the calendar (ILM 110).

Mary, Mother of the Church

On the day after Pentecost, the faithful observe a memorial of Mary, Mother of the Church. With the approval of Pope Francis, the Congregation for Divine Worship and the Discipline of the Sacraments added this day to the universal calendar in 2018.[83] The decree was dated February 11, the anniversary of the first apparition of Our Lady of Lourdes.

---

83. Congregation for Divine Worship and the Discipline of the Sacraments, "Decree on the Celebration of the Blessed Virgin Mary Mother

Decades earlier the revisers had considered adding this day. Some particular calendars had already introduced the observance on the day after Pentecost.[84] Pope Paul had promoted this title of Mary and encouraged devotion to it.[85] This led to a Votive Mass of Mary Mother of the Church in the second edition of the Missal.

The celebration now calls for obligatory readings at Mass, rare for a memorial. The two options for the first reading can be found among the Commons of the Blessed Virgin Mary, but the specific psalm verses and the gospel are unique to this celebration. Although the books used to proclaim the readings are to be "worthy, dignified and beautiful" (ILM 35), this gospel cannot be found in the Lectionary and has to be read from a Bible or a printed sheet that the USCCB makes accessible.[86]

During this week the previous calendar held the octave of Pentecost with its array of antiphons, prayers, and readings. In some places around the world, the days after Pentecost are civic holidays.

The Most Sacred Heart of Jesus

The Table of Liturgical Days groups solemnities of the Lord with other solemnities at its third tier. Highly popular among these is the Most Sacred Heart of Jesus, the third Friday after Pentecost. It always falls on a weekday, even though the revisers once proposed moving it to the third Sunday after Pentecost.

---

of the Church in the General Roman Calendar," https://www.vatican.va /roman_curia/congregations/ccdds/documents/rc_con_ccdds_doc_2018 0211_decreto-mater-ecclesiae_en.html.

84. Bugnini, pp. 318–19.

85. Paul VI, "Apostolic Exhortation *Signum magnum*, on Mary, Mother of the Church," 13 May 1967, DOL 463 (3880), p. 1198.

86. USCCB, "Monday after Pentecost, the Blessed Virgin Mary, Mother of the Church," https://www.usccb.org/resources/mother-of-the-church -readings.pdf.

The devotion rests on the visions of St. Margaret Mary Alacoque († 1690) at Paray-le-Monial in France. In 1765 Pope Clement XIII approved a liturgical feast of the Sacred Heart for the bishops of Poland and the Archconfraternity of the Sacred Heart in Rome. Paul VI noted that the feast was also kept by "the bishops and the queen of France, the superior and members of the Society of Jesus."[87] On the two-hundredth anniversary of this approval, Pope Paul encouraged devotion to the Sacred Heart throughout the church.

In 1995, Pope John Paul II accepted the suggestion of the Congregation for the Clergy that every diocese celebrate a day of prayer for the Sanctification of Priests on the solemnity of the Sacred Heart or on another day suited to local needs. He wrote that priests have a duty to strive for holiness and to serve as ministers of holiness to those in their pastoral care.[88] The USCCB adopted the suggestion, naming the solemnity of the Sacred Heart as one of its national days of prayer.[89]

The Immaculate Heart of Mary

The last of the days depending on the date of Easter is the memorial of the Immaculate Heart of Mary. The revisers thought it should merely be included among Votive Masses, as this would allow people to celebrate it on a day of their own choosing, reducing the number of devotional observances. They grouped it with the former feasts of the most holy name of Mary and of Mary the Queen, all of which they thought

87. Paul VI, "Apostolic Epistle '*Investigable divitias Christi*,' marking the second centenary of the feast, on the liturgical cult of the Sacred Heart," 6 February 1965, DOL 453 (3850), p. 1184.

88. John Paul II, "Letter to Priests for Holy Thursday 1995," https://www.vatican.va/content/john-paul-ii/en/letters/1995/documents/hf_jp-ii_let_25031995_priests.html.

89. USCCB Clergy, Consecrated Life & Vocations, "World Day of Prayer for the Sanctification of Priests," https://www.usccb.org/committees/clergy-consecrated-life-vocations/world-day-prayer-sanctification-priests.

duplicated celebrations of the Nativity of Mary, the Immaculate Conception, and the Assumption of the Virgin.

Upon review in 1968, the Congregation for the Doctrine of the Faith argued that this popular devotional feast should be retained in the calendar. A compromise was reached by making this an optional observance near the celebration of the Sacred Heart of Jesus. Several years later, Pope Paul listed the Immaculate Heart of Mary among the celebrations "that are evidence of strong currents in contemporary devotion."[90]

Formerly observed on August 22, it entered the revised calendar as an optional memorial on the day after the Sacred Heart of Jesus. In 1996 it became obligatory.[91] In years when it coincides with another memorial, both become optional.[92]

90. Paul VI, "Apostolic Exhortation *Marialis cultus*, on rightly grounding and increasing Marian devotion," 2 February 1974, DOL 467 (3906), p. 1209.

91. Congregation for Divine Worship and the Discipline of the Sacraments, "Prot. 2376/95/L, Decretum de celebratione Immaculati Cordis beatae Mariae Virginis in Calendario Romano Generali," *Notitiae* 362, vol. 32, no. 9 (September 1996): 654–56.

92. Congregation for Divine Worship and the Discipline of the Sacraments, "Notification De Occurrentia Memoriae Obligatoriae Immaculati Cordis beatae Mariae Virginis una cum Altera Memoria eiusdem Gradus," 8 December 1998, https://www.vatican.va/roman_curia/congregations/ccdds /documents/rc_con_ccdds_doc_20000630_memoria-immaculati-cordis -mariae-virginis_lt.html.

Chapter Five

Proper of Saints

The calendar of saints begins in January. In the previous Missal, it began in late November to synchronize with Advent. However, the calendar of saints flows independent of the liturgical year, so the Missal now frames it with the civic year. Integrated below are national and universal special days of prayer not explicitly found in the Proper.

January

2 Saints Basil the Great and Gregory of Nazianzen, Bishops and Doctors of the Church

In the previous calendar, Basil was observed on June 14, though he died on January 1 († 379), the octave of Christmas and now the solemnity of Mary the Mother of God. Gregory of Nazianzen had been celebrated on May 9. However, his *dies natalis* was January 25 († 389 or 390), the Conversion of St. Paul.

Basil was a founder of monasticism in the East, but the revisers first categorized him as a Doctor of the Church.[1] Basil had been listed in the Roman calendar since the thirteenth century,

---

1. Schemata, n. 132, p. 19. Throughout this chapter, the revisers' first categorizations come from this Schemata, pp. 8–22.

and Gregory since the year 1500.[2] The revisers proposed their collective commemoration "by reason of the friendship between them, who cannot be honored on their own day," making it an obligatory memorial "because of the importance of these doctors in the Church."[3]

At first the revisers wanted to move their day to January 26. In the end, the two were moved off the day following Gregory's *dies natalis* and onto the day following Basil's. This opened January 26 for the memorial of Timothy and Titus, while giving some deference to Basil, whose presence on the calendar is older.

Basil is named in the Litany of the Saints among early doctors of the church. In the solemn profession of religious women, his sister Macrina, a consecrated virgin who died the same year he did, is also invoked. During the Consecration of Virgins, Macrina replaces Basil in the litany, perhaps to increase the number of women without unduly lengthening the list.

3 The Most Holy Name of Jesus

The revisers discontinued the Most Holy Name of Jesus. They believed that its significance was already assumed on January 1, when the gospel recounts the bestowal of Jesus' name. The group asked,

> Is it appropriate to give this day [January 1] the title of the name of Jesus or of the imposition of the name of Jesus?
>
> From the biblical point of view, it seemed impossible to put in the foreground the imposition of the name of Jesus in the title, letting the circumcision pass in silence, the mention of

---

2. Schemata, n. 188, p. 10. Throughout this chapter, the dates for the death of saints and their addition to the Roman calendar come from this Schemata, pp. 9–28, unless otherwise noted.

3. Schemata, n. 188, p. 10.

which had been suppressed in 1961; the two acts are recalled in the same event.[4]

Furthermore, if they retained the Holy Name of Jesus, "The gospel of January 2 would be a repetition of the one on January 1."[5]

Nonetheless, in 2002, the Most Holy Name of Jesus returned to the calendar and Missal as an optional memorial. Perhaps its devotional appeal prompted the Holy See to restore it. January 2 now honored two great doctors of the church, but January 3 stood within the range of the former observance. The *Supplement* to the Lectionary includes alternative readings (510/1).

4 Saint Elizabeth Ann Seton, Religious

In the United States, the calendar includes an obligatory memorial of Elizabeth Ann Seton. Born in New York City just before the nation's independence, she is considered the first saint born in the country. January 4 was her *dies natalis* († 1821). Pope John XXIII beatified her in 1963, and she was added to the particular calendar in the United States with an opening prayer.[6] Paul VI canonized her in 1975, so the propers expanded with antiphons, suggested readings, and prayers over the gifts and after communion.[7] These all remain in the Missal, unusual for a memorial.

The *Book of Blessings* offers a service for visiting a cemetery on All Souls' Day. In the United States, Elizabeth's name is part of the short litany of saints (1746).

---

4. Schemata, n. 260, p. 47.

5. Schemata, n. 260, p. 47.

6. *The Roman Missal: The Sacramentary* (New York: Catholic Book Publishing, 1974), p. 599.

7. *The Roman Missal: The Sacramentary* (New York: Catholic Book Publishing, 1985), p. 598.

5 Saint John Neumann, Bishop

The next day of the calendar also has an American saint. John Neumann discerned a missionary vocation in his native Bohemia. Ordained for the Diocese of New York, he became the bishop of Philadelphia. He died on January 5, 1860.

Pope Paul beatified him in 1963 and canonized him in 1977. The *Sacramentary* in the United States first had an opening prayer for Blessed John Henry Neumann. After his canonization it added other prayers, antiphons, and recommended readings.[8] An undated sheet of paper, folded as if mailed in an envelope, added an Old Testament reading, "Isaiah 52:7-10 (Lectionary no. 1), for Canonization only—chosen for missionary zeal of Neumann," and said of the responsorial Psalm 96 that it was "chosen because of life of Neumann in announcing salvation to all."[9] These antiphons and prayers remain in the Missal, unusual for a memorial.

6 Saint André Bessette, Religious

Another saint appears on the American calendar for the third consecutive day. Holy Cross brother André Bessette was Canadian, but spent some of his early years in the United States. He died on January 6, 1937. He was beatified in 1982 and added to the calendar in the United States that year along with Kateri Tekakwitha and Marie Rose Durocher.[10] He was canonized in 2010.

As Blessed André, he first appeared in the texts for Mass with an opening prayer.[11] The saint's collect now in the Missal is a lightly edited version of the same prayer. However, unlike Elizabeth and John, in keeping with the more common usage

8. *The Sacramentary* (1974), p. 600; *The Sacramentary* (1985), p. 599.

9. The author has the sheet inside his 1974 *Sacramentary*.

10. "Confirmation of Calendar Change and Additions," *Newsletter* XIX (March 1983): 854.

11. *The Sacramentary* (1985), p. 600.

of the Missal, the other presidential prayers, antiphons, and readings all come from the Commons.

7 Saint Raymond of Penyafort, Priest
Since 1671 the Roman calendar had assigned January 23 to Raymond of Penyafort. The revisers first categorized him as a confessor who was not a pope, not a doctor, and not a founder, considered him "of little importance,"[12] and omitted him from the early drafts. A month after the second draft, he was reinserted as an optional memorial, probably because of his significance in the history of canon law.

All the drafts assigned a new date, January 7, which remains in force. Raymond died on January 6, 1275, so his actual *dies natalis* would coincide with Epiphany in many countries.

13 Saint Hilary, Bishop and Doctor of the Church
On the Roman calendar since the thirteenth century, Hilary was formerly honored on January 14. His *dies natalis* was January 13, 364, which used to coincide with the Baptism of the Lord. In the revisions, the Baptism moved to a Sunday, allowing Hilary to be remembered on this day. The drafts listed him as an optional memorial, as he remains.

17 Saint Anthony, Abbot
On the Roman calendar since the thirteenth century, Anthony's *dies natalis* has been celebrated on this date in Eastern Rites since the fifth century. He was considered "the father of all monks."[13] The revisers first categorized him among founders of orders, obligatory since the first draft. All the drafts included him, and his day remains an obligatory memorial.

12. Schemata, n. 132, p. 17. All further references to this phrase come from this Schemata.
13. Schemata, n. 188, p. 9.

18–25 Week of Prayer for Christian Unity

Among its Days of Prayer and Special Observances, the USCCB keeps the Week of Prayer for Christian Unity from January 18–25.[14] Originally this bridged the traditional day for the start of Peter's ministry in Rome with the day marking the conversion of Paul. On unimpeded weekdays, the priest may use the Mass "For the Unity of Christians."

20 Saint Fabian, Pope and Martyr
20 Saint Sebastian, Martyr

Fabian and Sebastian appeared on the former calendar as a single feast. They were listed separately in the earliest listing of saints, the Chronography of Filocalus from 354.[15] Both shared the same *dies natalis*, but Fabian died in 250 and Sebastian died about 304. From the first draft, they embraced a single celebration, but they separated due to tradition and their distinct generations.

Both are optional memorials. Fabian is probably listed first because he was a pope and predates Sebastian.

21–27 Sunday of the Word of God

Pope Francis established the Third Sunday in Ordinary Time as the Sunday of the Word of God. The USCCB lists it among its days of prayer and offers a variety of resources.[16] On this day some priests bless those who proclaim the readings.[17]

---

14. USCCB Ecumenical & Interreligious Affairs, "International Week of Prayer for Christian Unity," https://www.usccb.org/committees/ecumenical-interreligious-affairs/international-week-prayer-christian-unity.

15. *The Chronography of 354 AD*, Part 12: Commemorations of the Martyrs, "Item Depositio Martirvm," https://www.tertullian.org/fathers/chronography_of_354_12_depositions_martyrs.htm.

16. USCCB Divine Worship, "Sunday of the Word of God," https://www.usccb.org/committees/divine-worship/sunday-word-god.

17. *Book of Blessings*, nos. 1827–33.

21 Saint Agnes, Virgin and Martyr

This traditional date for the *dies natalis* of Agnes remains untouched because of devotion to this saint, "in whom are honored all the virgin martyrs."[18] She is listed in the Chronography of 354. The revisers considered her life certain, but her biography fictitious. Still, all the drafts kept her day obligatory. She appears in all versions of the Litany of the Saints.

Agnes receives special treatment in the Liturgy of the Hours. The Office of Readings and Morning Prayer have special hymns in her honor, the first by Blessed Alphonsus of Salerno, OSB († 1085), and the second attributed to St. Ambrose († 397), which is repeated at Evening Prayer.[19] At Morning Prayer the psalms come from Sunday of the first week, each with a special antiphon. The psalms of Evening Prayer come from the Commons and have proper antiphons. The readings for Morning and Evening Prayer are those from the Common of a Martyr, but each is copied into the texts for January 21 because of the succeeding unique responsory. Agnes has special antiphons for the *Benedictus* and *Magnificat*. This expanded treatment underscores that in Agnes all the virgin martyrs are honored.

22 Day of Prayer for the Legal Protection of Unborn Children

The Supreme Court legalized abortion in the United States on January 22, 1973, prompting the bishops to call for the legal protection of unborn children. Although the case has been struck down, the day of prayer that the bishops established remains.

18. Schemata, n. 188, p. 9.
19. *The Divine Office Hymnal* (Chicago: GIA Publications, 2023), pp. 351–54.

The Missal in the United States gives a particularly full guidance for celebrating the day:

> In all the Dioceses of the United States of America, January 22 (or January 23, when January 22 falls on a Sunday) shall be observed as a particular day of prayer for the full restoration of the legal guarantee of the right to life and of penance for violations to the dignity of the human person committed through acts of abortion. The liturgical celebrations for this day may be the Mass "For Giving Thanks to God for the Gift of Human Life" (no. 48/1 of the Masses and Prayers for Various Needs and Occasions), celebrated with white vestments, or the Mass "For the Preservation of Peace and Justice" (no. 30 of the Masses and Prayers for Various Needs and Occasions), celebrated with violet vestments. (GIRM 373)

The *Supplement* to the Lectionary suggests readings from the Mass "For Peace and Justice." It also provides a sweeping set of alternate readings for its Mass "For Giving Thanks to God for the Gift of Human Life"—three from the Old Testament, two of which are quite long (947A); five from the New Testament as additional options for the first reading (947B); two responsorial psalms (947C), three gospel acclamations (947D), and seven options for the gospel (947E).

23 Saint Vincent, Deacon and Martyr

The USCCB moves the optional memorial of St. Vincent to January 23 because of the conference-wide day of prayer on January 22, the proper *dies natalis* of this Spanish martyr († 304). The drafts first categorized Vincent as a non-Roman martyr of little importance, even though Augustine testified that this saint had been revered throughout the church since the beginning of the fifth century. The drafts kept Vincent as an alternative to Fructuosus and companions, martyred on January 21 († 259). The revisers had removed many martyrs of whom they knew "only the name alone or fictitious biographies."[20] They unsuccessfully proposed adding this group, whose biographies were indeed reliable.

In the ordination of deacons, the Litany of the Saints adds Vincent right after Lawrence (OBPD 203). The *Supplement* to the Lectionary offers particular readings from the Common of Martyrs.

23 Saint Marianne Cope, Virgin

Marianne Cope was added to the United States calendar in 2013.[21] German by birth, she became a Sister of St. Francis in Syracuse, New York, and moved to Hawaii, where she continued the work of Damien de Veuster.

A proper collect and second reading for the Office of Readings are on the USCCB website, and the *Supplement* to the Lectionary recommends readings from the Commons of Those Who Work for the Underprivileged (517A). If January 23 is a Monday, then the impeded day of prayer transfers to this day, and neither Vincent nor Marianne are observed. Marianne died on August 9 († 1918), but her optional memorial is the anniversary of her birth.

24 Saint Francis de Sales, Bishop and Doctor of the Church

On the calendar since 1666 and originally on January 29, Francis de Sales is now honored on the day his remains were placed in Annecy, France, in 1623. He died on December 28, 1622, when the church honors the Holy Innocents. The drafts kept Francis optional on the same day as Timothy and Titus,

---

20. Schemata, n. 138, p. 2; n. 154, p. 4; and Consilium ad Exsequendam Constitutionem de Sacra Liturgia, Schemata, n. 154 addendum, De Calendario, 9—Addenda, 3 May 1966, p. 2.

21. USCCB, "St. Marianne Cope," https://www.usccb.org/prayer-and-worship/liturgical-year-and-calendar/saint-marianne-cope.

but those saints moved to a new date, and Francis received an obligatory memorial.[22]

Initially listing his day as obligatory, the revisers favored making Francis optional because of an abundance of doctors. The Congregation for the Doctrine of the Faith thought the number of saints had diminished too much in the drafts, and Paul VI personally wanted Francis promoted to an obligatory memorial, which happened.

Francis is the patron saint of journalists. On this day the pope delivers his annual message anticipating World Communications Day.

Catholic Schools Week

The USCCB designates the last week of January as Catholic Schools Week. This makes an appropriate time for the blessing of students and teachers (*Book of Blessings*, nos. 522–50.) The week spans the memorial of Thomas Aquinas.

25 The Conversion of Saint Paul the Apostle

Although the actual date of Paul's conversion is unknown, this day traditionally holds its observance. The drafts all kept it and categorized it as a feast.

Because this is a feast of an apostle, if a bishop is ordained on this day, the prayers and readings are those of the Conversion of St. Paul. Paul is among the saints always implored in the litany, even in the shorter version for infant baptism (OBC 48).

26 Saints Timothy and Titus, Bishops

The dates of death for these disciples of Paul are unknown. They appeared separately in the calendar since the thirteenth century—Timothy on January 24 and Titus on February 6.

---

22. Schemata, n. 237, p. 5, for example.

The drafts united their observance; they received Paul's three Pastoral Epistles.

The revisers tested January 22, January 23, or January 24 as optional observances, the last as an alternative with Francis de Sales. The Congregation for the Doctrine of the Faith did not object to joining the two disciples on one day, but preferred an obligatory observance. In the end, Francis received an obligatory memorial, Titus joined Timothy, and their combined observance neared Timothy's former feast on January 24.

The first reading at Mass is proper. The Lectionary offers a choice between a passage from Paul's Second Letter to Timothy and his Letter to Titus. A proper reading is rare on a memorial, but both saints are in the Bible (ILM 83). The psalm is not proper, but the one for Timothy and Titus coheres with the first reading.

27 Saint Angela Merici, Virgin

The foundress of the Ursulines, Angela Merici, died on this day in 1540. Pope Pius VII canonized her in 1807, and she was added to the calendar in 1861. Her original feast day was May 31, her *dies natalis* having already been assigned to John Chrysostom. In 1955 Pius XII put the Queenship of Mary on May 31, displacing Angela to June 1. Moving John Chrysostom's observance closer to his day of death, the revisers kept Angela as an optional memorial on her *dies natalis.*

28 Saint Thomas Aquinas, Priest and Doctor of the Church

For many centuries the church observed the feast of the Dominican Thomas Aquinas († 1274) on his *dies natalis*, March 7. That day often falls during Lent. The Ambrosian Rite, the Dominicans, and the people of Toulouse already honored Thomas on January 28, in commemoration of the day in 1369 that the principal relic, his head, was moved from the place of his death, Fossanova, Italy, to the mother church of the Dominicans in Toulouse, France. The revisers kept his day obligatory throughout the drafts and moved it here.

Thomas has long been honored as a Doctor of the Church, but the drafts named him simply as a priest. The Congregation for the Doctrine of the Faith called Thomas one of the most influential doctors. Catholic Schools Week in the United States always includes this date.

31 Saint John Bosco, Priest

The previous Missal observed John Bosco on his *dies natalis*, January 31. Having died in 1888, John was added to the calendar in 1936. The revisers kept his memorial obligatory throughout the drafts, "because of the importance of this saint in the apostolate among the youth."[23]

In the solemn religious profession of men, John Bosco's name is included in the Litany of the Saints. As founder of the Oratorians, he completes a short list of male founders, following Vincent de Paul.

February

2 The Presentation of the Lord

The previous Missal called this the feast of the Purification of the Blessed Virgin Mary. The revised Missal made it a feast of the Lord. When it falls on a Sunday, it replaces the Fourth Sunday in Ordinary Time. Pope Paul called this feast a combined remembrance of Son and Mother:

> For it is a celebration of the mystery of salvation accomplished by Christ with Mary at his side as Mother of the suffering Servant . . . , as the one fulfilling the charge belonging to ancient Israel, and as the prototype of the new people of

---

23. Schemata, n. 225, p. 10.

God, who again and again are afflicted in their faith and hope by torment and persecution (see Lk 2:21-35).[24]

The revisers never considered moving this observance to a different date, though they immediately changed the title to focus on Christ. Other Rites had made this change, including the Roman Rite in 1960. The 1962 Missal kept the title referring to Mary but noted beneath it that the day was held as a feast of the Lord.

The revisions preserved some of the traditional chants and an appropriate prayer. Revisers added an explanatory introduction, and recommended the blessing take place at the external gates, the door, or the vestibule. As noted above concerning Palm Sunday, the Missal permits the blessing of ashes outside Mass, but not of palms and candles, which are strictly connected to the procession or solemn entrance.

2–8 World Day of Prayer for Consecrated Life

John Paul II instituted February 2 as a day of prayer for those in religious life. However, the USCCB moved the World Day of Prayer for Consecrated Life to the following Sunday, the Fourth or Fifth Sunday in Ordinary Time. The bishops provide a selection of resources.[25]

3 Saint Blaise, Bishop and Martyr

Although Blaise has occupied a place on this date since the twelfth century, the revisers considered his biographical data fictitious. They said only his name was reliable. Although the

---

24. *Marialis cultus* 7, DOL 467 (3905), p. 1208.

25. USCCB Clergy, Consecrated Life & Vocations, "World Day for Consecrated Life," https://www.usccb.org/committees/clergy-consecrated -life-vocations/world-day-consecrated-life.

first drafts omitted Blaise, his day remains an optional memorial "because of popular devotion in many regions."[26]

That devotion includes a blessing of throats. According to legend, Blaise miraculously dislodged a fishbone from the throat of a young boy. In the United States, the blessing of throats may take place within Mass, within a celebration of the Word of God, or in a shorter rite (*Book of Blessings*, nos. 1622–55).

3 Saint Ansgar, Bishop

The revisers added some overlooked saints, such as Ansgar and Columban, non-martyr bishops from the early Middle Ages. As the apostle who converted many Swedes and Danes to Christ, Ansgar has an optional memorial on his *dies natalis* († 865).

5 Saint Agatha, Virgin and Martyr

Since the time of Gregory the Great († 604), Agatha has been commemorated on this date. She remained in the first draft, but as an alternative to "the Japanese martyrs."[27] The revisers later proposed moving her observance to February 6, giving Paul Miki and Companions this day, which is linked to their martyrdom. However, Agatha maintains her long association with February 5.

The revisers kept her day optional, probably because her devotion centered in Italy. However, it became an obligatory memorial at the request of the Congregation for the Doctrine of the Faith.

Memorials of the Saints in Lent

February 5 is the first saint's day that may fall on a weekday inside Lent. When this happens, even an obligatory memorial

---

26. Schemata, n. 109, p. 4; Schemata, n. 188, p. 11.
27. Schemata, n. 109, p. 4; Schemata, n. 138, p. 3.

becomes optional. In the Liturgy of the Hours, the saint may be observed as a commemoration. This applies to all upcoming memorials through Martin I on April 13. The last possible weekday of Lent outside Holy Week is April 17.

6 Saint Paul Miki and Companions, Martyrs

When the revisers first considered adding saints, they explicitly mentioned the martyrs of "Japan, Canada [Isaac Jogues and Companions] and Uganda [Charles Lwanga and Companions]."[28] The list soon expanded to include Peter Chanel of Oceania, "so that the universality of the holiness of the Church may be more openly evident."[29]

The drafts put Paul Miki and Companions on February 5, their *dies natalis* in Nagasaki, as an obligatory memorial "because these twenty-six martyrs are the canonized protomartyrs of the entire Far East, and many of them were in the nation of Japan."[30] The revisers proposed moving Agatha off her traditional date and making her optional. Eventually, they switched the dates, and both became obligatory.

The Congregation for Divine Worship corrected an error in the first edition of the calendar for this day.[31] Initially, Paul Miki was listed as "priest," but that title has been removed. He was a Jesuit missionary, but never ordained.

National Marriage Week

Among its special days of prayer, the USCCB honors February 7–14 as National Marriage Week.[32] The second Sunday of

28. Schemata, n. 75, p. 5.

29. Schemata, n. 132, p. 22.

30. Schemata, n. 188, p. 11.

31. Sacred Congregation for Divine Worship, "Corrigenda," *Notitiae* 47, vol. 5, nos. 7–8 (July–August 1969): 303.

32. USCCB Marriage and Family Life Ministries, "National Marriage Week," https://www.usccb.org/topics/marriage-and-family-life-ministries/national-marriage-week.

February is World Marriage Day, popularized by Worldwide Marriage Encounter,[33] and the week culminates with Valentine's Day.

8 Saint Jerome Emiliani

Honored in the previous calendar since 1769 on July 20, Jerome Emiliani († 1537) founded the Somascan Fathers. The revisers initially considered him of little importance and left him off an early draft of the calendar. They quickly restored him, moving the observance to his *dies natalis*.

As with Paul Miki, the Congregation for Divine Worship realized that the published version erroneously called Jerome a priest. The title was removed.[34] His day remains an optional memorial.

8 Saint Josephine Bakhita, Virgin

Canonized in 2000, Josephine was added to the calendar for the third edition of the Missal as an optional memorial. The USCCB includes this day among its special observances as the International Day of Prayer and Awareness Against Human Trafficking.[35] The *Supplement* to the Lectionary suggests readings (529A).

10 Saint Scholastica, Virgin

Scholastica, the sister of Benedict, founded the Benedictine sisters. Listed as optional through most of the drafts, her day became obligatory at the request of the Congregation for the

---

33. Worldwide Marriage Encounter, "World Marriage Day," https://wwme .org/community/sponsored-events/world-marriage-day/.

34. "Corrigenda."

35. USCCB Administrative, "February 8th: International Day of Prayer and Awareness Against Human Trafficking," https://www.usccb.org/committees /administrative/february-8th-international-day-prayer-and-awareness-against -human.

Doctrine of the Faith. Scholastica has occupied this date since the twelfth century. It was her *dies natalis* in 543.

In the solemn profession of religious women, Scholastica's name is added to the Litany of the Saints. In the Liturgy of the Hours, even though her day is only a memorial, it has a proper antiphon for the gospel canticle at Morning Prayer. No similar antiphon appears at Evening Prayer. This draws attention to the first Latin word of the morning canticle, *Benedictus*, which is also the name of Scholastica's brother.

11 Our Lady of Lourdes

In honor of the apparitions of Our Lady of Lourdes to Bernadette Soubirous in 1858, this feast entered the calendar in 1907. The revisers kept it optional, calling it "a devotional feast in honor of the Blessed Virgin Mary under an extremely popular title."[36]

They wanted another option, Saturninus and the martyrs of Abitina in North Africa († February 11, 304). When persecutors banned the Eucharist, these "martyrs of the Sunday assembly" declared that they could not live without the Mass.[37] This option did not endure.

The Congregation for the Doctrine of the Faith wanted Our Lady of Lourdes to be obligatory, but the Consilium preferred making it optional, to diminish the number of days associated with the Blessed Virgin Mary. It remains an optional memorial, though Paul VI listed it among local observances that had universal appeal.[38]

On the memorial of Our Lady of Fátima in 1992, John Paul II appointed the following year's memorial of Our Lady

36. Schemata, n. 188, p. 11.
37. Schemata, n. 188, p. 12.
38. *Marialis cultus* 8, DOL 467 (3906), p. 1209.

of Lourdes as the first annual World Day of the Sick.[39] The USCCB keeps this among its special days of prayer.

14 Saints Cyril, Monk, and Methodius, Bishop

The revisers removed the Roman martyr Valentine from the general calendar because his historical evidence is doubtful. He remains in the Martyrology on this day.

The brothers Cyril and Methodius had been celebrated together on July 7 since 1880. Although the previous calendar listed both as bishops, "Historically it seems that Cyril was not a bishop, but was always named in the first place in the liturgical books."[40] Cyril died on February 14, 869, and Methodius on April 6 around 885. The revisers recommended an obligatory memorial because of the apostolate that these saints conducted among the Slavs. They were considered "preachers of the Gospel" together with Boniface and Francis Xavier.[41]

Pope Paul chose February 14 to promulgate the new calendar in 1969,[42] the eleventh centenary of the death of Cyril. Pilgrims gathered for the celebration in Rome probably did not realize that the pope had just transferred the memorial of these saints from July 7 to that very day.

17 The Seven Holy Founders of the Servite Order

These founders had been honored since 1887 on February 12 in the previous calendar, but the revisers initially deemed

39. John Paul II, "Lettera di Giovanni Paolo II al Cardinale Fiorenzo Angelini, Presidente del Pontifico Consiglio della Pastorale per gli Operatori Sanitari per l'Istituzione della Giornata Mondiale del Malato," https://www.vatican.va/content/john-paul-ii/it/letters/1992/documents/hf_jp-ii_let_13051992_world-day-sick.html.

40. Schemata, n. 188, p. 12.

41. Schemata, n. 225, p. 7.

42. Paul VI, "Motu Proprio *Mysterii Paschalis*: On Liturgical Year and New Universal Roman Calendar," https://www.vatican.va/content/paul-vi/en/motu_proprio/documents/hf_p-vi_motu-proprio_19690214_mysterii-paschalis.html.

them of little importance. These saints appeared in only one of the early drafts, on February 11, as an option to Our Lady of Lourdes and the martyrs of Abitina. Otherwise they were among some thirty non-martyr saints removed from the calendar.

The last draft reinserted them, now on the *dies natalis* of the lay brother, Alexis Falconieri († 1310). The day is an optional memorial.

21 Saint Peter Damian, Bishop and Doctor of the Church

Adopted onto the Roman calendar in 1823, Peter Damian had died on February 22, 1072, now the Chair of Peter; the previous calendar observed Peter Damian's day on February 23. The revisers gave that date to Polycarp and moved Peter Damian's observance to February 21. From the beginning of the drafts, his day remained as an optional memorial, as it still is.

22 The Chair of Saint Peter the Apostle

This feast had already been observed on this date in Rome since the year 354, when it appeared in the Chronography. The revisers never challenged the date; it is observed as a feast.

For many centuries, January 18 marked the Chair of Peter in Rome, while February 22 celebrated his chair at Antioch. The first of these was removed in 1960 and absorbed into the second without reference to the location of the chair.[43]

If the ordination of a bishop takes place on the feast of an apostle, the antiphons, prayers, and readings of the feast take precedence. That would apply to this day.

23 Saint Polycarp, Martyr

Added to the calendar in the thirteenth century, Polycarp died on February 23 in either 156 or 177. The revisers moved

43. Sacred Congregation of Rites, *Rubricae Breviarii et Missalis Romani et Documenta adnexa, cum Indice Analítico* (Vatican City: Typis Polyglottis Vaticanis, 1960), pp. 100 and 119.

his observance here from January 26, which opened space for Timothy and Titus. Polycarp was part of the plans from the beginning, appearing first in a list of non-Roman martyrs.

In the drafts, his status oscillated between obligatory and optional. Pope Paul wanted it obligatory, as it remains.

27 Saint Gregory of Narek, Doctor of the Church

Widely esteemed by the Armenian church, Gregory was named a Doctor of the Church in 2015. Pope Francis added him to the calendar in 2021, together with John of Ávila and Hildegard of Bingen.[44] New to the calendar, this day was never affected by leap year, as explained below concerning Matthias.

The USCCB published guidelines for those choosing to celebrate Gregory's day.[45] It is an optional memorial.

March

3 Saint Katharine Drexel, Virgin

"Mother" Katharine Drexel († March 3, 1955), canonized in 2000, is an optional memorial in the United States, where she is the first saint born a citizen. The Missal and the Liturgy of the Hours in the United States use a collect that elaborates her achievements and other texts from the Common of Virgins.

---

44. Congregation for Divine Worship and the Discipline of the Sacraments, "Decree on the Inscription of the Celebrations of Saint Gregory of Narek, Abbot and Doctor of the Church, Saint John De Avila, Priest and Doctor of the Church, and Saint Hildegard of Bingen, Virgin and Doctor of the Church, in the General Roman Calendar," https://www.vatican.va/roman_curia/congregations/ccdds/documents/rc_con_ccdds_doc_20210125_decreto-dottori_en.html.

45. USCCB, "St. Gregory of Narek," https://www.usccb.org/prayer-and-worship/liturgical-year-and-calendar/saint-gregory-of-narek.

4 Saint Casimir

Also on this date in the previous Missal, Casimir came under scrutiny by the revisers, who first categorized this Polish layman as a non-bishop confessor of local importance. He was among the saints an early draft moved into February on the same date to avoid Lent. The remaining drafts kept him as an optional memorial. He died on March 4, 1484, and was added to the calendar in 1621.

The Polish bishops had requested that at least one of their saints—Casimir, Stanislaus, Hedwig, or John of Kanty—be named an obligatory memorial and included in the Litany of the Saints.[46] However, Casimir remains optional and unnamed in the litany.

7 Saints Perpetua and Felicity, Martyrs

These two martyrs from Carthage appeared in the Chronography of 354 on this date. The previous Missal honored them on March 6, leaving March 7 for Thomas Aquinas. By moving Thomas outside Lent, the revisers restored these martyrs to their *dies natalis* († 202 or 203). Some drafts tried moving their observance a full month earlier to February 7 to avoid Lent. They also added their martyr companions. The revisers initially categorized them as "holy matrons," not even among the martyrs.[47]

The drafts vacillated between making this day optional or obligatory. Pope Paul requested that it become obligatory, as it remains.

The first eucharistic prayer mentions these martyrs, though their names are reversed. There was a Roman martyr Felicity († 165). Possibly, the Roman Canon first adopted her name, and later someone confused that Felicity with the Carthaginian martyr and added Perpetua, thinking she was missing.

---

46. Bugnini, p. 318.
47. Schematas, n. 109, p. 4; n. 132, p. 22.

Both are in the Litany of the Saints. They are omitted in the religious profession of men and women, presumably because both were married women.

8 Saint John of God, Religious

The revisers first categorized John of God as a founder of little importance. His date was omitted from the first draft but then kept as an optional memorial, as it stands today. John died on this date in 1550, which has been observed on the calendar since 1714.

9 Saint Frances of Rome, Religious

Present in the calendar on this date since 1647, Frances of Rome died on March 9, 1440. Early drafts moved her observance to February 9 to avoid Lent, but that plan did not proceed. The revisers first categorized Frances among women who founded religious orders. They recategorized her as a widow, but she was quickly renamed mother of a family, and now is called a religious. Her day is an optional memorial.

17 Saint Patrick, Bishop

When discussing Patrick, one of the most popular saints on the calendar, the revisers lamented that it fell during Lent.[48] Having categorized him initially as a bishop confessor who was neither a doctor nor a founder, they tried moving his observance to February 17 to limit its occurrence during Lent. This attempt failed, and the date remained March 17, his *dies natalis* in 461.

The Congregation for the Doctrine of the Faith and Pope Paul both wanted Patrick raised to an obligatory memorial, but because of Lent, he could only be observed as an optional memorial and commemoration under the rules of the revision. Patrick had been on the calendar since 1687, and his

---

48. Bugnini, p. 311.

association with this date extends beyond popular piety into the secular sphere.

18 *Saint Cyril of Jerusalem, Bishop and Doctor of the Church*

Cyril died on this date in 386 but has been on the calendar on March 18 only since 1882. The revisers first categorized him as a Doctor of the Church and intended to make his day optional, as it remains. Early drafts tried moving his observance to February 18 because of Lent, but it remains on the traditional date.

19 *Saint Joseph, Spouse of the Blessed Virgin Mary*

One of only two solemnities on the general calendar during Lent, Joseph's day remains on its traditional date. March 19 was a day of obligation in some regions, so the revisers kept it, even when they tried moving other saints from March to February. Nonetheless, one draft moved his date to January 19, probably because even February 19 frequently falls during Lent. The traditional day remains, "however, with permission given to territorial authorities to transfer the entire feast to another day,"[49] which a further draft clarified would be "another day outside Lent."[50]

Before the revised calendar was finalized, a practical issue arose over the forthcoming March 19, 1967, which would be Palm Sunday. The next available weekday—beyond Holy Week and the octave of Easter—would be Monday, April 3. Many local ordinaries petitioned the Congregation of Rites to transfer Joseph's day to March 18 instead, and Pope Paul agreed.[51]

---

49. Schemata, n. 188, p. 13.

50. Schemata, n. 225, p. 14.

51. Sacred Congregation of Rites, "Decree (Urbis et Orbis) *Cum proximo anno,* on the feast of St. Joseph in 1967," 13 May 1966, DOL 471 (3952), p. 1231.

A similar problem arose in 1972, when March 19 fell on the Fifth Sunday of Lent. Ordinaries received permission again to move the date to Saturday, March 18, even to celebrate a Saturday evening Mass of St. Joseph that would fulfill the canonical obligation to participate at Sunday Mass.[52]

Now the rules state that if a conference observes March 19 as a holy day of obligation, and if it falls on Palm Sunday, it is to be moved back a day to March 18. However, where it is not a day of obligation, the conference of bishops may decide on a date for its observance, even outside Lent (UNLYC 56). The problem needed attention when the revised calendar first came out because the coincidence of these days would happen in 1978 and 1989. March 19 next falls on Palm Sunday in the year 2062. When March 19 falls on a weekday in Holy Week, it transfers to the Monday after the octave of Easter.

The area around the altar may not be decorated with flowers during Lent, except for solemnities like this (GIRM 305). Musical instruments such as the organ may only be used to support singing during Lent, but an exception applies to this day (GIRM 313). Joseph is one of the saints always invoked in the litany, even in the shorter version for the baptism of infants (OBC 48).

23 Saint Turibius of Mogrovejo, Bishop

Absent from the previous Missal, Turibius, archbishop of Lima, died on this day in 1606 and was added to the calendar because of "his importance in the restoration of ecclesiastical discipline throughout all of Latin America."[53] He shone among the newly introduced non-martyr saints of Latin America,

52. Sacred Congregation for Divine Worship, "Notification *Instructions de Constitution*, on the Roman Missal, the book of the Liturgy of the Hours, and the Calendar," 14 June 1971, DOL 216 (1776), p. 546.

53. Schemata, n. 188, p. 13.

together with Martin de Porres. As with other saints in March, the revisers considered moving his observance into February, then removing it altogether, before reinserting it on his *dies natalis*. His date almost always falls during Lent, so it is commonly observed as an optional memorial and commemoration.

25 *The Annunciation of the Lord*

Set exactly nine months before Christmas, this solemnity announces the incarnation of Christ in the womb of Mary. Formerly entitled the Annunciation of the Blessed Virgin Mary, its new name firmly categorizes it as a feast of the Lord. The revisers stated, "It is a feast of the Lord among all the Rites outside the Roman Rite. Nevertheless, the feast was introduced in Rome in the seventh century under the title proposed once again, as it appears in the Liber Pontificalis and in the ancient Roman Evangelary."[54] Pope Paul approved the new title, but he also remarked that the celebration "is really at the same time a festival of Christ and of the Virgin: a celebration honoring the Word who became the 'Son of Mary' (Mk 6:3) and the Virgin who became the Mother of God."[55]

The Annunciation of the Lord and Joseph's day are the only solemnities from the general calendar that may fall on weekdays in Lent. During the Creed, the faithful genuflect at the words of the incarnation—a custom repeated at Masses on Christmas (GIRM 137). Floral decorations and musical accompaniment are not to be used in Lent, but an exception is made for solemnities such as this one (305, 313).

In 2023, the Annunciation fell on a Saturday, so the rules pertaining to consecutive solemnities applied (UNLYC 60).[56] As the Fifth Sunday in Lent ranked higher, its Evening Prayer I

---

54. Schemata, n. 188, p. 13.
55. *Marialis cultus* 6, DOL 467 (3904), p. 1208.
56. "2023 Liturgical Calendar Advisories," *Newsletter* LIX (January 2023): 4.

took precedence over Evening Prayer II of the Annunciation. A regularly scheduled anticipatory parish Mass on Saturday became that of the Lent Sunday, but Masses scheduled at other times on Saturday could be for the Annunciation. A Ritual Mass was not permitted on either day, but a funeral Mass could have been celebrated on Saturday.

When March 25 falls on a Monday in Lent, Evening Prayer II for Sunday takes precedence over Evening Prayer I for the Annunciation. In 2024, March 25 fell on Monday of Holy Week, so it transferred to the nearest open date, the Monday after the octave of Easter, April 8.[57]

In the Litany of the Saints, Mary is always listed at the beginning as the Mother of God. In the ritual for the consecration of a virgin, her title divides into three: Holy Mary, Holy Mother of God, and Virgin of virgins. The Annunciation honors the birth of Jesus by a virgin.

April

Child Abuse Prevention Month

In the United States, April is Child Abuse Prevention Month. The USCCB includes this in its list of Days of Prayer and Special Observances and offers resources for education and prayer.[58] Some dioceses have a special Day of Prayer on a weekday this month in atonement for those harmed by sexual abuse.

2 Saint Francis of Paola, Hermit

First categorized among founders of religious orders, Francis de Paola was considered a saint of little importance whom

---

57. "2024 Liturgical Calendar Advisories," *Newsletter* LIX (November 2023): 44.

58. USCCB Communications, "Abuse Prevention Resources," https://www.usccb.org/committees/communications/abuse-prevention-resources.

all the drafts but two omitted. One of these scheduled his optional memorial with those of Isidore and Bernadette of Soubirous on April 16, the first open date outside of Lent and the octave of Easter. The previous Missal honored his *dies natalis*, April 2 († 1507), a date within a stretch when early drafts moved saints who could fall between Ash Wednesday and the octave of Easter.

The revisers explained Francis's exclusion by categorizing him among thirty non-martyr saints of some local interest. However, when the revised calendar was published, he received an optional memorial on this day.[59] He is the only hermit on the general calendar.

4 Saint Isidore, Bishop and Doctor of the Church

The previous and revised Missals have honored Isidore on this his *dies natalis*. He died in 636 and was added to the calendar in 1722. His name appears in all the drafts.

As noted above, the first draft considered moving his date to April 16 as an optional memorial, when people could choose Francis de Paola or Bernadette of Soubirous as alternatives. A later draft moved his date to May 4, part of a proposal to move most of the March saints into April on the same date. However, his date was restored to the *dies natalis* as an option, as it remains today. The revisers listed him first as a doctor and later as a bishop; the Missal recognizes him under both titles.

5 Saint Vincent Ferrer, Priest

Vincent died on this day in 1419 and was added to the calendar in 1702. As in the previous Missal, the revision kept him as an optional memorial.

---

59. Bugnini does not explain why, but he was possibly included in the list of saints recommended by the Congregation for the Doctrine of the Faith. See p. 313.

Vincent's date was another swept into the discussions of avoiding Lent and the early days of Easter. One early proposal moved him to April 17 as an optional memorial shared with Benedict the Black, the day after three other saints had been moved to secure them all a place during Easter Time. Some of the early drafts removed him from the calendar, especially because he had been categorized as a non-bishop confessor of little importance. However, he was restored to his *dies natalis*.

7 Saint John Baptist de la Salle, Priest

The previous Missal had John Baptist de la Salle on May 15, and the revisers, first categorizing him as a founder of a religious order, wanted to keep him as an optional memorial on this his *dies natalis*. Amid discussions about Lent and Easter, one draft proposed moving him to April 18 as an alternative to Peter the Martyr, the third of four consecutive dates when the revisers grouped saints into Easter weekdays. Another attempt moved his date exactly one month later to May 7.

Eventually the revisers made his day obligatory, but then changed it to optional. The Congregation for the Doctrine of the Faith wanted many of the optional saints obligatory, and Paul VI himself wanted John among them. John had died in 1719, and he was added to the Roman calendar in 1904. Because of Paul VI, he is now an obligatory memorial.

11 Saint Stanislaus, Bishop and Martyr

Stanislaus held May 7 in the previous calendar, but the revisers first categorized him as a non-Roman martyr of little importance. Still, in the early drafts they moved him to May 11, one month after his *dies natalis*, because of Lent and the octave of Easter. Stanislaus had died on April 11, 1079, and his feast had been part of the calendar since 1595, so the revisers gave him an optional memorial on this date.

As noted on March 4, the Polish bishops hoped that one of their countrymen would become obligatory on the calendar and the Litany of the Saints. In 1970, the Sacred Congregation for Divine Worship added Stanislaus to the litany for solemn supplications outside the standard baptismal litany, and not on the calendar. However, the Polish-born Pope John Paul II changed the status of this date from optional to obligatory in 1979, the first year of his pontificate, on the ninth centenary of the death of Stanislaus.[60]

13 Saint Martin I, Pope and Martyr

Although he was both pope and martyr, indeed the last person in history to have both these designations, Martin I was first categorized as a saint of little importance who could be removed. His date had been observed on November 12 since the eleventh century, but he had died on April 13, 656, according to a Greek biography, and was being celebrated on his *dies natalis* in the Byzantine Rite.

An early draft moved his date to April 19, the last of four consecutive days grouping saints into Easter Time. Another draft moved him to May 13, one month after his *dies natalis*, for the same reason. Eventually he received this date as an optional memorial. He is the last of the saints on the general calendar whose day could fall on a weekday of Lent.

21 Saint Anselm, Bishop and Doctor of the Church

Anselm died on April 21 in 1109, and his feast has been celebrated on this date since 1690. Categorized from the beginning as a Doctor of the Church, he remained on this date throughout the process as an optional memorial, as he does today.

---

60. Sacred Congregation for Sacraments and Divine Worship, "Circular Letter *Summus Pontifex* to presidents of the conferences of bishops and of national liturgical commissions, on the celebration of St. Stanislaus, Bishop and Martyr, 11 April in the General Roman Calendar," 29 May 1979, DOL 479 (3987), p. 1241.

23 Saint George, Martyr

Categorized from the beginning as a non-Roman martyr, George took a place in all the drafts as an optional memorial. He died on April 23 around the year 304, and his feast has been observed on this day since 682 or 683. His biography is apocryphal, which under the guidelines would have excluded him, but the revisers preserved his memorial "by reason of popular devotion in many regions especially among the Greeks and English."[61]

23 Saint Adalbert, Bishop and Martyr

The third edition of the Roman Missal added the optional memorial of Adalbert, whom John Paul II put on the calendar in 1995, together with Peter Julian Eymard and Peter Claver.[62] As he served as bishop of Prague, his addition broadens the representation of saints from around the world. He died on this date in 997.

24 Saint Fidelis of Sigmaringen, Priest and Martyr

The revisers first categorized Fidelis as a non-Roman martyr of little importance, so they were not initially moved to keep him where he had been listed on this date, his *dies natalis*, since 1771. However, all the drafts retained him as an option for April 24, as he remains.

25 Saint Mark, Evangelist

Consistently throughout the process, April 25 belonged to Mark. This evangelist had long held this date, though there is no reliable record for the day of his death. As noted in the section on Rogation Days, there used to be prayers and litanies

---

61. Schemata, n. 188, p. 14.
62. "New Saints Added to the General Calendar," *Newsletter* XXXII (May 1996): 1493.

associated with this day. Their removal freed Mark's day as a feast of full merit.

28 Saint Peter Chanel, Priest and Martyr

In the drafts from the beginning, Peter Chanel was among the martyrs whom the church was anxious to add. Listed as the representative of Oceania, he joined martyrs from Japan, Uganda, and Canada. When explaining the addition of John Fisher, Thomas More, and Maria Goretti to this group, the revisers wrote, "In order that the Roman calendar become universal, it seemed good in introduce into it feasts of martyrs who in some way represent all parts of the world."[63]

Peter died on April 28, 1841. "The memorial of the proto-martyr of Oceania is introduced so that the revised Roman calendar may be truly universal. It does not become [an obliga-tory] commemoration because St. Peter is not an indigenous martyr."[64]

28 Saint Louis Grignion de Montfort, Priest

The earliest draft listed Louis among optional observances on this day together with Peter Chanel. However, Louis later disappeared from consideration. He was ultimately added to the calendar and the third edition of the Missal. A decree numbered him among outstanding apostles of God, one who dedicated himself completely as a slave of Mary the Mother of God.[65] Pope John Paul devoted himself to Mary, adopting his motto "Totus tuus" from the writings of Louis.

63. Schemata, n. 225, p. 44.

64. Schemata, n. 188, p. 14.

65. Congregation for Divine Worship and the Discipline of the Sacra-ments, "Acts: On the Celebration of St. Louis Marie Grignion de Mont-fort, Priest, in the General Roman Calendar," *Notitiae* 362, vol. 32, no. 9 (September 1996): 657–58.

Louis died on April 28, 1716. The Missal offers two alternative collects, highly unusual for an optional memorial. The Montfort Missionaries have both a Proper Mass for Louis on April 28 and a Votive Mass for other days.[66] The Missal's two collects come from this tradition. The prayers were originally composed in Italian, and when the French province requested them, they had first to be translated into Latin. Both revised prayers ended up in the Missal.[67]

29 Saint Catherine of Siena, Virgin and Doctor of the Church

Honored on the calendar since 1461, Catherine held April 30 in the previous Missal, but she died on April 29, 1380. The drafts all moved her to that day. Her observance was made obligatory "because of the important action and writings of St. Catherine in the Church."[68]

First categorized as a non-martyr virgin, Catherine gained the status of Doctor of the Church in 1970. Pope Paul had already designated Teresa of Ávila as the first woman in this category. A week later, he added Catherine.[69] Catherine's name is among saints invoked in the standard litany, though in the solemn profession of a religious woman she shares an invocation with Clare of Assisi. In 1999 Pope John Paul named Catherine a co-patroness of Europe with Bridget of Sweden and Teresa Benedicta of the Cross.[70]

---

66. For example, https://www.montfort.org.uk/Documents/Mass%20for%20St%20Louis%20Marie%20de%20Montfort.pdf.

67. This information comes from personal correspondence with a Montfort father who tells the author that one of his confreres was working for the Congregation for Divine Worship at the time.

68. Schemata, n. 188, p. 14.

69. Paul VI, "Homily, on St. Catherine of Siena, Doctor of the Church," 4 October 1970, DOL 475 (3963), p. 1236.

70. Pope John Paul II, "Apostolic Letter Issued *Motu Proprio* Proclaiming Saint Bridget of Sweden, Saint Catherine of Siena, and Saint Teresa

30 Saint Pius V, Pope

The previous Missal honored Pope Pius V on May 5. He died on May 1, 1572, and was added to the calendar in 1713. The revisers first attempted to move his day to May 4, closer to his *dies natalis*, shared with Anthony the Florentine, both as optional memorials, and then to May 1, as an alternative to the optional memorial of Joseph the Worker. One draft had him on April 30, where he ultimately returned. His date is an optional memorial.

May

1 Saint Joseph the Worker

Pius XII instituted this date to counterbalance the secular workers' day in Europe. He added it to the calendar in 1955 as an obligatory observance, but the revisers thought otherwise. "It is reduced to an [optional] memorial because the so-called feast 'of work' [Labor Day], is not celebrated on the same day in all regions and does not have universal regard."[71]

Nonetheless, all the drafts put Joseph on May 1. One draft eliminated the designation "the worker" for the sake of countries without the secular holiday, and another attached the title "spouse of the Blessed Virgin Mary." He remains on May 1 as the worker. Joseph is always included in the Litany of the Saints, though without any further title.

2 Saint Athanasius, Bishop and Doctor of the Church

Athanasius died on May 2, 373, and has been honored since 1550 on this day. The revisers first categorized him as a Doctor

---

Benedicta of the Cross Co-Patronesses of Europe," 1 October 1999, https://www.vatican.va/content/john-paul-ii/en/motu_proprio/documents/hf_jp-ii_motu-proprio_01101999_co-patronesses-europe.html.

71. Schemata, n. 188, p. 14.

of the Church, and the drafts all kept his observance on May 2. He remains an obligatory memorial.

The Litany of the Saints invokes Athanasius. However, his name is missing when men and women make solemn profession in religious life, perhaps because he has no direct association with a religious order and to make room for saints who do. As the author of a discourse on virginity, he is included in the Consecration of Virgins.

3 Saints Philip and James, Apostles

Formerly observed on May 11, these two apostles now have May 3. The relics of both are kept at the Roman basilica of the Holy Apostles. Its dedication took place on May 1 around the year 570. Amazingly, to keep May 1 free for the more recently added optional memorial of Joseph the worker, and because Athanasius already occupied May 2, the revisers moved this feast to the closest available day, May 3. All the drafts placed it there, where it remains a feast.

If a bishop is ordained on this day, the liturgy of Philip and James takes precedence. Both saints are added to the litany at the ordination of a bishop, and James is listed first, as in the first eucharistic prayer. James preceded Philip in the Roman Canon even in the eighth-century Gelasian Sacramentary, without explanation.[72]

10 Saint John of Ávila, Priest and Doctor

Pope Benedict XVI declared John of Ávila († May 10, 1569) a Doctor of the Church in 2012.[73] In 2021 Pope Francis autho-

---

72. *Liber Sacramentorum Romanæ Æclesiæ Ordinis Anni Circuli (Sacramentarium Gelasianum)*, ed. Leo Cunibert Mohlberg (Rome: Casa Editrice Herder, 1981), n. 1246.

73. Benedict XVI, "Apostolic Letter Proclaiming Saint John of Avila, diocesan priest, a Doctor of the Universal Church," https://www.vatican.va/content/benedict-xvi/en/apost_letters/documents/hf_ben-xvi_apl_2012 1007_giovanni-avila.html.

rized his addition to the general calendar.[74] He is an optional memorial. The USCCB offers guidelines for those who elect to celebrate John on May 10.[75]

10 Saint Damien Joseph de Veuster of Moloka'i, Priest

A Belgian priest of the Congregation of the Sacred Hearts of Jesus and Mary, Damien served as a missionary in the Hawaiian Islands. He departed voluntarily to minister in the leper colony at Moloka'i on May 10, 1873.[76] He died on April 15, 1889, the date when the Martyrology inscribes his name. However, he is on the particular calendar in the United States as an optional memorial for the day commemorating his selfless acceptance of this ministry. Optional readings are in the *Supplement* to the Lectionary (561A).

12 Saints Nereus and Achilleus, Martyrs
12 Saint Pancras, Martyr

Nereus and Achilleus were martyred on May 12 around the year 304, as was Pancras. "These martyrs are honored separately in the ancient Roman liturgical books."[77]

In the previous Missal, Domitilla took her place together with Nereus and Achilleus. However, the revisers knew the names of the other three from the writings of Damasus, whereas they considered the evidence for Domitilla's life doubtful. Pancras disappeared from only one draft; otherwise,

74. Decree of inscription, 02.02.2021, https://press.vatican.va/content /salastampa/en/bollettino/pubblico/2021/02/02/210202b.html.

75. USCCB, "Saint John of Avila," https://www.usccb.org/prayer-and -worship/liturgical-year-and-calendar/saint-john-of-avila.

76. St. Jozef Damien De Veuster (1840–1889), https://www.vatican.va /news_services/liturgy/saints/2009/ns_lit_doc_20091011_de-veuster_en .html.

77. Schemata, n. 188, p. 15.

the revisers kept all three as optional memorials on their traditional date, as they remain today.

13 Our Lady of Fátima

Devotion to Our Lady of Fátima shares popularity with devotion to Our Lady of Lourdes; however, Fátima went unnamed in the previous calendar. On February 11, the day of the appearances at Lourdes, the former Missal commemorated the Apparition of the Blessed Virgin Mary, but the prayers never mentioned the site. Consequently, the day embraced other apparitions, such as the one at Fátima. The revisers never considered adding this date.

Nonetheless, Pope John Paul, who had a great devotion to Mary under this title, and who survived an assassination attempt on May 13, 1981, added this optional memorial to the third edition of the Missal. Optional readings are suggested in the *Supplement* to the Lectionary (563A).

14 Saint Matthias, Apostle

Since the eleventh century, Matthias had been honored in the church on February 24. The revisers proposed "the transfer of the feast of St. Matthias out of the month of February, where it often falls during Lent, to Easter Time, when the Acts of the Apostles is read."[78] At first they proposed May 27, a date that would appear after the Ascension of the Lord, when Matthias took up his service. They also considered May 15 before settling on May 14, a suitable date "in Easter Time, when 'he was numbered together with the eleven Apostles' (Acts 1:26)."[79]

The previous Missal held an alternative date for Matthias, February 25, observed in leap year. In the early Roman system

78. Schemata, n. 188, p. 15.
79. Schematas, n. 154 addendum, p. 6; and n. 225, p. 15.

of dates, still visible in the left column of the Missal's General Roman Calendar, three days anchored each month: calends, nones, and ides. The other dates were counted back from one of those three inclusive. For example, the Ides of March is on the 15th, so the third day before the Ides is March 13. Matthias had been celebrated on the sixth day before the calends of March, which in most years is February 24, but changes to February 25 in a leap year. As will be seen, these calculations also affect the Nativity of John the Baptist.

The ordination of a bishop on this day would take the readings and prayers of Matthias. In the same liturgy, Matthias is invoked in the Litany of the Saints.

15 Saint Isidore

In the United States, Isidore is honored on May 15, his *dies natalis* († 1130). He occupied this date in the previous Missal's collection of regional observances, not in the general calendar. In the revision, the USCCB added this patron of farmers as an optional memorial.

18 Saint John I, Pope and Martyr

The Roman calendar added John in the twelfth century, and the previous Missal kept his day on May 27. He had been martyred on May 18, 526, so the drafts all moved the remembrance to John's *dies natalis*, where it remains as an optional memorial.

20 Saint Bernardine of Siena, Priest

The previous Missal honored Bernard on this day, the anniversary of his death in 1444. He had been added to the calendar in 1657. The revisers first categorized him among non-pope confessors. All the drafts assigned this date as an optional memorial, as it remains.

21 Christopher Magallanes, Priest, and Companions, Martyrs

The revisers added selected regional martyrs, and the third edition of the Missal added more. Among those are the Mexican martyrs of the Cristero War, represented by Christopher, who died on this day in 1927. Among the companions are two founders of religious orders, José María de Yermo y Parres and María de Jesús Sacramentado Venegas. Pope John Paul had canonized this group in 2000 before they were added to the Missal as an optional memorial.[80] The *Supplement* to the Lectionary suggests readings (566A).

22 Saint Rita of Cascia, Religious

Absent from the previous general calendar, Rita was recognized as a saintly widow among the former Missal's regional celebrations on this day, her *dies natalis* († 1457). The third edition of the Missal added her observance for the first time to the general calendar as an optional memorial. The *Supplement* to the Lectionary suggests readings (566B).

22 National Day of Prayer and Remembrance for Mariners and People of the Sea

The USCCB recognizes among its Days of Prayer and Special Observances this day for mariners. "National Maritime Day is commemorated on May 22 as an opportunity to recognize the hardworking men and women of the U.S. Merchant Marine, seafarers, fishers, port personnel, and all who work or travel on the high seas for the vital services they provide in support of our nation's economic well-being and national

---

80. "Homily of his holiness Pope John Paul II, Canonization of 27 New Saints," https://www.vatican.va/content/john-paul-ii/en/homilies/2000 /documents/hf_jp-ii_hom_20000521_canonizations.html.

security."[81] Although not directly associated with this date, a liturgy for the Blessed Virgin Mary, Star of the Sea, is on the USCCB website.[82]

24 World Day of Prayer for the Church in China

Benedict XVI added this day of prayer in 2007. He chose May 24 because it "is dedicated to Our Lady, Help of Christians, who is venerated with great devotion at the Marian Shrine of Sheshan in Shanghai."[83] On May 24, 1814, Pius VII regained his throne after his unjust capture and imprisonment. He established Our Lady, Help of Christians, on this day. Texts for that Mass can be found in the *Collection of Masses of the Blessed Virgin Mary* (42).[84]

25 Saint Bede the Venerable, Priest and Doctor of the Church

Bede died on this day in 735, but he was added to the Roman calendar only in 1899. The previous Missal honored him on May 27, and the drafts first assigned him May 24 to free the following day for Gregory VII. The later drafts moved him to May 25, where he remains as an optional memorial.

---

81. USCCB, "National Day of Prayer and Remembrance for Mariners and People of the Sea, May 22, 2022," https://www.usccb.org/events/2022/national-day-prayer-and-remembrance-mariners-and-people-sea.

82. USCCB, "The Blessed Virgin Mary, Star of the Sea, Liturgy Guide, Mass and Liturgy of the Hours," https://www.usccb.org/resources/Stella%20Maris%20Liturgy%20Guide.pdf.

83. "Letter of the Holy Father Pope Benedict XVI to the Bishops, Priests, Consecrated Persons and Lay Faithful of the Catholic Church in the People's Republic of China," https://www.vatican.va/content/benedict-xvi/en/letters/2007/documents/hf_ben-xvi_let_20070527_china.html.

84. *Collection of Masses of the Blessed Virgin Mary* (Collegeville, MN: Liturgical Press, 2012).

25 Saint Gregory VII, Pope

Gregory died on this day in 1085, and his feast has been on the calendar since 1729. The previous Missal honored him on this his *dies natalis*. The drafts kept the day, the early ones making it an obligatory memorial, but the later an optional one, as it remains.

25 Saint Mary Magdalene de' Pazzi, Virgin

In the former Missal on May 29, Mary Magdalene de' Pazzi died on May 25, 1607, and was added to the calendar in 1670. The revisers first considered her of little importance. She appeared in the first draft as an option on May 24, closer to her *dies natalis*, but was removed from the next ones. She later reappeared as an optional memorial on May 25, as she remains. On this day the Missal offers a rare selection from three optional memorials.

25–26 World Day of Children

Pope Francis designated May 25–26, 2024, as the first World Day of Children.[85] As it fell on the weekend of Trinity Sunday, it had no direct impact on the liturgy. However, prayers for or by children would be fitting.

26 Saint Philip Neri, Priest

Philip died on this day in 1595 and was added to the calendar in 1657. The previous Missal also kept his observance on May 26. The revisers first moved his memorial to May 28, freeing the two previous days for other saints whom they named obligatory: Augustine of Canterbury and Matthias. However, both of them received other dates, and Philip retained his *dies natalis*. The drafts envisioned this as an optional

---

85. Pope Francis, "Angelus: Solemnity of the Immaculate Conception of the Blessed Virgin Mary, 8 December 2023," https://www.vatican.va /content/francesco/en/angelus/2023/documents/20231208-angelus.html.

memorial, but Pope Paul wanted Philip obligatory, as he now stands.

27 Augustine of Canterbury, Bishop

Augustine died on May 26 in 604 or 605, and his feast had been observed on May 28 since 1882. Early on, the revisers listed him among bishop confessors who were neither doctors nor founders of orders, and they recommended keeping his date on May 28, or moving him to May 26, displacing Philip Neri to May 28. Later, both of these saints, who share the same *dies natalis*, appeared as optional memorials on May 26. However, after Pope Paul stated his preference that Philip's memorial become obligatory, Augustine needed a new date. This was the next one available.

29 Saint Paul VI, Pope

Pope Francis declared Pope Paul VI among the blessed in 2014 and a saint in 2018. Then in 2019, Francis added Paul to the general calendar.[86] Paul had died on August 6, 1978, the feast of the Transfiguration, so his *dies natalis* was not available. May 29 was his ordination anniversary, so that became the date for his optional memorial. In the Ambrosian Rite, celebrated in Milan where Paul had served as cardinal archbishop, May 29 was already occupied by Sisinnius, Alexander and Virgil, so Paul is observed in the Ambrosian calendar on May 30, the next available date to the one chosen for the Roman calendar.

31 The Visitation of the Blessed Virgin Mary

In the previous calendar, the Visitation had been observed on July 2, and the Blessed Virgin Mary, Queen, on May 31.

---

86. "Decree on the Inscription of the Celebration of Saint Paul VI, Pope, in the General Roman Calendar," https://press.vatican.va/content/salastampa/it/bollettino/pubblico/2019/02/06/0103/00210.html.

Early drafts of the revision kept this arrangement, listing the first among the mysteries connected to Mary's life, and the second among the feasts of devotion. Eventually the revisers proposed that May 31 "become the feast of the Visitation of the Blessed Virgin Mary, that is between the Annunciation of the Lord and the Nativity of St. John the Baptist, and to crown the month of special prayers in honor of the Blessed Virgin Mary."[87] The Congregation for the Doctrine of the Faith wanted to keep both observances from the previous Missal as obligatory, but the Consilium successfully argued in favor of moving the Queenship of Mary to August 22 "as complement and crown of the Assumption," and transferring the Visitation to May 31.[88]

June

1 Saint Justin, Martyr

The day of Justin's death is unknown, but the year was around 165. "His memory is already celebrated on this day among the Byzantines since the ninth century."[89] His feast has been on the calendar since 1882, but on April 14 in the previous Missal. The transfer of his date to June 1 achieves an ecumenical consensus. The drafts all kept the observance obligatory, the Congregation for Doctrine of the Faith concurred, and so it remains.

2 Saints Marcellinus and Peter, Martyrs

The previous Missal observed these martyrs on this date together with the bishop martyr Erasmus. Since the year 354, Pope Damasus had recorded the martyrdom of Marcellinus and Peter on June 2, 304, though not Erasmus, so these two

87. Schemata, n. 188, p. 16.
88. Bugnini, pp. 311 and 312.
89. Schemata, n. 188, p. 16.

saints continue to be remembered on this date. Marcellinus and Peter are among the Roman martyrs named in the first eucharistic prayer.

Throughout the drafts, June 2 also honored martyrs from Lyon: Pothinus, Blandina and companions. The revisers considered their biographies reliable. They had died on this date in 177, and they had a popular following. The addition of the Lyon martyrs, who were not in the previous Missal, had been mentioned in one of the earliest meetings. They held an optional place in all of the drafts, but they were not included in the final calendar.

3 Saints Charles Lwanga and Companions, Martyrs

Among the first new martyrs from diverse regions of the world, these saints were added "to show the universality of the Church" and to avoid making the Roman calendar a "Mediterranean calendar." Certain saints "must be inserted: for example, the Japanese, Canadian and Ugandan martyrs."[90] Charles and his companions appeared throughout all the drafts on this day.

Charles died on June 3, 1886. "The commemoration of the protomartyr saints of black Africa is proposed for the same reason as the commemoration of the protomartyr Japanese saints on February 5."[91] They were first categorized among lay martyrs.

5 Saint Boniface, Bishop and Martyr

The previous Missal observed Boniface on this date. Among non-Roman martyrs, some are "spurious or legendary, nothing is known of many except their name," and only a few "are of some importance for the whole Church."[92] Of these

90. Schemata, n. 75, p. 5.
91. Schemata, n. 188, p. 16.
92. Schemata, n. 132, p. 14.

last, Boniface shared space with Polycarp, Ignatius, Irenaeus, Cyprian, Stephan, and the Holy Innocents. The revisers also listed him among preachers of the gospel together with Cyril and Methodius, as well as Francis Xavier.

Nearly all the drafts made his day obligatory "because of the importance that he had in the evangelization of Germany and in the restoration of ecclesiastical discipline among the Franks."[93] He died on this day in 755, and his feast has been on the calendar since 1874.

6 Saint Norbert, Bishop

Norbert has been on the calendar since 1620. The previous Missal also kept his observance on this date, his *dies natalis* (†1134). The revisers first categorized him among founders of orders of little importance. Still, he appeared in all the drafts and remains an optional memorial.

9 Saint Ephrem, Deacon and Doctor of the Church

According to the Chronicle of Edessa in 540, Ephrem "the wise" died on this day in 378,[94] but the previous Missal observed him on June 18. He was added to the calendar in 1920. Nearly all the drafts included him, and he remains an optional memorial. In the ordination of a deacon, Ephrem is invoked in the Litany of the Saints.

11 Saint Barnabas, Apostle

The Byzantine church had observed June 11 as Barnabas's feast since the ninth century, and he was added to the Roman calendar in the eleventh century. The previous Missal also observed him on this date, and all the drafts kept it.

---

93. Schemata, n. 188, p. 16.
94. "The Chronicle of Edessa," *The Journal of Sacred Literature, New Series* [=Series 4], vol. 5 (1864), pp. 28–45, https://www.tertullian.org /fathers/chronicle_of_edessa.htm.

Barnabas, not one of the Twelve, is an obligatory memorial. Acts of the Apostles calls him an apostle because of the nature of his ministry. The first reading at Mass, which mentions Barnabas (Acts 11:21b-26; 13:1-3), is proper (GIRM 357).

In the Liturgy of the Hours, this day has proper antiphons for the invitatory, *Benedictus*, and *Magnificat*. Barnabas also has proper readings and responsories for the three offices of Daytime Prayer, most unusual for a memorial, but more common on feasts such as those honoring the Twelve. Barnabas is among the saints named in Eucharistic Prayer I.

13 Saint Anthony of Padua, Priest and Doctor of the Church

One of the most popular saints, Anthony died on this day in 1231 and was added to the calendar the following year. The previous Missal also honored him on June 13. The revisers first categorized him among Doctors of the Church and never altered his date. The final drafts made the day optional, but the Congregation for the Doctrine of the Faith wanted it obligatory, as it now is.

19 Saint Romuald, Abbot

In the previous calendar on February 7, Romuald died on this day in 1027 and was added to the calendar in 1595. The previous Missal had several other martyrs on June 19: Juliana Falconieri, and Gervase and Protasius. The drafts frequently referred to one or two of them as an alternative optional memorial to Romuald, whom the revisers considered of little importance. Romuald disappeared from some of the drafts, but reappeared near the end as an optional memorial, as he remains, without the other saints.

Gervase and Protasius are patrons of Milan, and, on June 19, 386, Ambrose had their recently discovered relics interred in the church now known as St. Ambrose. This started the custom of honoring the relics of saints just before placing them in a newly constructed church (ODCA II:10).[95]

21 Saint Aloysius Gonzaga, Religious

The previous Missal honored Aloysius on this same day, his *dies natalis* († 1591). He has been on the calendar since 1842. The revisers first categorized him among non-bishop confessors who were neither doctors nor founders. One draft categorized him as an acolyte because he had received that minor order.

All the drafts recommended June 21 as an optional observance. However, Pope Paul personally sided with the Congregation for the Doctrine of the Faith and thought that Aloysius should become an obligatory memorial, as his rank remains.

22 Saint Paulinus of Nola, Bishop
22 Saints John Fisher, Bishop, and Thomas More, Martyrs

Paulinus of Nola died on this date in 431 and has been inscribed in the calendar since the twelfth century. John Fisher was martyred on this date in 1535, as was Thomas More on June 6 that same year. "A memorial of these two illustrious martyrs is proposed, who were killed in the sixteenth century because of their faithfulness toward the Catholic Church."[96]

The revisers had first categorized Paulinus among bishop confessors who were neither doctors nor founders. As noted on April 28, John Fisher and Thomas More appeared as "martyrs of a more recent age,"[97] together with several others.

95. Paul Turner, *New Church, New Altar: A Commentary on the Order of Dedication of a Church and an Altar* (Collegeville, MN: Liturgical Press, 2021), pp. 21–22.
96. Schemata, n. 188, p. 17.
97. Schemata, n. 225, p. 44.

The revisers listed Paulinus, John, and Thomas as optional memorials throughout the drafts, and they remain that way in the Missal.

22–29 Religious Freedom Week

Because both John Fisher and Thomas More defended their faith amid political opposition, the USCCB designates the week beginning on their optional memorial as Religious Freedom Week. The website offers ideas for preaching and prayer on the Twelfth or Thirteenth Sunday in Ordinary Time.[98]

24 The Nativity of John the Baptist

The calendar retains this time-honored date for the birth of John the Baptist. All of the drafts had done the same. The actual date is unknown, but, at the annunciation, the archangel Gabriel told Mary that John's mother Elizabeth was in her sixth month of pregnancy (Luke 1:36). The date for John's birth has therefore been observed exactly six months before Christmas.

As noted on May 14, the general calendar still acknowledges the early Roman calendar, which computes dates based on the calends, ides, and nones of the month. The birth of Jesus falls on the eighth day before the calends of January, and the birth of John is therefore observed on the eighth day before the calends of July. In the modern calculation, June 24 appears to be six months and one day before December 25, but in the old reckoning the dates on those two months are identical.

John's birth may coincide with important moveable days. Foreseeing the problem, Jounel summarized the acting principle, recalling the resolution a few years before:

98. USCCB Religious Liberty, "Religious Freedom Week," https://www.usccb.org/committees/religious-liberty/religious-freedom-week.

Priority has been given to fixed solemnities over moveable solemnities, for these are older and more popular. It follows that the feast of the apostles Peter and Paul takes precedence over that of the Sacred Heart, without needing an intervening decree from the Sacred Congregation of Rites, as happened in 1962.[99]

However, the principle was not followed in 1973 when June 24 fell on a Sunday. As noted above, the Sacred Congregation for Divine Worship decreed that the Nativity of John the Baptist would transfer to Saturday, June 23, in those conferences that moved the solemnity of the Body and Blood of Christ to a Sunday.

A similar resolution was made in 2022 when the Nativity of John the Baptist coincided with the Most Sacred Heart of Jesus. John's birth moved to June 23.[100]

In 2023, the Nativity of John the Baptist fell on Saturday before the Twelfth Sunday in Ordinary Time. As the Nativity ranks higher, its Evening Prayer II took precedence over Evening Prayer I of Sunday. However, a regularly scheduled Saturday evening Mass used the liturgy for the Twelfth Sunday in Ordinary Time. A special Mass on Saturday evening could have been for the Nativity of John the Baptist. A Ritual Mass was permitted on Sunday, though not on Saturday, and a funeral Mass could be celebrated on either day.[101]

In 2024, the Nativity of John the Baptist fell on a Monday. In the Liturgy of the Hours, Evening Prayer I of the Nativity took precedence over Evening Prayer II of the Twelfth Sunday in Ordinary Time; however, in celebrations with the people,

99. Schemata, n. 237, p. 3.

100. USCCB Committee on Divine Worship, "Liturgical Calendar for the Dioceses of the United States of America 2022," p. 7, https://www.usccb.org/resources/2022cal.pdf.

101. "2023 Liturgical Calendar Advisories," *Newsletter* LIX (January 2023): 4.

Evening Prayer II could have been used. A regularly scheduled parish Mass on Sunday evening was that of Ordinary Time; however, an extra Mass could have used the prayers and readings for John the Baptist.[102]

In the Liturgy of the Hours for this day, some psalms come from the Common of Holy Men. The Litany of the Saints always includes an invocation to John the Baptist. He is also always mentioned in Eucharistic Prayer I.

27 *Saint Cyril of Alexandria, Bishop and Doctor of the Church*

The previous Missal observed Cyril's day on February 9. He died on this day in 444, and had been on the Roman calendar since 1882. His observance was therefore moved to his *dies natalis*. The revisers kept his day optional throughout almost all the drafts, as it remains.

28 *Saint Irenaeus, Bishop, Martyr, and Doctor of the Church*

Pope Francis named Irenaeus a Doctor of the Church in 2022.[103] He is the only martyr on the general calendar so designated. Formerly observed on July 3, and part of the calendar since 1921, Irenaeus was martyred on June 28, 202, so the revisers moved his observance here.

The revision retained a selection of saints from different categories. Irenaeus was listed among bishops such as Martin and Leo the Great, rather than among martyrs such as Ignatius of Antioch and Cornelius and Cyprian. The drafts kept his memorial obligatory, as it remains.

---

102. "2024 Liturgical Calendar Advisories," *Newsletter* LIX (November 2023): 44.

103. "Decree of the Holy Father for the conferral of the title of Doctor of the Church on Saint Irenaeus of Lyon, 21.01.2022," https://press.vatican .va/content/salastampa/en/bollettino/pubblico/2022/01/21/220121b.html.

29 Saints Peter and Paul, Apostles

This solemnity had a place in the Chronography from 354, making it one of the oldest observances. Legend has it that on June 29 († 64) these two great apostles met for a final embrace on Rome's Ostian Way before departing toward their martyrdoms, Peter to the Vatican Hill, and Paul outside the city walls. The drafts show no disagreement over the date and its importance.

As noted on June 24, fixed feasts were to take priority over moveable feasts, but devotional observances have in fact displaced some of the fixed days. In 1973, the same year that the Nativity of John the Baptist conflicted with the Most Holy Body and Blood of Christ in some conferences, the solemnity of Peter and Paul coincided everywhere with the solemnity of the Sacred Heart. That year, the Congregation transferred Sacred Heart to the following Sunday, except in places that had already transferred Peter and Paul to a Sunday.[104]

In 2024, June 29 fell on a Saturday. That evening, normally scheduled parish Masses were to be the Thirteenth Sunday in Ordinary Time. Other Masses could celebrate Peter and Paul. In the Liturgy of the Hours, Saturday required Evening Prayer II of Peter and Paul, rather than Evening Prayer I of Sunday.

Ritual Masses are not permitted on solemnities such as this, so weddings and confirmations, for example, take place within the readings and prayers of this Mass. The ordination of a bishop on June 29 would use the prayers and readings of Peter and Paul. Both these apostles are invoked in the Litany of the Saints. Eucharistic Prayer I always mentions them.

30 The First Martyrs of the Holy Roman Church

The revised calendar includes the protomartyrs of Rome. "The feast of the martyrs killed near the Vatican in the per-

---

104. Sacred Congregation of Divine Worship, "Notification *Instructione de Constitutione*, on the Roman Missal, the book of the Liturgy of the Hours, and the Calendar," 14 June 1971, DOL 216 (1777), p. 546.

secution of Nero has been celebrated in Rome since the year 1923. An insertion in the Roman calendar is proposed for the memory of the Roman protomartyrs, whose passion is attested by the most certain, even secular tombs."[105]

Many names had been removed because of a lack of verifiable information, yet many Christians spread the faith by giving their lives. The drafts added this optional memorial on the day after Peter and Paul, the two most important martyrs of early Christian Rome.

The revisers had planned on other martyrs from the primitive church, "of whom are preserved authentic biographies or significant testimonies. The celebration of their memory may have a pastoral value even today; the reading of such biographies in fact contributes much to the spiritual formation of those who recite the Divine Office."[106] The proposed names included martyrs from Tarragon, Spain; Lyon, France; and Scilla in Africa. The only ones preserved were these protomartyrs of Rome.

July

1 Saint Junípero Serra, Priest

In the United States the evangelical fervor of Junípero Serra garnered him a date on the national calendar. Pope Francis canonized him in the United States in 2015.[107] This optional memorial takes place on the anniversary of the day that Junípero arrived in San Diego in 1769 to begin his work as a Franciscan missionary. His *dies natalis* is August 28 († 1784), the day

---

105. Schemata, n. 188, p. 18.
106. Schemata, n. 260, p. 61.
107. "Homily of his Holiness Pope Francis, National Shrine of the Immaculate Conception, Washington D.C., Wednesday, 23 September 2015," https://www.vatican.va/content/francesco/en/homilies/2015/documents/papa-francesco_20150923_usa-omelia-washington-dc.html.

honoring Augustine. The *Supplement* to the Lectionary proposes readings (592A).

3 *Saint Thomas, Apostle*

For centuries people celebrated Thomas during Advent. This probably explains the location of his name in the first eucharistic prayer. After the more prominent apostles—Peter, Paul, James, and John—he leads the list in order of their appearance on the former calendar.

> St. Thomas has been celebrated in Rome on December 21 since the ninth century, and, in some churches, even since the seventh century.
>
> In the Syro-Malabar, Syro-Antiochene, and Syro-Chaldean Rites, and also in the Ambrosian liturgy, he is celebrated on July 3, when the transfer of his body is commemorated at Edessa.
>
> It is proposed that this day be chosen also in the Roman calendar because the feast in December takes place among the important weekdays of Advent.[108]

If the ordination of a bishop takes place on July 3, the antiphons, prayers, and readings of Thomas take precedence. His name is included in the litany of saints for the same ritual.

4 *Independence Day*

For Independence Day in the United States, the Missal carries special antiphons and presidential prayers, including a preface. The Gloria is said and a solemn blessing may be given, even though this is an optional Mass, because of the day's significance. The Lectionary recommends readings from Masses for Various Needs and Occasions. The anomaly of finding the Mass for Independence Day inside the Proper of Saints demonstrates the now-expansive purpose of the Proper.

---

108. Schemata, n. 188, p. 18.

5 *Saint Elizabeth of Portugal*

Since 1694 Elizabeth has held a place on the general calendar, where she is remembered on her *dies natalis*, July 4 (†1336). In the United States, that is Independence Day, so her optional memorial moves a day later. In the previous Missal, she was honored on July 8, and the revisers considered her of little importance. Still, they included her in all the drafts save one. The *Supplement* to the Lectionary proposes readings (594).

5 *Saint Anthony Zaccaria, Priest*

Occupying the same date as Elizabeth in the United States, Anthony is remembered on the anniversary of his death in 1539. The previous Missal honored him on this day since he joined the calendar in 1897. Almost all the drafts kept his observance on this day, even though the revisers first considered him of little importance.

6 *Saint Maria Goretti, Virgin and Martyr*

Added to the calendar only in the last drafts, "The memorial of this holy martyr is proposed because of popular devotion and the importance of her witness in our times."[109] As indicated on April 28, the revisers introduced martyrs from around the world. That list included Maria Goretti.

Maria died on this date in 1902, but the late drafts listed it as 1906. After the calendar was published in 1969, the Sacred Congregation for Divine Worship issued a correction.[110] Maria is included in the Litany of the Saints during the Consecration of Virgins.

109. Schemata, n. 225, p. 19.
110. "Corrigenda," *Notitiae* 5 (47, July–August 1969): 303.

9 Saints Augustine Zhao Rong, Priest, and Companions, Martyrs

Martyrs of China were added to the calendar in 2000 and appear as an optional memorial in the third edition of the Missal. Augustine Zhao heads the list of over one hundred clergy, religious, and lay faithful killed between 1648 and 1930.[111] Two bishops were martyred on July 9, 1900, and their *dies natalis* became associated with the entire group.

Augustine was a Chinese convert to Christianity who was ordained a priest, arrested, tortured, and martyred in 1815. The name of this indigenous saint appears in the Missal, rather than those of the bishops, who were missionaries. The *Supplement* to the Lectionary suggests readings (596A).

11 Saint Benedict, Abbot

Benedict died about the year 543 on March 21, the day observed in the former calendar and Missal. The revisers favored moving saints' days to their *dies natalis*, but Benedict marks an exception. They moved him off that date, honored since the eleventh century. "In sacramentaries of the eighth century, the heavenly birthday of Saint Benedict is on July 11. It is proposed that that date be accepted because March 21 always falls during Lent."[112]

Most of the drafts accepted this, though one mistakenly assigned July 10, and another kept him on March 21. The revisers first categorized Benedict among founders of religious orders and among monks, along with Anthony and Bernard.

111. "Agostino Zhao Rong (+1815) and 119 Companions, Martyrs in China (+1648–1930)," https://www.vatican.va/news_services/liturgy/saints/ns_lit_doc_20001001_zhao-rong-compagni_en.html.

112. Schemata, n. 188, p. 18.

In 1964, Pope Paul named Benedict patron of Europe.[113] Benedict's name is invoked in the standard Litany of the Saints.

13 Saint Henry
The previous Missal honored Henry on this same date, his *dies natalis* († 1024). He was added to the calendar in 1668. The revisers considered him a non-bishop confessor of local interest and once listed his date as July 15. However, most of the drafts retained this day as an option, and Henry's memorial remains optional today.

14 Saint Kateri Tekakwitha, Virgin
The USCCB honors Kateri on July 14, the day in 1677 when she fled her abusive home to find solace and faith at a mission in Canada. There she developed her young Christian faith and received her First Communion.[114] She died on April 17, 1680, and the church in Canada honors her on that day. Pope Benedict canonized her together with several other saints in 2012 after the publication of the third edition of the Roman Missal in English.[115]

In 2023 the Dicastery for Divine Worship and the Discipline of the Sacraments confirmed texts for a Mass in Kateri's honor in the United States, where she is observed as an obligatory memorial. These include a revised collect and expanded

---

113. Pope Paul VI, "Pacis Nuntius," AAS 56 (1964), pp. 965–67, https://www.vatican.va/content/paul-vi/la/apost_letters/documents/hf_p-vi_apl_19641024_pacis-nuntius.html.

114. Br. Joseph, M.I.C.M., "Saint Kateri Tekakwitha," https://catholicism.org/kateri-tekakwitha.html.

115. "Homily of his Holiness Pope Benedict XVI," https://www.vatican.va/content/benedict-xvi/en/homilies/2012/documents/hf_ben-xvi_hom_20121021_canonizzazioni.html.

proper antiphons and prayers.[116] The *Supplement* to the Lectionary offers readings (599A).

15 Saint Bonaventure, Bishop and Doctor of the Church

Honored as one of the doctors of the church with a feast on the calendar since 1483, Bonaventure appeared in the previous Missal on July 14. However, he died on July 15, 1274, so the revisers moved his observance here. All the drafts made Bonaventure an optional memorial, but he ultimately became obligatory.

16 Our Lady of Mount Carmel

Added to the calendar in 1726, this day appeared in the previous Missal and remains on the same date. The revisers first made it a Votive Mass, removing it from the calendar, but later reinserted it. Pope Paul named this among days that originated within religious communities but had attained universal appeal.[117]

18 Saint Camillus de Lellis, Priest

On the general calendar since 1762, Camillus is celebrated as an optional memorial on July 14, the date of his death in 1614. In the United States, where that day is an obligatory memorial, Camillus moves to July 18—not the first available date closest to his *dies natalis*, but the date used in the previous Missal.

20 Saint Apollinaris, Bishop and Martyr

The revisers considered the first-century Apollinaris of Ravenna one of the non-Roman martyrs for optional reten-

116. USCCB, "Saint Kateri Tekakwitha," https://www.usccb.org/prayer-worship/liturgical-year/saint-kateri-tekakwitha.

117. *Marialis cultus* 8, DOL 467 (3906), p. 1209.

tion. The previous Missal honored him on July 23. The revisers found his biography credible but thought his importance more regional than universal. All but one of the drafts omitted him, he was listed among thirty-two non-Roman martyrs to be removed,[118] and the 1969 calendar did not include him.

However, Apollinaris was restored to the third edition of the Missal on a new date, July 20. The Martyrology notes both dates—the traditional date of his death, July 23, and the date of its liturgical observance, July 20. The *Supplement* to the Lectionary suggests readings (601B).

21 Saint Lawrence of Brindisi, Priest and Doctor of the Church

On the calendar only since 1959, Lawrence died on July 22 in 1619. The previous Missal also honored him on July 21, probably due to the longstanding association of July 22 with Mary Magdalene. Several drafts proposed making both these saints optional on July 22, but that idea did not prevail.

22 Saint Mary Magdalene

Originally on the revised calendar as an obligatory memorial, Mary Magdalene's day now ranks as a feast, complete with its own newly composed preface for the Mass.[119] The previous Missal gave her the title "Penitent," showing the long confusion of the penitent woman with this saint who encountered the risen Christ. The revisers struggled to find an appropriate title, listing her first among the "holy matrons" with saints such as Perpetua and Felicity, Frances of Rome, and Monica, even categorizing Mary Magdalene as a saint of little

118. Schematas, n. 225, p. 43; and n. 260, pp. 57–58, which raised the number of this group to 33.

119. Congregation for Divine Worship and the Discipline of the Sacraments, "Decree" Pro. N. 257/16, https://www.vatican.va/roman_curia /congregations/ccdds/documents/sanctae-m-magdalenae-decretum_en.pdf.

importance. This probably influenced the attempt to make her optional with Lawrence of Brindisi, whose *dies natalis* is July 22. Now Mary shares the same rank as the apostles; indeed, as the first bearer of the news of the resurrection, she is called the apostle to the apostles.

Mary Magdalene had been celebrated on this day among the Byzantines since the ninth century, and also by the Copts. She has been inscribed in the Roman calendar since the twelfth century. The revisers commented about her inclusion, "About thirty saints are honored with an obligatory memorial: among those it seemed necessary to place those who equally played a role in all the ages from the primitive church (for example, Saint Mary Magdalene) up to our times (for example, St. Pius X)."[120]

Mary Magdalene is one of the few women invoked in the standard Litany of the Saints. The *Supplement* to the Lectionary has the readings for her feast (603).

23 Saint Bridget, Religious

In the previous Missal on October 8, Bridget now has July 23, the day she died in 1373. She has been on the calendar since 1673. The revisers kept her day optional throughout the drafts, though they noted that she is both the foundress of a religious order and a holy matron. One draft called her Mother of a Family. Some early drafts removed her observance, but she returned.

Jounel offered the transfer of this date as one example of the efforts to restore saints' days to the anniversary of each one's death. "One should not then be surprised at the numerous changes brought to the dates. For example, it thus happens that St. Vincent de Paul († 27 September 1660) moves from July 19 to September 27, St. Bridget († 23 July 1373) from

120. Schemata, n. 225, p. 7.

October 9 [*sic*] to July 23."[121] As noted on April 29, Pope John
Paul II named her a co-patroness of Europe.

24 Saint Sharbel Makhlūf, Priest

The third edition of the Missal added Sharbel as an optional
memorial. Paul VI had canonized him in 1977 shortly after
publishing the second edition of the Missal. Sharbel died on
Christmas Eve, 1898, making his *dies natalis* inappropriate for
observance. He had been ordained a priest on July 23, 1859.
The Maronites honor him on the third Sunday in July, and the
Roman Church chose a date near his ordination anniversary.
The *Supplement* to the Lectionary suggests readings for this
Lebanese saint (604A).

25 Saint James, Apostle

The previous calendar and Missal listed James on this date,
and the revisers never proposed a change. In the previous
Missal, though, he shared this day with the popular patron
saint of travelers, Christopher. The revisers had listed him
among non-Roman martyrs whose biographies were doubtful.
Christopher is still in the Martyrology, but not on the calendar.

The ordination of a bishop on this day requires the antiphons, prayers, and readings of the apostle. James is added to
the litany of saints in the same ceremony. He is also numbered
among the apostles in the first eucharistic prayer.

National Family Planning Awareness Week

The USCCB sets aside National Family Planning Week. The
dates begin on a Sunday and always embrace the July 25 anniversary of Paul VI's encyclical *Humanae vitae*, as well as July

---

121. Sacred Congregation for Divine Worship, "Studia De Quibusdam
Animadversionibus ad Calendarium Romanum Instauratum: E Conferentia
Rev. Prof. Jounel ad Scriptores diariorum et periodicorum," *Notitiae* 47,
vol. 5, nos. 7–8 (July–August 1969): 297.

26, the date honoring the grandparents of Jesus. The USCCB offers a page with suggestions for prayer and the liturgy.[122]

26 Saints Joachim and Anne, Parents of the Blessed Virgin Mary

The previous Missal honored Anne on this date and Joachim on August 16, but the revised calendar joined Joachim to Anne. Anne has been on the calendar since 1584, Joachim since 1738, but the revisers proposed a single obligatory memorial "of the father and the mother of the Blessed Virgin Mary, as has happened in the Benedictine calendar since the year 1915."[123] All the drafts kept them together on this day.

29 Saints Martha, Mary, and Lazarus

Since the thirteenth century, Martha alone appeared on this date. All the drafts kept it, as had the previous Missal. The first draft omitted the observance, and subsequent drafts added Mary, giving both of them the title Sisters before restoring the day to Martha alone. The day was optional throughout. Pope Paul intervened, so Martha became an obligatory memorial. In 2021, after the publication of the third edition of the Missal, Pope Francis added Mary and Lazarus. According to the Decree,

> The traditional uncertainty of the Latin Church about the identity of Mary—the Magdalene to whom Christ appeared after his resurrection, the sister of Martha, the sinner whose sins the Lord had forgiven—which resulted in the inclusion of Martha alone on 29 July of the Roman Calendar, has been resolved in recent studies and times, as attested by the current Roman Martyrology, which also commemorates Mary and

122. USCCB Natural Family Planning, "Prayer and Liturgy," https://www.usccb.org/topics/natural-family-planning/prayer-and-liturgy.
123. Schemata, n. 188, p. 19.

Lazarus on that day. Moreover, in some particular calendars, the three siblings are already celebrated together.[124]

At Mass, the gospel of the day is proper (GIRM 357), but the first reading may come from the weekday. The USCCB made other texts available for the Mass and the Liturgy of the Hours.[125] The updated memorial comes with a new second reading for the Office of Readings, drawn from the *Sermons* of the abbot Bernard.

30 Saint Peter Chrysologus, Bishop and Doctor of the Church

In the previous Missal, Peter was observed on December 4. He died on July 31, 451, "according to more recent authors,"[126] and this was the nearest available date. The calendar has included his observance since 1729. The revisers listed Peter among the doctors of the church and assigned him this date throughout the drafts as an optional memorial, as he remains.

31 Saint Ignatius of Loyola, Priest

Ignatius died on July 31, 1556, and his date has been observed on the calendar since 1644. The previous Missal honored him on this date, as did all the drafts. The drafts gave the day obligatory status, as it remains. The revisers first categorized him among the founders of religious orders. He is listed among examples in that category with Francis of Assisi

124. "Decree of the Congregation for Divine Worship on the Celebration of Saints Martha, Mary and Lazarus, in the General Roman Calendar" (26 January 2021), https://press.vatican.va/content/salastampa/en/bollettino /pubblico/2021/02/02/210202c.html.

125. USCCB, "Saints Martha, Mary and Lazarus," https://www.usccb.org /prayer-and-worship/liturgical-year-and-calendar/saints-martha-mary-and -lazarus.

126. Schemata, n. 188, p. 19.

and Dominic. At a solemn profession to religious life, this Ignatius is added to the Litany of the Saints, whereas Ignatius of Antioch is removed.

August

1 Saint Alphonsus Mary Liguori, Bishop and Doctor of the Church

Alphonsus has been on the calendar since 1839, and the revisers moved his optional observance from August 2 to August 1, the date on which he died in 1787. They noted his role as a founder of a religious order, the Redemptorists, but categorized him first as a Doctor of the Church.

They wanted another option on this day, the Maccabee brothers, in keeping with the previous Missal and indeed the traditional observance since the fourth century in almost all regions both East and West. They also proposed a third option, Eusebius of Vercelli, who died on this date.

The Congregation for the Doctrine of the Faith feared that too many doctors were being removed, and that Alphonsus ranked with Thomas Aquinas and Francis de Sales. Pope Paul wanted Alphonsus obligatory, which then happened, removing the day's optional memorials. The change gave Alphonsus the same rank as Ignatius the previous day. The Maccabees, who would have been the only Old Testament figures in the revision, were removed.

2 Saint Eusebius Vercelli, Bishop

Honored in the previous calendar on December 16, Eusebius was considered optional because of his regional appeal. He had died on August 1, 370 or 371, and was added to the calendar in 1602. All the drafts kept his *dies natalis* as an alternative to Alphonsus. Once Alphonsus's memorial became obligatory, Eusebius moved to the next available day.

2 *Saint Peter Julian Eymard, Priest*

The revisers never considered adding Peter Julian, nor did the previous Missal assign him a day. He died on August 1, 1868, but like Eusebius, who shared this *dies natalis*, his optional memorial moved one day later due to the obligatory memorial of Alphonsus.

As noted on April 23, Peter Julian was added to the calendar in 1995. The third edition of the Roman Missal includes his day.

4 *Saint John Mary Vianney, Priest*

In the previous Missal on August 8, John Mary Vianney moved to August 4. He died on this date in 1859 and has been on the Roman calendar since 1928. The revisers first listed him among non-bishop confessors who were neither doctors nor founders. The drafts made him sometimes obligatory, sometimes optional. A late draft concluded, "His memorial becomes obligatory by reason of the importance of this saint as patron and example of pastors."[127] He remains an obligatory memorial. His name is invoked in the standard Litany of the Saints.

5 *The Dedication of the Basilica of St. Mary Major*

The previous Missal called this the dedication day of "Our Lady at the Snows," and the revisers intended to suppress it, in accord with the council (SC 111), as a celebration of local interest. Tradition holds that snow amazingly fell in Rome on this day in August on a spot where Mary requested the construction of a church in her honor. The revisers first considered this a devotional feast of little importance, though it marks the anniversary of the dedication of the Basilica of St.

---

127. Schemata, n. 225, p. 22.

Mary Major, the oldest church in the West dedicated to the Blessed Virgin.

A late draft restored the date, recalling that the feast had been on the Roman calendar since 1568, where it appeared in an edition of the Martyrology of Jerome as the dedication of the basilica of St. Mary. After its inclusion, Pope Paul called it an example of a local devotion that had spread to many people.[128]

6 *The Transfiguration of the Lord*
This feast has had a place on the calendar since 1456, but the revisers considered moving it to a different time of year. Dirks wrote of the 1965 discussion:

> In addition, a question under consideration has been proposed about inserting the feast of the Transfiguration of the Lord into the Time of Epiphany.
>
> Eventually, as to the feast of the Epiphany, the faculty has been requested on behalf of the Conferences of Bishops of transferring this feast either to the following Saturday or Sunday.[129]

The proposal never entered the drafts, which retained August 6 throughout. This displaced the observances of several saints who died on August 6: Pope Sixtus II and companions, Dominic, and Pope Paul VI.

As a feast of the Lord, whenever August 6 falls on a Sunday it replaces the Eighteenth Sunday in Ordinary Time. When it falls on a Saturday, Evening Prayer II of the Transfiguration takes precedence over Sunday's Evening Prayer I, but as Sunday is a day of precept, the scheduled Saturday evening Mass is that of Sunday, for the benefit of the faithful. When

---

128. *Marialis cultus* 8, DOL 467 (3906), p. 1209.
129. Schemata, n. 93, p. 2.

the Transfiguration falls on a Monday, its Evening Prayer I replaces Sunday's Evening Prayer II, unless a celebration with a congregation argues in favor of Sunday's, or if the conference or local bishop determines otherwise.

In the Liturgy of the Hours, Evening Prayer features a canticle from the First Letter to Timothy. Its only other occurrence is on the Epiphany (GILH 137).

7 Saints Sixtus II, Pope, and Companions, Martyrs

These martyrs enjoy one of the earliest references in the Roman calendar, appearing in the Chronography of 354 on August 6, the day of their death in 258. The previous Missal kept them on that date with the Transfiguration of the Lord. The revisers opted to move the martyrs to August 7 as an optional memorial, so that those who wished could celebrate them unimpeded by the more important observance of the Transfiguration. One draft moved the date to August 5 as an alternative to the dedication of St. Mary Major, but these martyrs stand now as an optional memorial on August 7.

7 Saint Cajetan, Priest

Cajetan died on this date in 1547, and his feast has appeared here in the calendar since 1673. The revisers first categorized him among founders of orders but considered him of little importance. The early drafts did not include him, but he was reinserted on this day.

Cajetan was surprisingly moved to August 8 in the revised calendar. Dominic had replaced Cajetan on August 7. The Dominicans appealed for an exchange of these two dates, and the Holy See granted the concession.[130] Cajetan moved back to his traditional date of August 7 as an optional memorial.

---

130. "Variations in 'Calendarium Romanum' inductae: Calendarium Romanum Generale," *Notitiae* 54, vol. 5, no. 5 (May 1970): 192.

8 *Saint Dominic, Priest*

In the previous Missal, Dominic was observed on August 4. As with Sixtus and companions, he had died on August 6, now the Transfiguration, though in the year 1221, and was added to the calendar rather quickly in 1254. When one draft removed Our Lady of the Snows from August 5, it placed Dominic on that date. However, when the dedication of St. Mary Major returned on August 5, Dominic moved to August 7, where he first appeared in the published revision.

This changed in 1970, as noted in the entry above for August 7. "A light transfer has been made in the feasts of St. Cajetan and St. Dominic, at an agreement made between the religious families of the Dominicans and the Clerics Regular, and accepted by the Holy See for pastoral reasons."[131] The Congregation of the Clerics Regular, the Theatines, was founded by Cajetan.

As a result, Dominic occupies August 8 as an obligatory memorial, and Cajetan shares August 7 with Sixtus and his companions as optional memorials.

In the standard Litany of the Saints, Dominic shares an invocation with Francis, whose name appears first. In the ordination of a deacon, the two are invoked separately, again with Francis first. In the Consecration of Virgins, the two are invoked together, but Dominic comes first, possibly due to the tradition that the Virgin Mary appeared to give him the rosary.

9 *Saint Teresa Benedicta of the Cross, Virgin and Martyr*

Canonized by Pope John Paul in 1998,[132] Teresa was added to the calendar and Missal as an optional memorial. Born Edith

131. Gottardo Pasqualetti, Sergio Bianchi, "Variations in 'Calendarium Romanum' inductae: Calendarium Romanum Generale," *Notitiae* 54, vol. 5, no. 5 (May 1970): 192.

132. "Homily of John Paul II for the Canonization of Edith Stein, Sunday, 11 October 1998," https://www.vatican.va/content/john-paul-ii/en /homilies/1998/documents/hf_jp-ii_hom_11101998_stein.html.

Stein and known as a German philosopher, she joined the Carmelites and accepted the name Teresa Benedicta of the Cross. Put to death at Auschwitz-Birkenau on this day in 1942, she is listed as both virgin and martyr. As noted on April 29, Pope John Paul II named her a co-patroness of Europe. The Supplement to the Lectionary offers optional readings (617A).

10 Saint Lawrence, Deacon and Martyr

Celebrated as a feast, Lawrence enjoys immense popularity especially in Rome, which is said to have more churches named for him than for any other saint except Mary. His death on this date in 258 was noted in the Chronography of 354, making him one of the most continuously honored saints in history. The previous Missal celebrated him on this same day, and the drafts never wavered. Lawrence is invoked in the standard Litany of the Saints.

11 Saint Clare, Virgin

First categorized by the revisers as a founder of a religious order, Clare of Assisi appeared in the previous Missal on August 12. She died on August 11, 1253, so the drafts uniformly moved her to this date. She was canonized in 1255, astonishingly quickly after her death. Put forward as an optional memorial, her day became obligatory at the request of Paul VI.

Clare is added to the litany of saints at the solemn profession of religious women. An early follower of Francis, she is invoked together with Catherine of Siena. Clare's name comes first, preceding Catherine in chronological order and echoing the pairing of Francis and Dominic in the standard litany.

12 Saint Jane Frances de Chantal, Religious

Added to the calendar in 1779, Jane appeared in the previous Missal on August 21, though she had died on December 13, 1641. The revisers, who first categorized her among founders of religious orders and holy matrons, initially either omitted her observance or placed it on her *dies natalis* as an optional memorial shared with Lucy. When the calendar was first published, Lucy's day became obligatory, so Jane moved to December 12, close to the date of her death.

In 1971 the USCCB added Our Lady of Guadalupe as an obligatory memorial on December 12, impeding Jane's day. In 1988 the memorial of Our Lady of Guadalupe was raised to a feast in the United States, and in 1989 the Holy See granted the American bishops' petition to transfer Jane to August 18, as recommended by the Visitation Sisters, whom she founded. When the third edition of the Missal was published, Our Lady of Guadalupe appeared for the first time on the general calendar as an optional memorial. Because of the importance of that day throughout the Americas, the Missal moved the optional observance of Jane again, this time to August 12, when she is now observed in the United States as well.[133]

The *Supplement* to the Lectionary offers optional readings (623A). Jane's name is added to the Litany of the Saints in the solemn profession of religious women.

13 Saints Pontian, Pope, and Hippolytus, Priest, Martyrs

These martyrs are among the saints in the earliest calendar, the Chronography of 354. The previous Missal celebrated them separately: Hippolytus with Cassian on August 13, and Pontian on November 19. The revisers reunited Pontian with Hippolytus, naming the pope first, on the day from the Chronography, August 13. Both had died in 235, and their bodies were brought some years later to the catacombs in Rome on this day. This is an optional memorial, as it was throughout the drafts.

---

133. "Memorial of Saint Jane Frances de Chantal: Which Date is Correct?," *Newsletter* XLV (May–June 2009): 24, https://www.usccb.org/upload/divine-worship-newsletter-mayjune2009.pdf.

13 Blessed Michael McGivney, Priest

The beatified founder of the Knights of Columbus is respected highly throughout the United States. Originally from the Archdiocese of Hartford, Connecticut, Michael's day is an optional memorial there.

In the past, the Holy See allowed conferences of bishops to put blesseds on the particular calendar. Indeed, this happened in the United States on January 3, 4, and 5. Such permission is more commonly granted now only for local calendars, not national ones.

However, each bishop may permit groups of Knights to venerate Michael on this day. If he is ultimately canonized, the conference may request his entry on the national calendar. The USCCB's explanation and presentation of liturgical texts is on the website of the Knights of Columbus.[134]

14 Saint Maximilian Mary Kolbe, Priest and Martyr

This Polish Franciscan priest was imprisoned in Auschwitz during World War II and gave his life so that another prisoner could be spared. He died on this day in 1941. His countryman Pope John Paul canonized him in 1982 and added him to the general calendar the following year as an obligatory memorial.[135] An English translation of the texts for the Mass and the Liturgy of the Hours first appeared in 1984.[136]

---

134. Committee on Divine Worship, "Memorandum," August 5, 2021, https://www.kofc.org/en/resources/events/father-mcgivney-beatification/memoradum-usccb-committee-divine-worship.pdf.

135. "Memorial of Saint Maximilian Maria Kolbe, Priest and Martyr," *Newsletter* XIX (June/July 1983): 865.

136. "Saint Maximilian Mary Kolbe," *Newsletter* XX (June/July 1984): 915–16.

15 The Assumption of the Blessed Virgin Mary

Pope Paul called the day of Mary's Assumption "the festival honoring the fullness of blessedness that was her destiny, the glorification of her immaculate soul and virginal body that completely confirmed her to the risen Christ."[137] The date of Mary's passing to the next life is unknown, but August 15 is when the church has celebrated it, and where it remained throughout the drafts. The revisers first categorized this among four feasts connected with the mysteries of Mary's life, along with the Immaculate Conception, her Nativity, and the Visitation. The Assumption ranks as a solemnity and is numbered among potential holy days of obligation that conferences may establish.

This is a holy day in the United States, but if August 15 falls on a Saturday or a Monday, the obligation is lifted. If a Saturday, evening prayer remains that of the Assumption, but the afternoon or evening Mass in the parish is that of the Twentieth Sunday in Ordinary Time. When Sunday is August 14, Evening Prayer I of the Assumption takes precedence, but Sunday evening Masses remain those of Ordinary Time.

On particular calendars that honor Mary under a title not included in the general calendar, the patronal celebration may take place on this day, which is honored as Mary's *dies natalis*. However, a local devotion or shrine with a long history of a different date may keep it.[138]

16 Saint Stephen of Hungary

Occupying a place on the Roman calendar since 1686 and in the previous Missal on September 2, Stephen has moved to August 16, closer to the date of his death, August 15 († 1038). The revisers first categorized him as a non-bishop confessor, neither a doctor nor a founder of a religious order, and the

---

137. *Marialis cultus* 6, DOL 467 (3904), p. 1208.
138. *Calendaria particularia* 35, DOL 481 (4030), p. 1253.

previous Missal gave Stephen the title King. He remains an optional memorial without any further designation.

19 Saint John Eudes, Priest

John Eudes died on this day in 1680, has had a feast on the Roman calendar since 1928, and enjoyed this same date in the previous Missal. First categorized as a founder of a religious order, he remains as an optional memorial. Nearly all the drafts held his date in place.

20 Saint Bernard, Abbot and Doctor of the Church

On the calendar since the thirteenth century, Bernard died on this date in 1153. The previous Missal held his observance on the same day, as did all the drafts. The revisers first categorized him among the doctors of the church and listed him among monks, together with Anthony and Benedict. "Because of the importance of the life and writings of St. Bernard in the Church,"[139] they kept his date obligatory, as it continues to be. In the solemn profession of religious men and women, this abbot's name is added to the Litany of the Saints after Benedict and before Francis and Dominic.

21 Saint Pius X, Pope

As noted on July 22, the revisers honored about thirty saints with an obligatory observance, representing the span of ages from the primitive church to the present, citing Mary Magdalene and Pius X at the extremes. This day remained obligatory throughout the drafts. Pius X died on August 20, 1914, and was added to the Roman calendar in 1955. In the previous Missal on September 3, his observance was moved to an open date close to his *dies natalis*.

---

139. Schemata, n. 225, p. 23.

22 The Queenship of the Blessed Virgin Mary

Pope Paul, alluding to the collect for the Mass of this day, wrote, "The solemnity of the Assumption is continued on into the celebration of the Queenship of Mary on the octave day. She who is enthroned next to the King of Ages is contemplated as the radiant Queen and interceding Mother."[140]

The previous Missal devoted May 31 to Mary under this title, which Pius XII had added to the calendar in 1954. The revisers first categorized it as an optional devotional feast to conclude the month of May. The early drafts kept it, but later ones moved the Visitation there from July 2, recommending the Queenship of Mary as a Votive Mass. The revisers reasoned that her queenship was already present in Mary's Assumption. However, the Congregation for the Doctrine of the Faith wanted to keep a number of days devoted to Mary obligatory, including May 31 with this title. The revisers reached a compromise by moving the observance to the octave of the Assumption, previously the Immaculate Heart of the Virgin Mary, another of the days that the Congregation hoped to retain. In the end, the Visitation moved to May 31, where it concluded May and formed a bridge between the Annunciation on March 25 and the Nativity of John the Baptist on June 24. The Queenship of Mary moved to this date, and the Immaculate Heart of Mary moved nearer to the Sacred Heart of Jesus.

23 Saint Rose of Lima, Virgin

First categorized by the revisers among virgins who were not martyrs, Rose of Lima had been on the previous calendar on August 30. She had died on August 24, 1617, the feast of Bartholomew, and was added to the calendar in 1727. The revisers initially moved her to August 23, then to August 25,

---

140. *Marialis cultus* 6, DOL 467 (3904), p. 1208.

and eventually back to August 23, close to her *dies natalis*. This is an optional memorial.

Rose took a vow of virginity. At the solemn profession of religious women, her name is added to the litany of saints.

24 Saint Bartholomew, Apostle

Bartholomew has long been associated with this date, honored here in the previous Missal and in all the drafts. He is one of many apostles whose feasts fall near the end of the month in what may have been a lost attempt to insert each of the Twelve into a similar slot throughout the year. Bartholomew is named in the first eucharistic prayer and in the litany of saints for the ordination of a bishop. If a bishop is ordained on this day, the ceremony takes place inside the Mass for Bartholomew.

25 Saint Louis

As with Stephen of Hungary, Louis appeared in the previous Missal designated as King. The revisers first categorized him among non-bishop confessors who were neither doctors nor founders. The revised calendar removed secular titles, so Louis appears under the simple but nonetheless exalted title of Saint. He died on this day in 1270, and his feast has been on the calendar since 1297. The previous Missal honored him on this date, as did all the drafts. He remains an optional memorial.

25 Saint Joseph Calasanz, Priest

The revisers first considered Joseph a founder of a religious order of little importance. He had occupied August 27 in the previous Missal. He died on August 25, 1648, so the drafts uniformly moved him to this day, nearly always as an optional memorial, as it remains.

27 Saint Monica

The revisers initially categorized the mother of Augustine among holy matrons. The day of her death in 387 is unknown.

Her feast had been observed on May 4 since the fifteenth century because the Hermits of St. Augustine celebrated the following day as the feast of the Augustine's conversion. Because the conversion was removed from the general calendar, the revisers proposed "that the memorial of St. Monica become the day that precedes the commemoration of St. Augustine."[141]

All the drafts moved her to August 27. She was listed alternatively as a widow, a matron, or a mother of a family. The revisers proposed keeping her day optional, but the Congregation for the Doctrine of the Faith wanted it obligatory, and so it stands.

28 Saint Augustine, Bishop and Doctor of the Church

A pivotal figure in Christianity, Augustine died on this day in 430, and his feast has been on the calendar since the eighth century. The revisers first categorized him among the doctors of the church and proposed that the traditional date of his observance be kept obligatory. The previous Missal honored him on August 28, and all the drafts kept the date, which stands as an obligatory memorial.

Augustine is invoked in the standard Litany of the Saints among the doctors of the church, chronologically between Gregory and Athanasius. In the solemn profession of religious men or women, the doctors give way to those who helped establish a rule for those in religious life. Gregory and Athanasius are removed, and Basil, who wrote on asceticism, remains. Augustine follows Basil, moving him out of bishops and doctors and into priests and religious, just ahead of Benedict, highlighting Augustine's authorship of a monastic rule.

29 The Passion of John the Baptist

The Roman calendar has commemorated the martyrdom of John the Baptist on this day since the seventh century. The

141. Schemata, n. 188, p. 21.

previous Missal and all the drafts kept the date. Formerly called the "Beheading," it is now called the "Passion" to show the likeness of his death to that of Christ, and to distinguish John's *dies natalis* among that of other martyrs. This day stands as an obligatory memorial.

John is one of only a few saints appearing twice in the calendar, which commemorates both his birth and his death. He is invoked in the standard Litany of the Saints, even in its abbreviated form at the baptism of a child.

At Mass the gospel of the day, recounting his passion, is proper (GIRM 357), but the first reading is usually that of the weekday. In the Liturgy of the Hours, this memorial receives special treatment, probably because of its significance in the gospels. The office includes a unique invitatory, hymns, antiphons, readings, and intercessions.

September

1 *World Day of Prayer for the Care of Creation*

In 2015 Pope Francis assigned the first day of September as the World Day of Prayer for the Care of Creation,[142] and in 2016 he endorsed it as the beginning of a season of creation within the church, culminating with the memorial of Francis of Assisi on October 4.[143] The USCCB lists September 1 among its Days of Prayer and Special Observances, and its

---

142. "Letter of His Holiness Pope Francis for the Establishment of the 'World Day of Prayer for the Care of Creation,'" https://www.vatican.va/content/francesco/en/letters/2015/documents/papa-francesco_20150806_lettera-giornata-cura-creato.html.

143. "Message of his Holiness Pope Francis for the Celebration of the World Day of Prayer for the Care of Creation, 1 September 2016," https://www.vatican.va/content/francesco/en/messages/pont-messages/2016/documents/papa-francesco_20160901_messaggio-giornata-cura-creato.html.

department of Justice, Peace, and Human Development offers reasons for the season.[144]

3 Saint Gregory the Great, Pope and Doctor of the Church

In the previous calendar Gregory the Great was honored on March 12, his *dies natalis* in 604. He had entered the Roman calendar in the eighth century. However, "As the date of St. Gregory's death always falls during Lent, it is proposed that his commemoration be made on the day of his ordination,"[145] which took place on September 3, 590. All the drafts placed him there, except for one that chose September 1. Gregory's day remained September 3 as an obligatory memorial.

Gregory is invoked in the standard Litany of the Saints. However, at the solemn profession of religious men and women, he and fellow Doctor of the Church Athanasius are replaced by saints who composed a rule for religious life. The omission of Gregory, a monk who became pope, perhaps dissuades religious men from aspiring to hierarchical achievement through religious profession.

7–13 World Day for Grandparents and Elderly

Pope Francis established the fourth Sunday of July as the World Day for Grandparents and Elderly. This put the observance close to the day when the church honors the grandparents of Jesus, Joachim and Anne. However, in the United States, the bishops have transferred the observance to the weekend after Labor Day to coincide with National Grand-

144. "The Season of Creation: September 1–October 4," https://www.usccb.org/issues-and-action/human-life-and-dignity/environment/upload/WDPCC-Bulletin-Insert.pdf.

145. Schemata, n. 188, p. 22.

parents Day. Resources are available for the Twenty-Third or Twenty-Fourth Sunday in Ordinary Time.[146]

8 *The Nativity of the Blessed Virgin Mary*

The date of Mary's birth is unknown, but the church has long honored this date for her Nativity. The revisers considered this among the important feasts connected to the mysteries of Mary's life, along with her Immaculate Conception, Visitation, and Assumption. The previous Missal kept this date, as did all the drafts. This day ranks as a feast. Mary is always invoked in the Litany of the Saints.

9 *Saint Peter Claver, Priest*

A Spanish Jesuit who ministered to enslaved persons in Colombia, Peter died on September 8, 1654, and was canonized in 1888. The previous Missal listed him on September 9, the closest available date to his *dies natalis*, among its regional celebrations, not on the general calendar.

A saint of the New World, Peter's obligatory memorial has been kept in the United States from the beginning of the revisions. As noted on April 23, Pope John Paul added Peter to the general calendar in 1995. The third edition of the Missal has him as an optional memorial throughout the world, but obligatory in the United States. The *Supplement* to the Lectionary offers optional readings (636A).

9 *Day of Prayer for Peace in our Communities*

In 2021, "in light of recent incidents of violence and racial tension in communities across the United States,"[147] the

---

146. USCCB Marriage and Family Life Ministries, "Grandparents & Elderly," https://www.usccb.org/topics/marriage-and-family-life-ministries /grandparents-elderly.

147. USCCB, "Day of Prayer for Peace in Our Communities, September 9, 2021," https://www.usccb.org/events/2021/day-prayer-peace-our -communities.

USCCB added this as a day of prayer for peace within local communities. It provides resources through its Ad Hoc Committee Against Racism.[148] The day coincides with the optional memorial of Peter Claver, who ministered to and evangelized enslaved persons.

12 The Most Holy Name of Mary

The previous Missal included this observance, but the revisers removed it. The Congregation for the Doctrine of the Faith wanted to retain it among the obligatory days honoring Mary, but the Consilium stood its ground and suppressed it "since it is included in the feast of her Nativity" just a few days before.[149] The third edition of the Missal restored the texts for the day as an optional memorial, and the *Supplement* to the Lectionary offers readings (636B).

13 Saint John Chrysostom, Bishop and Doctor of the Church

First categorized by the revisers among the Doctors of the Church, John died on September 14, 407, and entered the Roman calendar in the thirteenth century. The previous Missal honored him on January 27, but he has moved closer to his *dies natalis*. The West Syrians use this day, though the Byzantines honor him on November 13.[150] All the drafts made him obligatory on September 13, as he remains. Both he and Cornelius died on September 14, though several decades apart, and are celebrated on proximate dates.

---

148. USCCB Ad Hoc Committee Against Racism, https://www.usccb.org /committees/ad-hoc-committee-against-racism.

149. Bugnini, p. 312.

150. Schemata, n. 188, p. 22, provides this information in a handwritten note on the extant copy.

14 The Exaltation of the Holy Cross

Among the feasts of the Lord, the Exaltation of the Holy Cross has occupied this date since the seventh century. Prior to the revised translation of the Missal, it was known in English as the Triumph of the Cross. The Latin title seems to refer less to the success of the cross and more to its purpose. According to tradition, the true cross was lifted up for display on this date after its discovery in fourth-century Jerusalem. The previous Missal and all the drafts kept it on this date without debate. As a feast of the Lord, when it falls on a Sunday, it takes precedence over the Twenty-Fourth Sunday in Ordinary Time.

15–21 Catechetical Sunday

The third Sunday in September is Catechetical Sunday in the United States. Some parishes incorporate a blessing for teachers and students into the celebration of Mass (*Book of Blessings*, nos. 491–550). The USCCB provides resources for the Twenty-Fourth or Twenty-Fifth Sunday in Ordinary Time.[151]

15 Our Lady of Sorrows

In the previous Missal this date honored the Seven Sorrows of the Blessed Virgin Mary, added to the calendar in 1814. In some countries the Friday before Palm Sunday was Our Lady of Sorrows, and some local customs persist. As noted in the final two weeks of Lent above, the third edition of the Missal added an alternative collect mentioning Mary on that day. But the revisers did not add her patronage to the Friday before Palm Sunday because that would have duplicated the traditional day in September. They only changed the title

151. USCCB, "About Catechetical Sunday," https://www.usccb.org/beliefs -and-teachings/how-we-teach/catechesis/catechetical-sunday/catechetical -sunday-about.

from the Seven Sorrows of the Blessed Virgin Mary to Our Lady of Sorrows.

The revisers preferred to keep this optional, but the Congregation for the Doctrine of the Faith favored making it an obligatory memorial. The Consilium conceded.

In the Liturgy of the Hours, the invitatory, hymns, antiphons, readings, and responsories are all proper. *Stabat mater*, a popular hymn at the Stations of the Cross, may be sung.

16 Saints Cornelius, Pope, and Cyprian, Bishop, Martyrs

The Chronography of 354 had placed Cyprian's observance on September 14, the day of his martyrdom in 258, before the feast of the Exaltation of the Cross was added to the calendar. The date of the death of Cornelius in 253 is unknown, but Gregory IX assigned the two to this date in the late fourteenth century, where they appeared in the previous Missal. One from Rome, the other from Carthage, they represent two different regions suffering the same persecution. All the drafts kept them on September 16 as an obligatory memorial, as they remain. Both are mentioned in the first eucharistic prayer.

17 Saint Robert Bellarmine, Bishop and Doctor of the Church

Honored in the previous Missal on May 13, Robert had died on September 17, 1621, so the revisers moved his observance here. He has been on the calendar since 1931. The drafts kept his observance optional, as it remains.

17 Saint Hildegard of Bingen, Virgin and Doctor of the Church

As noted on February 27, Pope Francis added the optional memorial of Hildegard to the general calendar in 2021. Absent from the previous Missal and all the drafts, Hildegard's inclusion shows a new appreciation of her writings and impact.

17–24 National Migration Week

The USCCB celebrates National Migration Week on the seven days anticipating the World Day of Migrants and Refugees.[152] The website provides resources for this day of prayer.[153]

19 Saint Januarius, Bishop and Martyr

Januarius has occupied this date since 1586. He died on September 19 around the year 304. Highly popular in Naples, Januarius remained here throughout the drafts. The early drafts commemorated him with companions, as the previous Missal had done, but regarded him as a non-Roman martyr of little importance. Some of the drafts omitted his observance. The final calendar without comment removed his companions from this optional memorial.

20 Saints Andrew Kim Tae-gŏn, Priest, Paul Chŏng Ha-sang, and Companions, Martyrs

Examples of global witness to Christ, even unto death, these martyrs of Korea were added to the calendar for the third edition of the Missal. Over a hundred faithful Catholics were killed over a period of about thirty years. Andrew, the first Korean to be ordained a priest, was among them, and Paul was a lay apostle.[154] Andrew was martyred on September 16, 1846, and this date falls close to his *dies natalis*. As these martyrs were native to Korea, their memorial is obligatory.

152. USCCB Migration, "National Migration Week," https://www.usccb.org/committees/migration/national-migration-week-2023.

153. USCCB Migration, "Catholic Ministries Serving Migrants and Refugees," https://www.usccb.org/migrationministries.

154. Dicastero delle Cause dei Santi, "Andrea Kim Taegon e 102 Soci († 1838–1867)," https://www.causesanti.va/it/santi-e-beati/andrea-kim-taegon.html.

21 Saint Matthew, Apostle and Evangelist

Another apostle on a late date of the month, Matthew has long been honored on September 21. The previous Missal celebrated him on this date, as did all the drafts. Matthew is mentioned in the first eucharistic prayer. In the ordination of a bishop, his name is added to the Litany of the Saints. If the ordination takes place on this day, the Mass of this apostle is celebrated.

23 Saint Pius of Pietrelcina, Priest

Pope John Paul canonized the man popularly called "Padre Pio" on June 16, 2002, about a month after the printing of the third edition of the Missal. At the Angelus that day, the pope announced the addition of Pius of Pietrelcina to the general calendar for September 23, his *dies natalis*.[155] In an instant, the new Missal was out of date. Subsequent translations have added Pius to the Proper of Saints. Since then, other saints have been added to the general calendar, leaving the Missal increasingly outdated. The *Supplement* to the Lectionary offers optional readings (643A).

The collect in English translates this saint's popular Italian first name from "Pio" to "Pius." It also eliminates his title, "Padre," by which he is equally well known. "Priest," not "Father," is the descriptor the calendar uses for many saints in this category, so it would be inconsistent to put the title "Padre" in the collect. Although saintly popes with the same name are known in English as "Pius," the names of some other saints in the Missal keep their original language, such as Thérèse and Juan Diego.

---

155. "Canonization of St. Pio of Pietrelcina, John Paul II, Angelus, Sunday, 16 June 2002," https://www.vatican.va/content/john-paul-ii/en/angelus/2002/documents/hf_jp-ii_ang_20020616.html.

24–30 World Day of Migrants and Refugees

The last Sunday in September is the World Day of Migrants and Refugees. The Vatican's department of Integral Human Development states that the day has been observed since 1914.[156] This Sunday concludes a week of prayer for migrants. In the United States this is also Priesthood Sunday, the Twenty-Fifth or Twenty-Sixth in Ordinary Time, when people often show appreciation for their priests.

26 Saints Cosmas and Damian, Martyrs

The previous Missal honored Cosmas and Damian on September 27, the anniversary of the dedication of their basilica near the Roman Forum, an event that took place about the year 530. Although these saints had occupied a place on the calendar since the sixth century, the revisers moved them to make room for Vincent de Paul, whose anniversary of death was known and who ranked as an obligatory memorial.

The revisers first categorized Cosmas and Damian as non-Roman martyrs whose biographies were unreliable, but whose names were known. The early drafts did not include them, but eventually they took a place near their traditional date, first on September 28, and then on September 26. The revisers noted, "The memorial is kept by reason of the popular devotion toward these martyrs."[157] Both are mentioned in the first eucharistic prayer.

27 Saint Vincent de Paul, Priest

The previous Missal honored Vincent on July 19, but the revisers moved his observance to his *dies natalis*, September 27 († 1660). Vincent entered the calendar in 1753. The revisers first categorized him as a founder of a religious order, and

156. Integral Human Development, "World Day of Migrants and Refugees," https://migrants-refugees.va/world-day-of-migrants-refugees/.

157. Schemata, n. 225, p. 25.

they kept his date on September 27 throughout the drafts. They made his date an obligatory memorial "because of the charitable deeds of this saint."[158] Jounel cited this as an example of a day that the revised calendar moved quite some distance from its traditional observance, due to the importance of the *dies natalis*.[159] Vincent remains an obligatory memorial.

At the solemn profession of religious men, Vincent is invoked in the litany of saints among founders of religious orders. In the solemn profession of religious women, his friend Louise de Marillac replaces him in the litany. Although the two of them founded the Daughters of Charity, Vincent is on the general calendar, and Louise is not.

28 Saint Wenceslaus, Martyr

The revisers first categorized Wenceslaus as a non-Roman martyr of little importance. Even so, he appeared in all the drafts as an optional memorial, as he remains. He died on this date in 929 and had been on the calendar since 1729, honored on this same date in the previous Missal.

28 Saint Lawrence Ruiz and Companions, Martyrs

Added to the third edition of the Missal, these sixteen Dominican-associated martyrs represent the spread of the faith to the Philippines, Taiwan, and Japan. Lawrence, a layman, died on September 29, 1637. As protomartyr of the Philippines, he is remembered with an optional memorial on a day close to his *dies natalis*, already taken by the feast of the archangels.[160]

---

158. Schemata, n. 225, p. 25.

159. "Studia De Quibusdam Animadversionibus," p. 297.

160. "Lawrence Ruiz, layman, Dominic Ibánez de Erquicia, O.P., James Kyushei Tomonaga, O.P., and 13 companions, Philippines, martyrs in Japan," https://www.vatican.va/news_services/liturgy/saints/ns_lit_doc_19871018 _ruiz-compagni_en.html.

Lawrence's 1981 beatification in Manila was the first such ceremony outside the Vatican.[161] The *Supplement* to the Lectionary offers optional readings (645A). John Paul II canonized the martyrs in 1987. The Philippine Conference of Bishops requested putting them onto the general calendar, and the pope did so in March 1988.[162]

29 Saints Michael, Gabriel, and Raphael, Archangels

The Basilica of the Holy Angels on Rome's Via Salaria was dedicated in the fifth century on this date. The previous Missal honored Michael on September 29, Gabriel on March 24, Raphael on October 24, and the Guardian Angels on October 2. The revisers offered a different approach:

> The feast has been celebrated at Rome since the seventeenth century as a feast of all angels, as is clear in the liturgical formulas (see especially the collect). The feast of all Guardian Angels was inscribed into the Roman calendar in the year 1670; the feasts of Saints Gabriel and Raphael in 1921. A return to the ancient Roman tradition is proposed.[163]

The drafts changed the title to the feast of St. Michael and All the Angels. The Congregation for the Doctrine of the Faith wanted to keep a memorial of Gabriel on March 24, and one of the drafts did so. In the end the names of all three archangels conjoined on this day. Michael and the Holy Angels of God are invoked in the standard Litany of the Saints.

161. "Holy mass for the Beatification of Lorenzo Ruiz: Homily of the Holy Father John Paul II," https://www.vatican.va/content/john-paul-ii/en/homilies/1981/documents/hf_jp-ii_hom_19810218_beatificazione-ruiz.html.
162. Congregation for Divine Worship, "Prot. 1215/87, Decree, 22 March 1988," *Newsletter* XXIV (April 1988): 1099.
163. Schemata, n. 188, p. 23.

30 Saint Jerome, Priest and Doctor of the Church

Jerome died on this date in 420 and has been on the calendar since the eighth century. The previous Missal and all the drafts retained him as an obligatory memorial on this day, as he remains.

October

Domestic Violence Awareness Month

In the USCCB's list of Days of Prayer and Special Observances, all of October is Domestic Violence Awareness Month. Resources include a sample homily for Mass.[164]

Respect Life Month

October is Respect Life Month. The USCCB's website offers a variety of resources.[165]

1–7 Respect Life Sunday

The first Sunday in October is Respect Life Sunday in the United States. Homily helps are available for the Twenty-Sixth or Twenty-Seventh Sunday in Ordinary Time.[166]

1 Saint Thérèse of the Child Jesus, Virgin and Doctor of the Church

First categorized by the revisers among non-martyr virgins, Thérèse was added to the calendar in 1927. The previous Missal honored her on October 3. She died on September 30,

---

164. USCCB Marriage and Family Life Ministries, "Domestic Violence," https://www.usccb.org/topics/marriage-and-family-life-ministries/domestic-violence.

165. USCCB Pro-Life Activities, "Respect Life Program," https://www.usccb.org/respectlife.

166. USCCB Respect Life, "Respect Life Month," https://www.respectlife.org/respect-life-month.

1897, the day of Jerome, so her observance stands closer to her *dies natalis*. All the drafts kept her on October 1 as an optional memorial, but the Congregation for the Doctrine of the Faith wanted her status obligatory, and the change was made.

Thérèse was canonized in 1925, just 28 years after her death. Pope John Paul named her a Doctor of the Church in 1997, a title enjoyed by only three previous women: Hildegard of Bingen, Catherine of Siena, and Teresa of Ávila.[167] The English translation of the Missal keeps the French spelling of her name, as many English-speakers pronounce it.

2 The Holy Guardian Angels

Attempting to gather all angels into a single observance on September 29, the early drafts removed the Guardian Angels from October 2, their date in the previous Missal. The Congregation for the Doctrine of the Faith wanted this to become an obligatory memorial, and one draft shows it that way. The Consilium complied.

At Mass, the gospel—in which Jesus states that angels behold the face of God—is proper, but the first reading may come from the weekday (GIRM 357). The Liturgy of the Hours treats this memorial with a special invitatory, hymns, antiphons, readings, and intercessions. The psalms of Morning Prayer are those of the first Sunday of the cycle, as happens with feasts and solemnities. Midday Prayer comes with special readings and responsories. The psalms of Evening Prayer were selected for their reference to angels. The litany of saints includes an invocation to the Holy Angels of God.

167. Apostolic Letter of His Holiness Pope John Paul II, "*Divini amoris scientia*: Saint Thérèse of the Child Jesus and the Holy Face Is Proclaimed a Doctor of the Universal Church," https://www.vatican.va/content/john -paul-ii/en/apost_letters/1997/documents/hf_jp-ii_apl_19101997_divini -amoris.html.

4 Saint Francis of Assisi

Francis died on October 3, 1226, and his feast entered the calendar only two years later. The previous Missal observed his date on October 4, and none of the drafts changed it. He remains an obligatory memorial. The revisers categorized him both as a founder of a religious order and, with Augustine, one of "a few saints whose long-lasting splendor has spread everywhere."[168]

In the Litany of the Saints, Francis pairs with Dominic, his contemporary and founder of another religious order. However, in the ordination of a deacon, Francis is invoked separately, according to the tradition that he served as a deacon of the church. In the Consecration of Virgins, the litany keeps them paired, but Francis takes the second spot.

5 Blessed Francis Xavier Seelos, Priest

Added to the proper calendar for the United States in 2014, Francis has special liturgical texts on the USCCB website and optional readings in the *Supplement* to the Lectionary (651A).[169] A German Redemptorist who labored in the United States, Francis died on October 4, 1867. His optional memorial is observed close to his *dies natalis*.

5 Saint Faustina, Virgin

Faustina died on this date in 1938, and Pope John Paul, a fellow Pole, canonized her in 2000. On the one hundredth anniversary of Pope John Paul's birth, the Congregation for Divine Worship and the Discipline of the Sacraments announced that Pope Francis had inscribed Faustina into the general cal-

---

168. Schemata, n. 225, p. 7.

169. USCCB, Blessed Francis Xavier Seelos, https://www.usccb.org/prayer-and-worship/liturgical-year-and-calendar/blessed-francis-xavier-seelos.

endar as an optional memorial.[170] The USCCB provides texts
for the Mass and Liturgy of the Hours on its website.[171]

6 *Saint Bruno, Priest*
The revisers first categorized Bruno as a founder of a religious order of little importance, but all the drafts kept him
on this day as an optional memorial. He died on October 6 in
1101 and entered the calendar in 1674. The previous Missal
also remembered him on this day, when he now appears as
an optional memorial.

6 *Blessed Marie Rose Durocher, Virgin*
Marie Rose died on this date in 1849 and was beatified by
Pope John Paul in 1982. Although she ministered primarily in
Canada, she founded the Holy Sisters of Jesus and Mary, who
also work in the United States. As noted above on January 6,
the USCCB added her to the calendar in 1982.

7 *Our Lady of the Rosary*
Marking the anniversary of Pius V's Holy League's naval
victory in the battle at Lepanto in 1571, this date traditionally demonstrates the power of the intercession of the Blessed
Virgin Mary, invoked through praying the rosary. The date was
added to the calendar in 1716 and observed on this date in
the previous Missal. The revisers sought to make it optional,
as it was a devotional feast rather than one connected to the
mysteries of Mary's life. The Congregation for the Doctrine
of the Faith preferred it as an obligatory memorial, and the

170. Congregation for Divine Worship and the Discipline of the Sacraments, "Prot. n. 229/20 Decree on the inscription of the celebration of Saint
Faustina Kowalska, virgin, in the General Roman Calendar," https://www
.vatican.va/roman_curia/congregations/ccdds/documents/rc_con_ccdds_doc
_20200518_decreto-celebrazione-santafaustina_en.html.

171. USCCB, Saint Faustina Kowalska, https://www.usccb.org/prayer
-worship/liturgical-year/saint-faustina-kowalska.

Consilium ultimately agreed. Paul VI numbered this day among those "that began as celebrations proper to religious communities, but then became so widespread that they were rightly regarded as ecclesial."[172]

The Liturgy of the Hours gives this memorial special treatment. A hymn, antiphons, readings, responsories, and intercessions are all proper, as are the psalms of the first Sunday of the cycle for Morning Prayer and the psalms from the Common of the Blessed Virgin Mary for Evening Prayer.

9 Saint Denis, Bishop, and Companions, Martyrs

At first the revisers removed Denis and his companions from the calendar because, among the non-Roman Martyrs, only their names were reliable. However, during the process they restored the martyrs as an optional memorial on the day when they appeared in the previous Missal. The martyrs are believed to have died on October 9, around the year 260, and they have been part of the Roman calendar since the eleventh century.

9 Saint John Leonardi, Priest

John died on October 9, 1609, and entered the calendar in 1940. He was honored in the previous Missal on this day, as were Denis and his companions, and both observances remain in the Missal as optional memorials. The revisers first categorized him among founders of religious orders of little importance, and some drafts omitted his observance, but he ultimately regained a place in the calendar and Missal.

11 Saint John XXIII, Pope

John XXIII died on June 3, 1963, a date already reserved for Charles Lwanga and his companions. John's memorial honors the anniversary of the opening of the first session of

---

172. *Marialis cultus* 8, DOL 467 (3906), p. 1209.

the Second Vatican Council, which he convened on October 11, 1962.

Pope Francis canonized John XXIII together with John Paul II on Divine Mercy Sunday in 2014. Both were added to the general calendar as optional memorials that same year.[173] The *Supplement* to the Lectionary provides optional readings (655A).

14 Saint Callistus I, Pope and Martyr

Honored on this day since the Chronography of 354, Callistus is believed to have died on October 14 in 222. The previous Missal kept his observance on this date, as did all the drafts. His day is an optional memorial.

15 Saint Teresa of Jesus, Virgin and Doctor of the Church

Also known as Teresa of Ávila, this saint was first listed among the founders of religious orders and virgins who were not martyrs. She died on the night in 1582 that the Gregorian calendar came into force, when October 4 was followed by October 15 in order to correct the imprecise calculation of previous leap years. As October 4 is the memorial of Francis, Teresa has had October 15 since 1644, even in the previous Missal.

Pope Paul declared her a Doctor of the Church, the first woman to receive the title. He noted that Pope Gregory XV had canonized her among an elite list including Ignatius of Loyola, Francis Xavier, Isidore the farmer, and Philip Neri. Pope Paul affirmed that he was not flouting the stern words of the apostle Paul, who commanded the silence of women in

173. Congregation for Divine Worship and the Discipline of the Sacraments, Prot. N. 309/14, "Decree," https://www.vatican.va/roman_curia /congregations/ccdds/documents/rc_con_ccdds_doc_20140529_decreto -calendario-generale-gxxiii-gpii_en.html.

churches (1 Cor 14:34). Instead, in naming Teresa a doctor, he affirmed the "sublime mission that women have as part of the people of God."[174]

Teresa is invoked near the end of the standard Litany of the Saints under the same title that appears in the Missal, Teresa of Jesus. All the drafts retained her memorial as obligatory, as do the present calendar and Missal.

16 Saint Hedwig, Religious

Hedwig died on October 15, 1243, and her observance entered the calendar in 1706. The previous Missal honored her on October 16. The revisers first categorized her as a holy matron of little importance, and they removed her from the early drafts. She was restored as an optional memorial.

The bishops of Poland hoped that she or one of her compatriots would be raised to obligatory status. "The secretariat proposed that St. Hedwig be given a higher rank," but the vote was negative.[175]

16 Saint Margaret Mary Alacoque, Virgin

In the year 1690, Margaret Mary died on October 17, the day now dedicated to Ignatius of Antioch, but also the day given her in the previous Missal. She was added to the calendar in 1929. The revisers categorized her among virgins who were not martyrs, at first proposing October 17 as her optional memorial, then omitting her from the calendar. The revisers finally restored an observance to this advocate for devotion to the Sacred Heart of Jesus, though on a new date, October 16.

Margaret's day is an optional memorial. Her name is invoked in the litany of saints in the Consecration of Virgins.

---

174. Paul VI, "Homily, on St. Teresa of Avila, Doctor of the Church, 27 September 1970," DOL 474 (3962), p. 1236.

175. Bugnini, p. 318.

17 Saint Ignatius of Antioch, Bishop and Martyr
The revisers first categorized Ignatius among the few non-Roman regional martyrs of some importance for the whole church. Their ranks of Christian saints opened with martyrs, naming Ignatius, as well as Cornelius and Cyprian, as examples. The previous Missal honored Ignatius on February 1, but the revisers declared, "Ignatius must be celebrated on his *dies natalis* (October 17)."[176] His martyrdom took place about the year 107, as recorded in "an Antiochene martyrology of the fourth century," and on October 17 as "celebrated in the Antiochene Rite."[177] The saint has been on the calendar since the twelfth century. All the drafts gave him obligatory status on October 17.

Ignatius is invoked in the standard Litany of the Saints, but he is omitted at the solemn profession of religious men and women. Perhaps this avoids confusion with Ignatius of Loyola, who is added to the same litany, and to call upon saints more directly related to religious life.

18 Saint Luke, Evangelist
The date of Luke's martyrdom is unknown, but he has been continually recognized on this date. The revised Missal kept October 18, the date from the previous Missal and retained throughout all the drafts. Luke's day is celebrated as a feast.

18–24 World Mission Sunday
The second to last Sunday in October is World Mission Sunday. Resources are available from the Society for the Propagation of the Faith and the Missionary Childhood Association.[178] Uniquely among these days of prayer, the Mass formula "For the Evangelization of Peoples" may replace the

176. Schemata, n. 132, p. 14.
177. Schemata, n. 188, p. 24.
178. Missio, "World Mission Sunday," https://www.missio.org/resources.aspx?localization=EN&activetab=world-mission-month.

antiphons, prayers, and readings assigned for this day, either the Twenty-Ninth or Thirtieth Sunday in Ordinary Time.[179] This replacement may happen on any Ordinary Time Sunday honoring the missions, such as when a visitor makes an appeal.

19 Saints John de Brébeuf and Isaac Jogues, Priests, and Companions, Martyrs

From the earliest discussions the revisers desired to insert saints from different regions to show holiness throughout the universal church. As noted above on February 6, adding martyrs from Japan, Uganda, and these from Canada diversified a calendar.

The drafts all included Isaac Jogues and Companions, the Canadian martyrs, among the "new feasts of saints."[180] They shared this recognition with others, as indicated above on April 28. The drafts alternated between making this an obligatory and an optional memorial.

Isaac and John de la Lande were martyred on October 18, 1647. "The memory of eight Canadian martyr saints is proposed to show the catholicity of the Roman calendar. Only an [optional] memorial is appropriate because it does not concern indigenous saints."[181]

In the United States this became an obligatory memorial. John de Brébeuf occupies the first position among the martyrs, as is the custom in Canada, where the day is celebrated as a feast on September 26.

20 Saint Paul of the Cross, Priest

In the general calendar, Paul is observed on October 19 as an alternative optional memorial to the Canadian martyrs, as some of the drafts had envisioned. Because that day is

---

179. Roman Missal: Masses and Prayers for Various Needs and Occasions, 18.

180. Schemata, n. 132, p. 22.

181. Schemata, n. 188, p. 24.

obligatory in the United States, Paul may be honored on the succeeding day, as the drafts making the Canadians obligatory had envisioned.[182]

The previous Missal placed Paul's observance on April 28. He died on October 18 († 1775), as had some of the Canadians († 1647), but since that date belongs to Luke, these saints moved to a day near their *dies natalis*. Paul has been on the Roman calendar since 1869.

22 Saint John Paul II, Pope

The pope who canonized more saints than any other in history himself has been recognized for his holiness of life. In 2014, just nine years after the death of John Paul II, Pope Francis canonized him together with John XXIII on Divine Mercy Sunday, a day and devotion dear to the Polish pope. Both John and John Paul were immediately added to the general calendar as optional memorials.[183] The *Supplement* to the Lectionary suggests readings (663A).

23 Saint John of Capistrano, Priest

The city where John was born is spelled "Capestrano" in the Table of Liturgical Days and "Capistrano" in the Proper of Saints. The revisers first categorized him as a non-pope confessor who was neither a doctor nor a founder of a religious order. They considered him of little importance, yet all the drafts but one placed him on this day. The previous Missal honored him on March 28, but the revisers moved him to his *dies natalis*.

John died in 1456 and has been on the calendar since 1890. His day is an optional memorial.

---

182. "Confirmation of Calendar Change and Additions," *Newsletter* XXVII (March 1991): 1244.

183. Congregation for Divine Worship and the Discipline of the Sacraments, Prot. N. 309/14, "Decree," https://www.vatican.va/roman_curia /congregations/ccdds/documents/rc_con_ccdds_doc_20140529_decreto- calendario-generale-gxxiii-gpii_en.html.

24 Saint Anthony Mary Claret, Bishop

The revisers first categorized Anthony Mary as a founder of little importance, but he appeared in nearly all the drafts on this day. He died on October 24, 1870, and was added to the Roman calendar in 1960.

The previous Missal assigned October 23 for his celebration, probably because October 24 was taken by the archangel Raphael. The revisers combined the archangels into a single observance on September 29, which opened this *dies natalis* for Anthony Mary. The day is an optional memorial, as it was through almost all the drafts.

28 Saints Simon and Jude, Apostles

Simon and Jude have occupied this date near the end of the month for many centuries. The previous Missal had them here, and the drafts all honored the date.

They are observed as a feast. If a bishop is ordained on this day, the antiphons, prayers, and readings of the apostles are used for the Mass, together with red vesture. In the Litany of the Saints for the same ordination, their names appear sequentially, not together. Both are named in the first eucharistic prayer.

November

Black Catholic History Month

In the USCCB's list of Days of Prayer and Special Observances, all of November is Black Catholic History Month—distinct from February, which is commonly observed as Black History Month. Resources include prayers, cards, and inspirational messages.[184]

---

184. USCCB African American Affairs, "Timely resources for Ministry with Catholics of African Descent," https://www.usccb.org/committees /african-american-affairs.

1 All Saints

The Solemnity of All Saints has long been celebrated on the first of November. The previous Missal and all the drafts kept it here. A conference of bishops may select it as a holy day of obligation. The obligation applies in the United States, but is lifted when November 1 falls on a Saturday or a Monday. When it is a holy day, a funeral Mass is not permitted, though a funeral without Mass is (GIRM 380). This implies that the mourners will return to church to celebrate the Mass of the holy day. A funeral Mass may take place in years when the obligation is lifted.

In the United States, if All Saints' Day falls on a Saturday, regularly scheduled anticipatory Masses are those of the Thirty-First Sunday in Ordinary Time. Evening Prayer, however, is of All Saints. When it falls on a Sunday, All Saints replaces the Ordinary Time liturgy. When All Saints falls on a Monday, Sunday's Evening Prayer II yields to Evening Prayer I of All Saints.

The Apostolic See permits a conference of bishops to choose a different date "that fits in better with local traditions or the culture of a people."[185] This applies to all solemnities of precept, but All Saints is given as a particular example.

2 All Souls

This day of prayer for all the faithful departed has enjoyed a long history on this date. The previous Missal honored it, and all the drafts maintained it. The Table of Liturgical Days lists it in the third tier after solemnities of the Lord, of Mary, or of the saints. Called a "commemoration," though not the same kind of "commemoration" as in the Liturgy of the Hours during privileged times, it ranks higher than proper solemnities and Sundays of Ordinary Time.

---

185. *Calendaria particularia* 36, DOL 481 (4031), p. 1253.

This was not clear in 1969 when November 2 fell on a Sunday, and a draft of the liturgical calendar for that year assigned the Twenty-third Sunday after Pentecost to that day, transferring All Souls' Day to November 3. The ranking now has the Mass of All Souls' Day replace that of the Thirty-First Sunday in Ordinary Time when they coincide.

The Liturgy of the Hours states on November 2 that when the day falls on a Sunday, the office is that of Sunday, not from the Common of the Dead. Nonetheless, in celebrations of Morning and Evening Prayer with the people, the office of the dead may be prayed on this Sunday. After the calendar was first published, the Consilium stated that the Mass for the Dead has a paschal character and may be celebrated on a Sunday, even with the clergy wearing white vestments, which the previous Missal did not allow on such occasions.[186]

The situation presented itself again in 1975, and the Holy See declared that evening Masses on Saturday November 1 had to be those of All Saints, which held a higher rank.[187] The declaration appeared on October 29, giving the church only three days' notice. However, as indicated above regarding consecutive solemnities, these rules were revised ten years later, and a regularly scheduled Saturday evening parish Mass on November 1 now celebrates All Souls.

The USCCB's Committee on Divine Worship states that on the evening of All Saints, after Evening Prayer II, for pastoral reasons, the faithful may also pray Evening Prayer of the dead, anticipating the next day. There is no Evening Prayer I for the dead, so the Evening Prayer assigned for November 2 could be offered in anticipation on November 1—after Eve-

186. Bugnini, p. 316.
187. Sacred Congregation for Sacraments and Divine Worship, "Communication *Domenica prossima*, on the evening Mass for 1 November in 1975," DOL 478 (3986), p. 1241.

ning Prayer II of All Saints.[188] The committee does not cite a source, indicating only that this may be done for pastoral reasons. It would be highly unusual to celebrate Evening Prayer twice on the same day, but the committee permits it in the United States on November 1.

Ritual Masses are forbidden on All Souls' Day (GIRM 372). Not even the Mass for the Dedication of a Church nor for the Dedication of an Altar may be celebrated on November 2. A wedding may take place outside Mass with the usual readings, but during Mass on November 2, a wedding uses the antiphons, prayers, and readings from the Mass for the Dead. Pastorally, this is not a good day for a wedding.

The previous Missal presented three completely distinct sets of Masses. The current Missal permits a priest to celebrate Mass three times on this day: one for a particular intention, which is the only Mass for which he may receive an offering, another for all the faithful departed, and a third for the intention of the pope.[189] The Missal presents three Masses, which may be used in succession. The readings formerly assigned to each Mass may be replaced by others from Masses for the Dead.

3 Saint Martin de Porres, Religious
4 Saint Charles Borromeo, Bishop

The revisers proposed adding two saints from Latin America unrecognized in the previous calendar: Turibius and Martin de Porres. Regarding Martin, "The memorial of this humble indigenous saint, extremely popular throughout all America,

---

188. "Liturgical Considerations for All Souls' Day 2013," *Newsletter* XLIX (January 2013): 4.

189. Citing Pope Benedict XV, "*Incruentum altaris,*" https://www.vatican.va/content/benedict-xv/it/bulls/documents/hf_ben-xv_bulls_19150810_incruentum-altaris.html.

is proposed."[190] Martin had died on November 3 in 1639, as Charles Borromeo had in 1584.

The previous Missal placed Charles's day on November 4; he had been on the calendar since 1652. In the revision, the drafts could not agree on making his date obligatory or optional.

Some of the drafts proposed celebrating Martin on November 4 and moving Charles from that date to November 3. Others proposed making them both optional on their shared *dies natalis*. Pope Paul wanted Charles Borromeo's memorial obligatory. Perhaps Martin was given his *dies natalis* because Charles had the succeeding day for so long. However it happened, Charles remained on November 4 as an obligatory memorial, and Martin is remembered on his *dies natalis*, November 3, as an optional memorial.

9 The Dedication of the Lateran Basilica

This feast has been on the Roman calendar since the eleventh century. The previous Missal called it the Dedication of the Archbasilica of the Most Holy Savior. The revisers kept it here, but proposed "the restoration of the most ancient title under which it is always designated as the Roman cathedral."[191]

This ranks as a feast of the Lord, as does the anniversary of the dedication of a parish church. As such, when it falls on a Sunday, it takes precedence over the liturgy of the Thirty-Second Sunday in Ordinary Time, both at Mass and in the Liturgy of the Hours.

10 Saint Leo the Great, Pope and Doctor of the Church

When the revisers gave examples of recognizable saints by category, they included popes among bishops, listing Leo the Great with Irenaeus and Martin. The drafts recognized Leo

190. Schemata, n. 188, p. 25.
191. Schemata, n. 188, p. 25.

as pope and doctor, and one example of saints moved to their *dies natalis*. Leo's case was significant: formerly in the Missal on April 11, his day transferred to November 10, the day on which he died in 461. The revisers explained, "The feast has been in the Roman calendar on June 28 (the transfer [of his relics to the Basilica of St. Peter]) from the eighth century, and on April 11 since the twelfth century."[192] They moved it again.

11 Saint Martin of Tours, Bishop

The revisers at first categorized Martin among bishop confessors who were neither doctors nor founders and wanted his day obligatory, along with Augustine of Canterbury, and Cyril and Methodius. When providing examples of a few recognizable saints by category, they included popes among bishops, listing Martin together with Leo the Great and Irenaeus. Martin had been in the calendar since the sixth century, honored on the day of the interment of his body, November 11, 397. The previous Missal had him on this day, and the drafts never wavered from it. "The memorial becomes obligatory by reason of the popular devotion to this saint, who was the first confessor inscribed in the Roman calendar (in the sixth century), and because of his importance in the apostolate of rural areas."[193]

The Liturgy of the Hours treats this memorial with special honor, perhaps because Martin entered the calendar so early as a mere confessor; that is, a non-martyr. Morning Prayer uses psalms of Sunday from the first week of the psalter, a privilege usually signaling feasts and solemnities. The invitatory antiphon, hymns, psalm antiphons, readings, and responsories are all proper. The *Magnificat* antiphon acclaims Martin equal to the martyrs, though he did not suffer a martyr's death. The traditional hymn for Morning Prayer calls him equal to the apostles who lived and died for his people. In the standard Litany of the Saints, Martin is always invoked.

---

192. Schemata, n. 188, p. 25.
193. Schemata, n. 225, p. 29.

12 Saint Josaphat, Bishop and Martyr

Josaphat died on this day in 1623 and was added to the Roman calendar in 1882. The former Missal honored him on November 14. The revisers categorized him among the non-Roman martyrs, who, though regional, held some importance for the entire church. They kept him as an optional memorial throughout the drafts. However, Pope Paul wanted this saint, whose body rests in St. Peter's Basilica, ranked as an obligatory memorial, as it now stands.

13–19 Sunday of the Poor

Pope Francis established the Thirty-Third Sunday in Ordinary Time as the Sunday of the Poor.[194] Set on the Sunday before the solemnity of Our Lord Jesus Christ, King of the Universe, it recalls that Christ identified himself with the little ones and the poor, who will judge individuals on their works of mercy. Not precisely a day of prayer "for" the poor, this is a day "of" the poor, in which the church recognizes their gifts.

13 Saint Frances Xavier Cabrini, Virgin

Mother Cabrini, founder of the Missionary Sisters of the Sacred Heart of Jesus, served Italian immigrants in the United States. In November 1971, the bishops of the United States voted to add several blesseds and saints to the calendar: Elizabeth Ann Seton, John Neumann, Isidore, Peter Claver, Isaac Jogues, John de Brébeuf and companions, Frances Xavier Cabrini, and Our Lady of Guadalupe.[195]

Frances died on December 22, 1917, an inconvenient *dies natalis* in the week before Christmas. In the United States

194. Francis, Apostolic Letter *Misericordia et misera*, https://www.vatican .va/content/francesco/en/apost_letters/documents/papa-francesco-lettera -ap_20161120_misericordia-et-misera.html.

195. "Liturgical Calendar for the United States," *Newsletter* 7, no. 12 (December 1971): 312.

she is honored with an obligatory memorial on November 13 instead, the day that Pius IX beatified her.

For All Souls' Day in the United States, the *Book of Blessings* includes a prayer service for visiting a cemetery. In the brief Litany of the Saints, Frances Xavier Cabrini is invoked, along with another American saint, Elizabeth Ann Seton (1746).

15 Saint Albert the Great, Bishop and Doctor of the Church

First categorized by the revisers among doctors of the church, Albert the Great was also honored on this day in the previous Missal. He died on November 15, 1280, and entered the Roman calendar in 1932. All the drafts retained his observance as an optional memorial, as it remains.

16 Saint Margaret of Scotland

The previous Missal honored Margaret the queen on June 10, but the revisers wanted her optional observance on her *dies natalis*, November 16 († 1093). She has been on the Roman calendar since the six hundredth anniversary of her death in 1693. The revisers had categorized her among matrons considered of little importance, so some of the drafts omitted her. She remains an optional memorial.

16 Saint Gertrude, Virgin

The revisers had first categorized Gertrude as non-martyr virgin of little importance. She died on November 17, 1302, and entered the Roman calendar in 1739. The previous Missal observed her day on November 16, where it remains, though the revisers attempted removing her or moving the day to her *dies natalis*. That day, though, would become occupied by an obligatory memorial.

17 Saint Elizabeth of Hungary, Religious

First categorized among the holy matrons worthy of optional observance, Elizabeth had been on the previous calendar since

1671 and in the Missal on November 19. The revisers initially thought she had died on November 16, 1231. They wanted her optional memorial on her presumed *dies natalis*, together with Margaret of Scotland, who had died the same day. However, the last draft entered the correct day of her death, November 17.

She was among the saints whom the Congregation for the Doctrine of the Faith wanted retained as an obligatory memorial, as it now stands. This caused the optional memorial of Gertrude, who died on November 17, to be retained on November 16.

18 The Dedication of the Basilicas of Sts. Peter and Paul, Apostles

The revisers first categorized this as a feast of the Lord of local interest. They kept it as an optional memorial, as it remains. The previous Missal honored the same date, but several of the drafts omitted the observance. It was restored in the final draft with a note that the feast had been on the Roman calendar since the twelfth century.

18 Saint Rose Philippine Duchesne, Virgin

Coming from France to the United States as a missionary, Rose Philippine ministered especially in Missouri. Anticipating her canonization in 1988, the bishops of the United States voted to include her in the proper calendar on November 17—possibly a typographical error.[196] She died on November 18, 1852, and the Martyrology lists her on that day. She is observed with an optional memorial.

21 The Presentation of the Blessed Virgin Mary

The revisers advised suppressing the feast of the Presentation of the Blessed Virgin Mary. It appears in none of the

196. "June Meeting of the Bishops' Committee on the Liturgy," *Newsletter* XXIV (May–June 1988): 1105.

drafts. They categorized it as a feast of devotion like the Seven Sorrows of Mary, the Holy Name of Mary, and the Blessed Virgin Mary of Mercy—all of which they recommended setting aside. They removed the Presentation "because it had been taken from the apocrypha."[197] "The spiritual object of this feast according to Eastern liturgies is almost equal to the Western celebration of the Immaculate Conception; that is, the holiness of Mary from the beginning of her life."[198]

The Congregation for the Doctrine of the Faith disagreed, wanting it kept and even made obligatory. Pope Paul explicitly concurred with the Congregation: "Let it be retained for ecumenical reasons, but let it have the same tonality it has in the Eastern liturgies; that is, let it express the unreserved surrender of the Virgin to God. Some texts from the Eastern liturgies might be used."[199] He later commented that this was a celebration "surrounded by venerable tradition, particularly dear to Eastern Christians."[200] Consequently, in spite of its apocryphal origins, the day remains where it was in the previous Missal, now an obligatory memorial.

22 Saint Cecilia, Virgin and Martyr

The revisers kept Cecilia on this day as in the previous Missal, but only as an optional memorial. Some of the drafts omitted her because of concerns over the validity of her biographies.

The revisers explained, "Whatever there may be concerning historical difficulties relevant to the person of Cecilia, the popular devotion toward the holy woman treated in the Passion of Saint Cecilia does not give license for removing her memorial from the Roman calendar, where it has been

197. Schemata, n. 188, p. 30.
198. Schemata, n. 225, p. 41.
199. Bugnini, p. 312.
200. *Marialis cultus* 8, DOL 467 (3906), p. 1209.

inscribed since the sixth century."[201] Defending the removal of dozens of saints "who present major historical difficulties," the revisers stated, "If historical arguments were strictly applied, to these names also the name of St. Cecilia should have been added, but whose memorial has nevertheless been retained because of popular devotion."[202]

Cecilia is among the saints whom the Congregation of the Doctrine of the Faith wanted obligatory. In spite of the difficulties, Cecilia keeps her place as an obligatory memorial.

Fourth Thursday: Thanksgiving Day

The United States sets the fourth Thursday of November as a day of gratitude. The Missal includes prayers and recommends readings, all giving thanks to God for the fruits of the nation. The prayer and collect first appeared in 1969,[203] and they were revised for the third edition of the Missal.

23 Saint Clement I, Pope and Martyr

Honored on the calendar since the sixth century, Clement remains on the day from the previous Missal. The early drafts made him obligatory, but his status changed to an optional memorial.

23 Saint Columban, Abbot

Columban died on this date in 615, and the revisers proposed adding him to the calendar "because of the importance of

201. Schemata, n. 188, p. 26. The wording varies slightly in Schemata, n. 260, p. 34: "Whatever there may be concerning historical difficulties relevant to the person of Cecilia, her ancient memorial is preserved because of the popular devotion toward the type of holiness that is treated in the Passion of Saint Cecilia (6th century)."

202. Schemata, n. 225, p. 41.

203. "Thanksgiving Day Mass," *Newsletter* 5, nos. 6–7 (June–July 1969): 183–84.

the apostolate of St. Columban and his monks."[204] While adding contemporary martyrs and saints from around the world,
they included two older "apostles," Columban and Ansgar, as
exceptional preachers of the gospel. The earliest draft placed
Columban on November 24 when Clement was obligatory on
November 23. Columban was omitted and finally reinserted
as an optional memorial on the same day as Clement.

23 Blessed Miguel Agustín Pro, Priest and Martyr

Miguel died by firing squad on this day in 1927, a martyr
of the Cristero War in Mexico. He was added to the calendar
in the United States in 1990 as an optional memorial on this
day, together with Juan Diego.[205] This is a rare day with three
optional memorials.

24 Saint Andrew Dũng-Lạc, Priest, and Companions, Martyrs

In 1988 John Paul II canonized a group of 117 Vietnamese
martyrs who died between the seventeenth and nineteenth
centuries. The priest Andrew Dũng Lạc († 1839) represents
them. The pope added them to the general calendar in 1989
as an obligatory memorial.[206]

Andrew died on December 21 during a week that now ex-
cludes obligatory memorials, so another date shared by three
of the martyrs was selected for the observance of them all.[207]
The *Supplement* to the Lectionary proposes readings (683B).

---

204. Schemata, n. 225, p. 29.

205. "Confirmation of Calendar Change and Additions," *Newsletter*
XXVII (March 1991): 1244.

206. "Saint Andrew Dung-Lac, priest and martyr, and companions, martyrs (November 24)," *Newsletter* XXV (August 1989): 1163–64.

207. Dicastery of the Causes of the Saints, "Chi muore per la fede sale in
cielo," https://www.causesanti.va/it/santi-e-beati/martiri-del-vietnam.html.

25 Saint Catherine of Alexandria, Virgin and Martyr

The revisers first categorized Catherine among virgin martyrs whose biographical information was doubtful. Although she occupied a place in the previous Missal on this day, none of the drafts included her.

The decision raised protests, especially from the East, where people venerated Catherine at least since the fifth century. Her body is revered in a monastery on the hallowed ground of Mount Sinai. However, she entered the Roman calendar only in the thirteenth century, nothing certain is known of her except her name, and other saints seemed more deserving of a place. "In these respects she may be compared to St. Cecilia, whose situation is more or less the same but who has been kept in the calendar 'because of the devotion of the people to her.' "[208]

Pope John Paul visited St. Catherine's Monastery in 2000,[209] and the third edition of the Missal, published shortly afterwards, reintroduced her day as an optional memorial. The *Supplement* to the Lectionary suggests readings (683C).

30 Saint Andrew, Apostle

Among apostles with a feast near the end of the month, Andrew has occupied this date for many centuries. The previous Missal and all of the drafts kept his obligatory observance on this day.

In the previous Missal, the Proper of Saints began on November 29 with Saturninus, followed by Andrew. This framed the saints' days within the liturgical year. The revised Proper

208. Bugnini, p. 318.

209. "Jubilee Pilgrimage of his Holiness John Paul II to Mount Sinai, Celebration of the Word at Mount Sinai: Homily of the Holy Father John Paul II," https://www.vatican.va/content/john-paul-ii/en/homilies/2000 /documents/hf_jp-ii_hom_20000226_sinai.html.

of Saints begins in January, as the dates have more to do with the saints than with the succession of liturgical times. Those accustomed to a typical calendar now find saints like Andrew easier to locate.

When a bishop is ordained on this day, the liturgy becomes that of the apostle. Andrew is listed in the standard litany of saints immediately after his brother Peter and Paul. Andrew appears in the first eucharistic prayer in a similar position, and his name is always pronounced, even when the priest abbreviates the list. Andrew's name is missing from the litany in the solemn profession of religious men and women, where Peter and Paul are invoked separately. The only other apostle in that litany is John. Perhaps this demonstrates a desire to manage the number of saints in the litany, adding a few religious, but retaining among the apostles only the two pillars of the church and the one who, as tradition holds, did not marry.

December

3 Saint Francis Xavier, Priest

Francis died on this day in 1552, and his feast entered the calendar in 1663. The revisers first categorized him among non-bishop confessors who were neither doctors of the church nor founders of religious orders, and among preachers of the gospel such as Boniface and Cyril and Methodius. They kept him obligatory throughout the drafts on the day from the previous Missal. It remains an obligatory memorial. His name is invoked in the standard Litany of the Saints.

4 Saint John Damascene, Priest and Doctor of the Church

The previous Missal honored John Damascene on March 27, which always falls during Lent or the octave of Easter. Entering the calendar only in 1890, he had died on December 4, 749. "He has been celebrated on that day in the Byzantine

Rite,"[210] so the revisers moved his date here for the sake of the liturgical year, ecumenism, and the *dies natalis*. He appeared here in all the drafts and remains an optional memorial.

6 Saint Nicholas, Bishop

The revisers first categorized Nicholas among bishop confessors who were neither doctors nor founders. He died on this day around the year 350, and his feast has been on the calendar since the twelfth century. The previous Missal and all the drafts kept him on December 6.

Nicholas remains an optional memorial, but the Congregation for the Doctrine of the Faith had vigorously discussed the suggestion that the day become obligatory. Nicholas was honored highly in some regions of the world, though not all. Little factual evidence about Nicholas had survived, which the revisers required for making a saint obligatory. Exceptions had been made for Cecilia, Agatha, and Lucy, honored in Rome since the time of Gregory the Great. "If a further exception were made for St. Nicholas, the door would be opened to a new conception of the revised calendar, and the very basis on which the revision was being made would be threatened."[211] In the end, the Congregation voted overwhelmingly to keep the day optional.

7 Saint Ambrose, Bishop and Doctor of the Church

The revisers first categorized Ambrose among doctors of the church and kept his date obligatory throughout the drafts on the day from the previous Missal. He had died on April 4, 397, Holy Saturday that year, and he entered the calendar in the twelfth century. His day has long been honored on the anniversary of his ordination as a bishop, December 7, 374.

---

210. Schemata, n. 188, p. 27.
211. Bugnini, p. 317.

The revisers made no attempt to change it, perhaps because April 4 could fall during Lent or the octave of Easter.

Ambrose remains an obligatory memorial. In the Consecration of Virgins, his name is added to the litany of saints; he authored one of the earliest treatises on Christian virginity.

8 The Immaculate Conception of the Blessed Virgin Mary

Paul VI declared that this solemnity "recalls the preparation for the Savior's coming at its origins (See Is 11:1 and 10) and also the happy beginning of the Church in its beauty without spot or wrinkle."[212] The celebration feels especially appropriate during Advent.

The date remains the traditional one, exactly nine months before the Nativity of Mary. The previous Missal honored Mary under this title on December 8, and all the drafts kept it. The revisers considered this one of four important feasts connected to the mysteries of the Virgin's life, together with her Nativity, the Visitation, and the Assumption.

This day is a solemnity on the general calendar, and a holy day of obligation in the United States, even when it falls on a Saturday or a Monday. Mary is patroness of the country under this title.

When December 8 falls on a Sunday, the observance transfers to Monday, December 9, and the obligation to participate at Mass transfers with it. Originally the revisers envisioned it differently, transferring it to the preceding Saturday. The Sacred Congregation for Divine Worship, foreseeing the first instance of this in 1974, legislated that the solemnity be observed on Saturday, December 7, that year. They permitted conferences of bishops to request replacing the Second Sunday of Advent with the Immaculate Conception, though "the homily and general intercessions are to stress the sense of the

212. *Marialis cultus* 3, DOL 497 (3901), p. 1206.

Advent season."[213] Replacing the Second Sunday of Advent with the Immaculate Conception does not fit the design of the revised liturgical year, but it still happens in Spain and some countries associated with it.[214]

When December 8 falls on a Saturday, a regularly scheduled parish evening Mass becomes that of Sunday. Many parishes have an anticipatory Mass for the holy day on December 7 to help the faithful participate twice. Evening Prayer I of the Second Sunday of Advent takes precedence, but the local bishop may judge otherwise. When December 8 falls on a Monday, any December 7 evening Mass and its Evening Prayer are those of the Second Sunday of Advent.

Throughout the year, the church permits Votive Masses of Mary under various titles, but not to commemorate the events associated with the mysteries of her life. An exception is made for the Immaculate Conception (GIRM 375).

Flowers and instrumental music are used in moderation during Advent. An exception is made for solemnities such as this (GIRM 305, 313).

9 Saint Juan Diego Cuauhtlatoatzin

The optional memorial of the man who reported visions of Our Lady of Guadalupe is observed on this date in the proper calendar of the United States. The *Supplement* to the Lectionary suggests readings (689A). According to *El Nican Mopohua*, Mary first appeared to Juan Diego on Tepeyac Hill on this date in 1531.[215]

---

213. Sacred Congregation for Divine Worship, "Note *Anno 1974*, on the solemnity of the Immaculate Conception in 1974," 20 January 1973, DOL 465 (3889), p. 1203.

214. Calendário Litúrgico España 2024, https://gcatholic.org/calendar /2024/ES-es.htm.

215. "Juan Diego Cuauhtlatoatzin (1474–1548)," https://www.vatican.va /news_services/liturgy/saints/ns_lit_doc_20020731_juan-diego_en.html.

In the Missal, if the first name is insufficient to identify the saint, the full name appears in the collect. This happens, for example, with John Damascene on December 4. There is only one Juan Diego in the calendar, winning the gratitude of many priests who find his full name unpronounceable. The collect simply refers to him as Juan Diego.

Pope John Paul beatified Juan Diego in 1990 and canonized him in 2002. After the beatification, the bishops of the United States petitioned the Congregation for Divine Worship and the Discipline of the Sacraments to add Juan Diego to the national calendar. The request was granted by the end of November 1990 and received in January 1991.[216]

Frequently, the calendar and missal present an anglicized version of the saint's name, as "Pius" for the familiar "Padre Pio." On this day the Spanish name remains in English, avoiding the infelicitous translation "Saint John Jim."

10 Our Lady of Loreto

On the memorial of Our Lady of the Holy Rosary in 2019, Pope Francis inscribed Our Lady of Loreto into the general calendar as an optional memorial on December 10. Although this runs counter to the plan of the revision to limit the number of devotional days, the Congregation for Divine Worship and the Discipline of the Sacraments noted the significance of the Holy House of Loreto in the spiritual lives of the faithful, and the Litany of Loreto, popular among various devotions to Mary.

In the city of Loreto, the feast is observed on this day, so Francis chose it for the observance. The USCCB makes available the English texts for the Mass and the Liturgy of the Hours.[217]

---

216. "Confirmation of Calendar Change and Additions," *Newsletter* XXVI (March 1991): 1244.

217. "Our Lady of Loreto," https://www.usccb.org/prayer-worship/liturgical -year/our-lady-of-loreto.

11 Saint Damasus I, Pope

Damasus died on this date in 384 and has been on the calendar since the twelfth century. The previous Missal honored him on this day, as did all the drafts. It remains an optional memorial.

12 Our Lady of Guadalupe

Completely missing from the previous Missal, Our Lady of Guadalupe now ranks as a feast in the United States. The third edition of the Missal added her observance as an optional memorial throughout the world, but the United States already had her on the proper calendar as an obligatory memorial, which the bishops unanimously wanted changed to a feast, a request approved in 1999.[218]

When December 12 falls on a Sunday, the liturgy remains the Third Sunday of Advent. If this happens, the USCCB permits customs, images, processions, music, and preaching that celebrate Guadalupe.[219] On a feast during Advent, floral decoration and music may reflect the degree of celebration (GIRM 305, 313).

13 Saint Lucy, Virgin and Martyr

Lucy died on this date around the year 304, and her feast has been on the calendar since the sixth century. She is much honored in piety and religious art. The previous Missal honored her *dies natalis*, and all the drafts did the same as an optional memorial. However, the Congregation for the Doctrine of the Faith wanted her day obligatory, and the revision has done so. Lucy is mentioned among the women martyrs in the first eucharistic prayer.

---

218. "Feast of the Blessed Virgin Mary of Guadalupe," *Newsletter* XXIII (December 1987): 1083; XXXIV (May–June 1999): 1639.

219. "Feast of Our Lady of Guadalupe," *Newsletter* XXXIV (July 1999): 1648.

14 Saint John of the Cross, Priest and Doctor of the Church

The previous Missal observed John's day on November 24. He died on this day in 1591, so nearly all the drafts moved him to December 14 as an optional memorial. He has been on the calendar since 1738. Pope Paul wanted him raised to an obligatory memorial, so the change was made.

21 Saint Peter Canisius, Priest and Doctor of the Church

The previous Missal observed Peter's day on April 27, but he died on December 21, 1597—a few years after John of the Cross. Peter was added to the calendar in 1926. As the apostle Thomas had moved from December 21 to July 3, Peter's *dies natalis* lay open. The revisers placed it there, even though it fell among the seven privileged last weekdays of Advent. One draft proposed moving him to December 16 to avoid the difficulty, but it remained here.

At Mass, if the priest desires to celebrate Peter, he may use only the collect (GIRM 355a). Everything else comes from the Advent weekday.

In the Liturgy of the Hours, Peter may be celebrated as a commemoration, as explained above. The English translation mistakenly assigns two antiphons to the *Benedictus* and *Magnificat*; they pertain to the closing prayer, as do the special antiphons for the commemorations of Lent.

23 Saint John of Kanty, Priest

John of Kanty died on December 24, 1473, and entered the calendar in 1770. In the previous Missal on October 20, he has moved closer to his *dies natalis*. The revisers first considered him a non-bishop confessor of little importance. Many of the early drafts omitted him, but he gained a spot as an optional memorial. A draft of the proposed 1969 calendar put him on December 22, apparently in error. John was among the saints whom the Polish bishops sought one obligatory memorial, but their appeal went unheeded until Stanislaus won the distinction in 1979.

At Mass the priest may use only the collect of this saint (GIRM 355a). The Liturgy of the Hours treats John as a commemoration. As on December 21, the English translation of the antiphons for Morning and Evening Prayer are mistakenly assigned to the *Benedictus* and *Magnificat*. They belong with the expanded closing prayer when the commemoration is observed.

26 Saint Stephen, the First Martyr

The revisers first listed Stephen among the few non-Roman martyrs of importance for the entire church, together with Polycarp, Ignatius, Boniface, Irenaeus, Cyprian, and the Holy Innocents. The previous Missal set December 26 within the octave of Christmas in the Proper of Time, and the drafts moved it to the Proper of Saints, always as an obligatory observance. Jounel's commentary on the proposed 1969 calendar noted, "The days in the octave of Christmas are all made similar, giving precedence to minor festive weekdays, whether the feasts of the universal church of December 26 and 27, or the days when the octave is celebrated (December 28–31)."[220]

Stephen's day is a feast. His name appears in the first eucharistic prayer and is invoked in the standard Litany of the Saints.

27 Saint John, Apostle and Evangelist

John remains on his traditional date. The previous Missal and all the drafts kept him here, though the Missal had included him in the Proper of Time during the Christmas octave.

If the ordination of a bishop takes place on this day, the Mass of this apostle is used. John is named in the first eucharistic prayer and in the standard Litany of the Saints.

---

220. Schemata, n. 237, p. 4.

28 The Holy Innocents, Martyrs

As with Stephen and John, the Holy Innocents appeared in the previous Missal within the Proper of Time during the Christmas octave. All the drafts retained the traditional date. The revisers first listed the Innocents among the non-Roman martyrs who, though regional, held importance for the entire church. Their day is a feast on the revised calendar.

29 Saint Thomas Becket, Bishop and Martyr

As with the other saints in the octave of Christmas, Thomas Becket appeared in the previous Missal within the Proper of Time. He was martyred on this day († 1170), and his feast was added to the calendar almost immediately, in 1173. The revisers first considered him a martyr of little importance, but he still appeared in the drafts. The early ones set his day on July 7, the date when his relics were transferred on the fiftieth anniversary of his death. The late drafts and the revised calendar honor his *dies natalis*.

Thomas is an optional memorial. At Mass, a priest may only use the collect of the saint (GIRM 355a). The Liturgy of the Hours offers Thomas as a commemoration, as explained above. The English translation mistakenly assigns the two antiphons that belong inside the concluding oration of Morning and Evening Prayer to the *Benedictus* and *Magnificat*.

One early draft proposed repeating the three Masses of Christmas on December 29, 30, and 31 respectively, and another draft wanted these as weekdays within the octave. However, the week proceeds on its own merits with the option of saints on December 29 and 31.

31 Saint Sylvester I, Pope

Sylvester appeared in the previous Missal within the Proper of Time in the octave of Christmas. Nearly all the drafts kept him on the list and on the same day, but the revisers moved him into the Proper of Saints, keeping him optional. Sylvester died on this day in 335, and his feast has been on the calendar since the sixth century.

Observing the optional memorial of Sylvester is limited to offering his collect (GIRM 355a). In the Liturgy of the Hours, he may be observed as a commemoration, as noted above. The English translation mistakenly reassigned the antiphon intended for the closing prayer to the *Benedictus*. There is no Evening Prayer for Sylvester because Evening Prayer I of the solemnity of Mary the Mother of God takes precedence, beginning the year anew.

Chapter Six

The Table of Liturgical Days

Introduction

Inside the Universal Norms on the Liturgical Year and Calendar is found the Table of Liturgical Days according to their order of precedence. The norms are in two chapters. The first is "The Liturgical Year," which subdivides into the Liturgical Days and the Cycle of the Year. The second is "The Calendar," which contains the Calendar and Celebrations To Be Inscribed in It, and the Proper Day for Celebrations. This last section introduces the table: "Precedence among liturgical days, as regards their celebration, is governed solely by the following Table" (UNLYC 59).

The table has three sections bearing numbers rather than titles. The first groups the first four ranks. The second section embraces ranks five through nine, and the third concludes with ranks ten through thirteen.

The Ranks

I

1. The Paschal Triduum of the Passion and Resurrection of the Lord.

The prominence given the paschal mystery in the Second Vatican Council finds expression in the first rank. Nothing takes priority over the Triduum from the Evening Mass of the Lord's Supper, through the Passion on Good Friday and the Easter Vigil, and Easter Sunday. Any solemnity falling within these days is moved, while the celebration of feasts and memorials is impeded.

2. The Nativity of the Lord, the Epiphany, the Ascension, and Pentecost.

Sundays of Advent, Lent, and Easter.

Ash Wednesday.

Weekdays of Holy Week from Monday up to and including Thursday.

Days within the Octave of Easter.

The second rank opens with four more days celebrating the mysteries of the Lord: his Nativity; his Epiphany, focusing on the visit of the magi; the Ascension of Jesus after his death and resurrection; and Pentecost, the celebration of the coming of the Holy Spirit upon Jesus' followers. Only the fourth of these falls universally on a Sunday. The second and third transfer to a Sunday if the conference does not list them among holy days of obligation. The first is always December 25, no matter the day of the week.

Following these come the privileged Sundays of Advent, Lent, and Easter Time. On these weeks the community explores the mysteries that unspool throughout the year. They take precedence over many other celebrations, including weddings.

Ash Wednesday shares the second rank. It replaces any other day that may conflict, from feasts such as the Chair of Peter to optional memorials such as Our Lady of Lourdes.

The first days of Holy Week and the days of the first week following Easter do not draw many Catholics to church, so it may surprise that these days rank high. So central is the paschal mystery to interpreting the liturgical year that the entire week before Easter—and the week following it—dispel all other observances.

The readings and prayers for Monday through Thursday morning prepare the faithful for the Triduum, and the week following Easter basks in joy. Feasts are impeded and solemnities must wait. At times the solemnities of Joseph and the Annunciation fall within these weeks, deferring their celebration.

3. Solemnities inscribed in the General Calendar, whether of the Lord, of the Blessed Virgin Mary or of Saints.

The Commemoration of All the Faithful Departed.

Other solemnities scattered throughout the year occupy the third rank. The solemnities of the Most Holy Trinity and of Our Lord Jesus Christ the King of the Universe, though Sundays in Ordinary Time, rank as solemnities of the Lord, as does the Most Holy Body and Blood of Jesus Christ, which transfers from a Thursday to a Sunday in the United States. Solemnities of the Lord that may or do fall on a weekday are the Annunciation and the Most Sacred Heart of Jesus.

Solemnities of Mary are Mary the Mother of God, the Assumption of the Blessed Virgin Mary, and the Immaculate Conception of the Blessed Virgin Mary. Joseph, Spouse of the Blessed Virgin Mary; the Nativity of John the Baptist; Peter and Paul; and All Saints are solemnities of the saints.

Such celebrations take precedence over others, such as a Ritual Mass of the sacrament of confirmation. A bishop may confirm at Mass on the Nativity of John the Baptist, but with the antiphons, prayers, and readings of the saint.

"All Souls' Day" is the popular title for the Commemoration of All the Faithful Departed. Its rank is significant especially when November 2 falls on a Sunday. It takes precedence over the Ordinary Time Mass, as well as Ritual Masses such as weddings.

4. Proper Solemnities, namely:

a) **The Solemnity of the principal Patron of the place, city or state.**

b) **The Solemnity of the dedication and of the anniversary of the dedication of one's own church.**

c) **The Solemnity of the Title of one's own church.**

d) **The Solemnity either of the Title**

    or of the Founder

    or of the principal Patron of an Order or Congregation.

Besides the general calendar, proper calendars are established. These are layered according to a region, a nation, a diocese, a religious order, or a parish.

The first category governing these concerns geographical areas named for something on the calendar. For example, parish churches within the city of St. Louis, Missouri, celebrate August 25 as a solemnity.

The next category applies to the anniversary of the dedication of the parish church. That day ranks as a solemnity for that parish every year. Some parishes are so old and their early records so poor that the dedication date has been lost. As noted above, the parish may choose a nearby Sunday in Ordinary Time or the Sunday preceding All Saints. If the day coincides with a day of higher rank, it moves to the nearest available day.

When a new church is to be dedicated, well-meaning organizers sometimes select a date that already has significance for the congregation, such as the church's title or ethnic patron. This creates the lamentable situation in which the popular date is removed from the local calendar in favor of the anniversary of the dedication. For example, if a parish named Our Lady of Guadalupe dedicates a new church on December 12, the anniversary of the dedication pushes the patronal feast to December 13 every year, which no one would want to do.

The title of the church ranks as a solemnity. Even a saint's day not on the general calendar becomes a solemnity in that parish church. For example, January 2 becomes a patronal solemnity for St. Munchin church, permanently replacing Basil the Great and Gregory of Nazianzen.

In religious communities the title of the order, its founder, or its principal patron is observed as a solemnity within the community. This does not affect a parish served by religious, unless the title of the church is the same.

II

5. Feasts of the Lord inscribed in the General Calendar.

Feasts of the Lord include the Holy Family, the Baptism of the Lord, the Presentation of the Lord, the Transfiguration of the Lord, the Exaltation of the Holy Cross, and the Dedication of the Lateran Basilica. As noted above, these have special significance, especially when they fall on a Sunday.

6. Sundays of Christmas Time and the Sundays in Ordinary Time.

Outside the United States the Second Sunday of Christmas ranks with Sundays in Ordinary Time. In the United States, where the Epiphany transfers to a Sunday, Holy Family is the only other Sunday of Christmas Time. It shares the rank of Sundays in Ordinary Time. Any celebration from the previous ranks falling on such a Sunday takes precedence, including, for example, the Baptism of the Lord and the title of the church.

7. Feasts of the Blessed Virgin Mary and of the Saints in the General Calendar.

The feasts of the Virgin include the Visitation and the Nativity of Mary. In the United States Our Lady of Guadalupe joins the list.

Feasts of the saints are the Conversion of St. Paul, the Chair of St. Peter, each of the apostles, Lawrence, the archangels, Luke, Stephen, and the Holy Innocents.

8. Proper Feasts, namely:

a) The Feast of the principal Patron of the diocese.

b) The Feast of the anniversary of the dedication of the cathedral church.

c) The Feast of the principal Patron of a region or province, or a country, or of a wider territory.

d) The Feast of the Title, Founder, or principal Patron of an Order or Congregation and of a religious province, without prejudice to the prescriptions given under no. 4.

e) Other Feasts proper to an individual church.

f) Other Feasts inscribed in the Calendar of each diocese or Order or Congregation.

Proper calendars include feasts. The principal patron of a diocese ranks first among these. Sometimes the patron already ranks as a feast or solemnity in the general calendar. Otherwise, the day with a lower rank in the general calendar rises to a feast in that diocese.

The anniversary of the dedication of the cathedral church is to be observed as a feast day in all parishes. This affects the daily Mass and the Liturgy of the Hours throughout the diocese.

If a wider territory falls under the patronage of a saint or title, then all the parishes within the territory celebrate that day as a feast. This would apply to December 13, for example, in the churches on the island of Santa Lucia.

In religious orders, those titles, founders, and patrons not observed as solemnities are feasts. Again, this applies to the community, but not to a parish it serves. For example, a Benedictine pastor from a monastery that retains March 21 as Benedict's solemnity observes the memorial on July 11 in the parish church.

An individual church, order, or diocese may have other proper feasts. For example, if a saint spent some time within its territory or community, the date may become a feast.

9. *Weekdays of Advent from December 17 up to and including December 24.*

Days within the Octave of Christmas.

Weekdays of Lent.

Weekdays immediately before and after Christmas, as well as those during Lent, rank higher than other weekdays. Saints who would normally be honored with a memorial become optional at Mass and commemorations in the Liturgy of the Hours. Not as important as the weekdays immediately before and after Easter, these weekdays still retain considerable value.

III

10. *Obligatory Memorials in the General Calendar.*

These are noted in the calendar simply as "memorials" with the implication that they are obligatory. The obligation is relative: Any memorial coinciding with a date from the first nine ranks is no longer obligatory and may be impeded. The revised calendar reduced the list of obligatory saints to those with truly universal importance for the church.

11. *Proper Obligatory Memorials, namely:*

a) **The Memorial of a secondary Patron of the place, diocese, region, or religious province.**

b) **Other Obligatory Memorials inscribed in the Calendar of each diocese, or Order or congregation.**

In addition to the memorials on the general calendar are those on proper calendars. A secondary patron of a diocese, for example, becomes an obligatory memorial—unless the patron already enjoys higher rank. A saint of some importance to a diocese, region, order, or congregation may be inscribed as obligatory.

12. Optional Memorials, which, however, may be celebrated, in the special manner described in the General Instruction of the Roman Missal and of the Liturgy of the Hours, even on the days listed in no. 9.

In the same manner Obligatory Memorials may be celebrated as Optional Memorials if they happen to fall on Lenten weekdays.

The creation of optional memorials was one of the greatest contributions to the revised calendar. They allowed the observance of certain days where they mattered most, omitting them where they mattered less. Some obligatory memorials become optional when they fall in the privileged times of the ninth rank.

13. Weekdays of Advent up to and including December 16.

Weekdays of Christmas Time from January 2 until the Saturday after the Epiphany.

Weekdays of the Easter Time from Monday after the Octave of Easter up to and including the Saturday before Pentecost.

Weekdays in Ordinary Time.

Other weekdays hold the final category on the table. The first ones come from the privileged times: Advent through December 16, Christmas between Mary the Mother of God and the Baptism of the Lord, and Easter between the Second Sunday and Pentecost. These all have relative unimportance when other local celebrations take place. All Lent weekdays have greater weight, sharing the ninth rank on the table.

The lowliest spot is given to weekdays in Ordinary Time. These have the greatest flexibility when a community wishes to celebrate something else.

Conclusion

The Table of Liturgical Days sums up the hard work devoted to revising the General Roman Calendar. It helps people discern the degree of celebration each liturgy deserves.

In the universal church, conferences of bishops, dioceses, parishes, and homes, the table helps the faithful observe each day according to its proper merit. It also points everyone to the central tenet of the faith they hold—the paschal mystery of Jesus Christ.

Appendix I

Alphabetical Listing of Days in the Proper of Time

Name	Date
Adalbert	April 23
Agatha	February 5
Agnes	January 21
Albert the Great	November 15
All Saints	November 1
All Souls	November 2
Aloysius Gonzaga	June 21
Alphonsus Mary Liguori	August 1
Ambrose	December 7
André Bessette	January 6
Andrew	November 30
Andrew Dũng-Lạc and Companions	November 24
Andrew Kim Tae-gŏn, Paul Chŏng Ha-sang, and Companions	September 20

Name	Date
Angela Merici	January 27
Annunciation of the Lord	March 25
Anselm	April 21
Ansgar	February 3
Anthony	January 17
Anthony Mary Claret	October 24
Anthony of Padua	June 13
Anthony Zaccaria	July 5
Apollinaris	July 20
Assumption of the Blessed Virgin Mary	August 15
Athanasius	May 2
Augustine	August 28
Augustine of Canterbury	May 27
Augustine Zhao Rong and Companions	July 9
Barnabas	June 11
Bartholomew	August 24
Basil the Great and Gregory the Great	January 2
Bede the Venerable	May 25
Benedict	July 11
Bernard	August 20
Bernardine of Siena	May 20
Blaise	February 3
Bonaventure	July 15

Name	Date
Boniface	June 5
Bridget	July 23
Bruno	October 6
Cajetan	August 7
Callistus I	October 14
Camillus de Lellis	July 18
Casimir	March 4
Catherine of Alexandria	November 25
Catherine of Siena	April 29
Cecilia	November 22
Chair of Saint Peter the Apostle	February 22
Charles Borromeo	November 4
Charles Lwanga and Companions	June 3
Christopher Magallanes and Companions	May 21
Clare	August 11
Clement I	November 23
Columban	November 23
Conversion of St. Paul	January 25
Cornelius and Cyprian	September 16
Cosmas and Damian	September 26
Cyril and Methodius	February 14
Cyril of Alexandria	June 27
Cyril of Jerusalem	March 18

Name	Date
Damasus	December 11
Damien Joseph de Veuster	May 10
Dedication of the Basilica of St. Mary Major	August 5
Dedication of the Basilicas of Sts. Peter and Paul	November 18
Dedication of the Lateran Basilica	November 9
Denis and Companions	October 9
Dominic	August 8
Elizabeth Ann Seton	January 4
Elizabeth of Hungary	November 17
Elizabeth of Portugal	July 5
Ephrem	June 9
Eusebius Vercelli	August 2
Exaltation of the Holy Cross	September 14
Fabian	January 20
Faustina	October 5
Fidelis of Sigmaringen	April 24
First Martyrs of the Holy Roman Church	June 30
Frances of Rome	March 9
Frances Xavier Cabrini	November 13
Francis de Sales	January 24
Francis of Assisi	October 4
Francis of Paola	April 2

Name	Date
Francis Xavier	December 3
Francis Xavier Seelos	October 5
George	April 23
Gertrude	November 16
Gregory of Narek	February 27
Gregory the Great	September 3
Gregory VII	May 25
Hedwig	October 16
Henry	July 13
Hilary	January 13
Hildegard of Bingen	September 17
Holy Guardian Angels	October 2
Holy Innocents	December 28
Ignatius of Antioch	October 17
Ignatius of Loyola	July 31
Immaculate Conception of the Blessed Virgin Mary	December 8
Irenaeus	June 28
Isidore of Seville	April 4
Isidore the Farmer	May 15
James	July 25
Jane Frances de Chantal	August 12
Januarius	September 19

Name	Date
Jerome	September 30
Jerome Emiliani	February 8
Joachim and Anne	July 26
John	December 27
John Baptist de la Salle	April 7
John Bosco	January 31
John Chrysostom	September 13
John Damascene	December 4
John de Brébeuf, Isaac Jogues, and Companions	October 19
John Eudes	August 19
John Fisher and Thomas More	June 22
John I	May 18
John Leonardi	October 9
John Mary Vianney	August 4
John Neumann	January 5
John of Ávila	May 10
John of Capistrano	October 23
John of God	March 8
John of Kanty	December 23
John of the Cross	December 14
John Paul II	October 22
John XXIII	October 11

Name	Date
Josaphat	November 12
Joseph Calasanz	August 25
Joseph the Worker	May 1
Joseph, Spouse of the Blessed Virgin Mary	March 19
Josephine Bakhita	February 8
Juan Diego Cuauhtlatoatzin	December 9
Junípero Serra	July 1
Justin	June 1
Kateri Tekakwitha	July 14
Katharine Drexel	March 3
Lawrence	August 10
Lawrence of Brindisi	July 21
Lawrence Ruiz and Companions	September 28
Leo the Great	November 10
Louis	August 25
Louis Grignion de Montfort	April 28
Lucy	December 13
Luke	October 18
Marcellinus and Peter	June 2
Margaret Mary Alacoque	October 16
Margaret of Scotland	November 16
Maria Goretti	July 6
Marianne Cope	January 23

Name	Date
Marie Rose Durocher	October 6
Mark	April 25
Martha, Mary, and Lazarus	July 29
Martin de Porres	November 3
Martin I	April 13
Martin of Tours	November 11
Mary Magdalene	July 22
Mary Magdalene de' Pazzi	May 25
Matthew	September 21
Matthias	May 14
Maximilian Mary Kolbe	August 14
Michael McGivney	August 13
Michael, Gabriel, and Raphael	September 29
Miguel Agustín Pro	November 23
Monica	August 27
Most Holy Name of Jesus	January 3
Most Holy Name of Mary	September 12
Nativity of John the Baptist	June 24
Nativity of the Blessed Virgin Mary	September 8
Nereus and Achilleus	May 12
Nicholas	December 6
Norbert	June 6
Our Lady of Fátima	May 13

Name	Date
Our Lady of Guadalupe	December 12
Our Lady of Loreto	December 10
Our Lady of Lourdes	February 11
Our Lady of Mount Carmel	July 16
Our Lady of Sorrows	September 15
Our Lady of the Rosary	October 7
Pancras	May 12
Passion of John the Baptist	August 29
Patrick	March 17
Paul Miki and Companions	February 6
Paul of the Cross	October 20
Paul VI	May 29
Paulinus of Nola	June 22
Perpetua and Felicity	March 7
Peter and Paul	June 29
Peter Canisius	December 21
Peter Chanel	April 28
Peter Chrysologus	July 30
Peter Claver	September 9
Peter Damian	February 21
Peter Julian Eymard	August 2
Philip and James	May 3
Philip Neri	May 26

Name	Date
Pius of Pietrelcina	September 23
Pius V	April 30
Pius X	August 21
Polycarp	February 23
Pontian and Hippolytus	August 13
Presentation of the Blessed Virgin Mary	November 21
Presentation of the Lord	February 2
Queenship of the Blessed Virgin Mary	August 22
Raymond of Penyafort	January 7
Rita of Cascia	May 22
Robert Bellarmine	September 17
Romuald	June 19
Rose of Lima	August 23
Rose Philippine Duchesne	November 18
Scholastica	February 10
Sebastian	January 20
Seven Holy Founders of the Servite Order	February 17
Sharbel Maklūf	July 24
Simon and Jude	October 28
Sixtus II and Companions	August 7
Stanislaus	April 11
Stephen	December 26
Stephen of Hungary	August 16

Name	Date
Sylvester	December 31
Teresa Benedicta of the Cross	August 9
Teresa of Jesus	October 15
Thérèse of the Child Jesus	October 1
Thomas	July 3
Thomas Aquinas	January 28
Thomas Becket	December 29
Timothy and Titus	January 26
Transfiguration of the Lord	August 6
Turibius of Mogrovejo	March 23
Vincent	January 23
Vincent de Paul	September 27
Vincent Ferrer	April 5
Visitation of the Blessed Virgin Mary	May 31
Wenceslaus	September 28

Appendix II

Table of Rubrics Governing Ritual Masses, Masses for Various Needs and Occasions, and Masses for the Dead[1]

Sigla

V1	Ritual Masses (GIRM 372) Masses for various needs and occasions and Votive Masses, in cases of graver need or pastoral advantage, at the direction of the diocesan bishop or with his permission (GIRM 374)
V2	Masses for various needs and occasions and Votive Masses, in case of real necessity or pastoral advantage, in the estimation of the rector of the church or the priest celebrant (GIRM 376)

1. This table is based on Appendix III of the Ceremonial of Bishops, updated with revised numbers from the GIRM and the revised English translation from the third edition of the Missal, with help from the Liturgy Office of England and Wales, https://www.liturgyoffice.org.uk/Calendar/Info/Rubrics.shtml.

V3	Masses for various needs and occasions and Votive Masses chosen by the priest celebrant in response to the devotion of the faithful (GIRM 373, 375)
D1	Funeral Mass (GIRM 380)
D2	Mass on receiving the news of a death, for the final burial, or the first anniversary (GIRM 381)
D3	"Daily" Mass for the dead (GIRM 381). When D1 and D2 are not permitted, neither is D3.

Are Ritual Masses, Masses for Various Needs and Occasions, and Masses for the Dead Permitted on These Days?

		V1	V2	V3	D1	D2	D3
1.	Solemnities of Precept	No	No	No	No	No	No
2.	Sundays of Advent, Lent, and Easter Time	No	No	No	No	No	No
3.	Holy Thursday, The Paschal Triduum	No	No	No	No	No	No
4.	Solemnities not of Precept, All Souls	No	No	No	Yes	No	No
5.	Ash Wednesday, Weekdays of Holy Week	No	No	No	Yes	No	No

		V1	V2	V3	D1	D2	D3
6.	Weekdays within the Octave of Easter	No	No	No	Yes	No	No
7.	Sundays of Christmas Time and of Ordinary Time	Yes	No	No	Yes	No	No
8.	Feasts	Yes	No	No	Yes	No	No
9.	Weekdays of Advent from December 17 to 24	Yes	No	No	Yes	Yes	No
10.	Weekdays within the Octave of Christmas	Yes	No	No	Yes	Yes	No
11.	Weekdays of Lent	Yes	No	No	Yes	Yes	No
12.	Obligatory Memorials	Yes	Yes	No	Yes	Yes	No
13.	Weekdays of Advent through December 16	Yes	Yes	No	Yes	Yes	No
14.	Weekdays of Christmas Time from January 2	Yes	Yes	No	Yes	Yes	No

		V1	V2	V3	D1	D2	D3
15.	Weekdays of Easter Time	Yes	Yes	No	Yes	Yes	No
16.	Weekdays in Ordinary Time	Yes	Yes	Yes	Yes	Yes	Yes

Index